THE LIVED CAREER I

AFRICAN AMERICAN LESBIAN MANAGERS: A

PHENOMENOLOGICAL STUDY

OF PROFESSIONAL ADVANCEMENT

by

Denalerie J. Johnson-Faniel


MARY BEMKER, DSN, PsyS, Faculty Mentor and Committee Chair

K. CANDIS BEST, PhD, Committee Member

RICH DEPARIS, DPA, Committee Member


Charles Tiffin, PhD, Dean, School of Public Service Leadership

A Dissertation Presented in Partial Fulfillment

Of the Requirements for the Degree

Doctor of Philosophy


Capella University

January 2011

© Denalerie J. Johnson-Faniel, 2011

ISBN 978-1-257-01992-2

Abstract

Homophobic discrimination and hate crimes faced by those that identify as gay might have an even greater impact on those African Americans females who proclaim themselves as lesbians and women of authority. Specifically, little work has been done to examine the effect of employment discrimination on the career development paths of African American women who see themselves as persons of authority and lesbians thus being considered as a triple-threat minority: Black, gay, and female. Thus this research study explored the lived experiences of eight African American self-identified lesbian managers. The study used a qualitative approach based on a phenomenological research design using a semi-structured interview process to address the questions posed to participants about their everyday lives and experiences with a specific focus on their career paths and professional development. It is hoped that the findings will show a need for further research in the area of vocational counseling relative to African American lesbians and expand on the social, cultural, and psychological literature in the field to address federal policy protection in cases of employment discrimination, career hindrances, including employment discrimination, denial of promotions, and lack of role models and mentors for this group. Strengths and limitations of the research design were identified and implications for organizations, employers, government and the general public are discussed in this research study.

Dedication

This work is dedicated to the beautiful gift of life. Life's experiences have shaped my view of the world, and have allowed me to be a part of how the world is viewed. Many want to take away the personal liberties and freedom of those that are 'different', not realizing that we are all the same. I am more than appreciative to everyone that has been with me during my journey and Ella Faye Ireland deserves to have her name forever imprinted in history. She is my mother and my biggest supporter, even in the afterlife. She had to leave us on 12/27/2003, and I held her hand as she took her last breath. I am overcome with emotion as I write this and my last words to her were "we all love you". Dear, you gave my mother life and you have saved us all- now we ask you to focus on saving yourself! As the foundation of this family you are my admired 's-hero'. Luk-Luk, you make our family holidays more than colorful and I appreciate those supportive corner talks you always manage to sneak in even in the midst of the joke. You are the essence of clean and always wise. Nelson, you are my father and I love your realness and spirit. You never left her side and you have always been the one I could count on when others doubted it. I pause and wipe away the tears now. Dinetta and Deondra, we rocked it out on the weekends as the '3Ds' and the performances were all the way live (Candy Coated Rain Drops)! Making calls to Aunt Olga and Aunt Ethel, and the many loved ones, dissecting pigs, gluing in burgundy hair, Timmy/Chimmy/Jimmy Chan's and Luby's, chasing after Ms. Kitty, messing up the cornbread, running out on "'Gram-Mow and Dan-Dan' when it was time to finally go home, washing dishes with only a drip of water, stepping on nails, bootsy shoes, hiding bundles of joy under sweaters, mother's gift of matching Mazda's…even though I didn't get one, Watkins/Weingarten/Standards, La Petite, Marlin waterfalls family reunions, "get out of my room", sleeping on the cot, mother's blue jean shirt and sweat pants, arranging canned goods, Mexican candy, Baybrook and Almeda Mall, the horse shaped mirror, Wilbert's 20 kids, Halloween parties, Askew and Codwell, Purple Pups and HSHP lab coats, Astroworld, feeding Zebras, spreading ashes in Galveston, yellow kitchen wall stripes, her gumbo and banana pudding recipes, moving Dear's mountains, the gray station wagon and green Monte Carlo, dollar movies and two for one tacos, family meetings, and giggling after the grasshopper drinks. Donye and Earl, the true men in my life,- if only. Tamiko and Wendy-la, you taught me pure friendship, respect, and sweet love-thank you. Salena, you were the one that experienced it all and helped me grow. We share so many memories and undying love. I thank you for being simply you and giving me your family as mine. You as my wife, it will never be replaced-just reframed. You will always be head cheerleader! Tamika, I took risks with you and eliminated a lot of the fear-I became an international executive and realized there is still so much more, because of you I am a top 40 under 40, and learned it was okay to sit still and focus on building wealth and family. It was you who saved my crashed dissertation draft…I thank my beautiful wife who has given me passion; I love you and the way we connect. To our wedding party, Dana, LaChanda, Tameka, Tarek, Reese, Jason, Cydney, and "true" friends-I love you. The Irelands, Gerri, Jeremy, Braden, Ms. Queen, Mama Debbie, Connie, Raven, Daddy Robert, Aunt Robyn, Aunt Princess, Ms. Jackie, Ms. Sadie, Mr. Serge, Grandma Elaine, Mama Leslie, Aunt Lisa, Aunt Sharon, Stanley, Brian, Matthew, Bobby,

Joshua, Osei, Crystal, Menelek, Asantewaa, Frog, Markeith, Freddy, Uncle Lorenzo, Aunt Gladys, and my extended families. I appreciate you all more than you know.

Acknowledgments

This work is for the fight for equality and dedicated to all of the women who love women, despite it all, and is inspired by the person who loved me most, my mother, Ella Faye Ireland. I miss you and I "am" because of you. Nathalie "Ashlee" Eve Simeon, you left us the day after the anniversary of my mother's death, but will never leave my heart. You were the epitome of what a true friend is and you are breathing life into me. You both supported my research even before it began. I send well wishes to nonprofits that are serious about the real business of uplifting… DFS and JW-thank you, "womyn" living the life, Black women in academe, Barbara Jordan's inspiration, the Howard and Columbia experience, and I give special thanks to my wife, friends, family, colleagues, and inner circle. I extend special greetings to Capella University for the support provided to me and the many community-based groups that have been more than dedicated to the needs of women of color. Fellow femmes, let's use those high heels to break that glass ceiling! Fellow women of color, claim your seat at the table! Younger 'womyn', please become pioneers to later be known as trailblazers! To all of 'us', embrace nonconformity and be the catalyst of change that is always willing to take risks. Never be afraid to follow your heart in an effort to create your own steps to success. What is your bridge from mediocre to exceptional? Without obstacles and the faith to ensure we will always be ordinary and Black women are not ordinary beings! Black women worldwide, we will indeed have our say and more opportunities for the head seat at the table. Those that presented challenges, your 'unspoken words and unhealthy actions' spoke volumes and moved me up as you pushed me out. I leave a legacy through Jaelyn and Julian and the millions of Black girls that will be Black women…nurture your well-being and never hide your true self. To those that did not want to see it in print: S.A.D. T.L. Faniel, my beloved, you came at the hardest period and made me realize that it was fine to let it all go. Every life experience has shaped my perspective, but above it all there was my grandmother's wisdom, Maya Angelou's words, Psalm 27 and faith. Thank you, Jesus! With that, I graciously express gratitude to my dissertation committee, mentor, and study participants. This work will continue and my life is calling. Dr. Bemker, you pushed me to succeed, despite the years! Capella University, Dr. DeParis, Dr. Best, and all that have encountered…you have changed my life. I thank you all. Hallelujah, Amen!!!

Table of Contents

    Acknowledgments      vi

CHAPTER 1. INTRODUCTION

    Introduction to the Problem      1

    Background of the Study      4

    Statement of the Problem      15

    Purpose of the Study      16

    Rationale      17

    Research Question      25

    Significance of the Study      26

    Definition of Terms      30

    Assumptions and Limitations      34

    Nature of the Study      40

CHAPTER 2. LITERATURE REVIEW

    Introduction to Employment Discrimination Based on Sexual Orientation      44

    General Overview of Employment Discrimination and the LGBT Community      46

    African American Lesbians in the Workforce      49

    The Role of Heterosexism in Employment Discrimination      68

    Early Attempts at Federal Legislation      71

    Equal Employment Non-Discrimination ACT (ENDA H.R. 2015)      74

    Corporate Equality      80

    Workplace Diversity Training Programs      95

| | |
|---|---|
| Employee Burnout and Job Productivity | 121 |
| Career Development Theory | 140 |
| The Effect of Employment Discrimination on African American Lesbian Career Development | 154 |

## CHAPTER 3. METHODOLOGY

| | |
|---|---|
| Methodology Introduction | 162 |
| Research Design | 167 |
| Sampling Approach | 177 |
| Participants | 184 |
| Instrumentation and Overview | 187 |
| Data Collection | 193 |
| Data Analysis Plan | 203 |

## CHAPTER 4. DATA COLLECTION AND ANALYSIS

| | |
|---|---|
| Overview | 222 |
| Demographics | 234 |
| Coding and Emerging Themes Process | 235 |
| Voices of the Participants | 243 |
| Confirmation of Validity and Reliability | 263 |
| Summary | 265 |

## CHAPTER 5. RESULTS, CONCLUSIONS, AND RECOMMENDATIONS

| | |
|---|---|
| The Discovered Phenomenon | 270 |
| Summary Discussion of Implications and Results | 278 |
| Recommendations and Future Research | 288 |

| | |
|---|---|
| Conclusion | 312 |
| REFERENCES | 318 |
| APPENDIX A. CONSENT LETTER AND DEMOGRAPHICS FORM | 369 |
| APPENDIX B. INTERVIEW GUIDE QUESTIONS | 377 |

CHAPTER 1. INTRODUCTION

Introduction to the Problem

Herr and Cramer (1996) stated "sexual preference should have an effect on career development and choice is, in many ways, repugnant" (p. 292). Yet the reality is that sexual minorities may be barred from certain careers and might find vertical mobility negligible because of sexual-orientation discrimination. The negative bias against lesbian, gay, bisexual, and transgendered (LGBT) people is often more intense than that directed at any other minority group, from both institutional and individual perspectives (Coleman, 1990). Since the passage of the 1964 Civil Rights Act, which does not include sexual orientation harassment protection, organizations have devoted considerable attention to policy and research related to employment discrimination (Buchanan & Fitzgerald, 2008). However, according to Buchanan and Fitzgerald (2008), most related empirical investigations focus on the negative consequences for women without considering the potential effects of race and sexual orientation. Likewise, research exploring race in the workplace has traditionally ignored how gender and sexual orientation might influence these experiences (Buchanan &

Fitzgerald, 2008). Thus, although facing increased exposure to both sex- and race-related workplace stressors, African American women and their harassment experiences have, until very recently, been absent from the research literature (Buchanan & Fitzgerald, 2008). Research inclusive of African American lesbian women is even more limited and as a result, little is known about the effects of experiencing multiple forms of discrimination or its contributions to vocational outcomes and career advancement.

Careful vocational and lifestyle planning might include, for example, preparing while young for an occupation in which there is a maximum of freedom from constraints such as stereotypes that are imposed by others. Vocational planning might involve restructuring one's income-producing activity later in life to enable such freedom (Shannon & Woods, 1991 and productive career development has a focus on systems or needs that do not deny, denigrate, or stigmatize forms of behavior, identity, relationship, or community that are not heterosexual (Lingiardi & Drescher, 2003). The current research indicated that although work and careers are critical for lesbians, the field of psychology has traditionally paid little attention to the career counseling issues with them (Gedro, 2006). Little attention has been paid to issues affecting lesbian careers and Bierema (2002) noted that as a discipline, human resources "has not vigorously studied diversity, equality, power, heterosexism, discrimination, sexism, racism, or other issues of oppression in organizations" (p. 245).

There was little research found on the lesbian labor force and its career development needs, and much of the related data was older and reflected timeframes of more than 10 years ago with a heavier reference to sexual harassment. In addition, minimal data were located on the uniqueness, or triple jeopardy, of those who identify as African American, lesbian, and female. The apparent lack of studies in empirical literature addressing African American lesbians points to the need for data relative to vocational mental health services for this group Van Puymbroeck (2002) found (a) that the effects on career development of ethnic or sexual minority status are not simply additive but interactive and (b) that gender plays a defining role. This additional data may lead to an understanding of the possible limitations of the glass ceiling (Redwood, 1996) and the effects of homophobia on career advancement.

History revealed limited career opportunities and discrimination toward minorities, including women and has an effect on African American lesbians' career advancement (Redwood, 1996). The existence of a glass ceiling in the workforce has been validated for many women and minorities of color (Redwood, 1996). Additional research is needed to begin to understand the barriers that are experienced by African American lesbians when trying to advance in their careers (Redwood, 1996).

A review of the literature shows that structural diversity for LGBT-related problems exists in many workplaces. Many gay men and lesbians fear that revealing their sexual orientation will inhibit their ability to remain employed or to advance in their organization (Irwin, 1999). In a 1993 study, the National Defense Research Institute found that many heterosexual individuals feel uncomfortable working alongside a gay person. However, the research to date fails to address possible effect of sexual orientation on career advancement, the penetration of the glass ceiling for women and minorities, or the "pink ceiling" for LGBT individuals. Sally Susman, Executive Vice President of Global Communications for Estée Lauder New York Companies Inc., stated that the pink ceiling is "that intangible barrier" that experts say keeps LGBT professionals out of the executive offices and boardrooms of corporate America (Slobodzian, 2006). According to Slobodzian (2006) the pink ceiling is described by experts as corporate culture that blocks women, African Americans, and other minorities from reaching the top executive jobs especially if they are LGBT because of its intangible barrier for sexual minorities.

Background of the Study

Employee morale and productivity are high in work environments where individuals believe that employers value their employees (Human Rights Campaign, 2006). According to a November 2005 Gallup poll, company diversity policies are strongly and positively related to employees' satisfaction and willingness to stay with their employer as well as their inclination to recommend the employer to others (Human Rights Campaign, 2006). In comparison with the private sector, the federal government does not appear to be moving as swiftly to extend equal benefits and job protection to LGBT Americans (Human Rights Campaign, 2006). The most recent federal related bill would not only deny protections to transgender people, but also fail to protect lesbian, gay and bisexual people such as effeminate men and masculine women (Human Rights Campaign Foundation, 2007). House action resulted in an unprecedented outpouring of anger and frustration from the LGBT community and over 350 organizations who oppose this ENDA version (Human Rights Campaign Foundation, 2007).

It is only recently that people have begun to hold candid discussions about homosexuality. Some individuals who self-identify as gay or lesbian have historically been reluctant to talk about their sexual identity (Chung, 2003). In the African American community, discussions of homosexuality were even less prevalent, and African American gay men and lesbians seemed to feel that silence would somehow alleviate the negative stigma attached to their sexual orientation (B. Greene, 1997). There is a lack of information concerning homophobia and heterosexism, in general, and heterosexism within the African American community, in particular. The effect and perception of heterosexism by gay African Americans, although vital to a total understanding of heterosexism as a phenomenon, has received only cursory treatment in the research to date. There is a need for more scientific attention to these areas of concern in an effort to understand the career advancement of African American lesbians and the possible effects of homophobia and heterosexism.

Psychosocial research regarding differing cultures, ethnicities, genders, and sexual orientation has become affirmative and less pathological over the years. However, little research specifically addressing lesbians' needs was found (B. Greene & Boyd-Franklin, 1996). Little research is available that addresses African American lesbians and how they manage their racial and sexual identity in their family and community of origin (Bowleg, Huang, Brooks, Black, & Burkholder, 2003). In fact, the literature that was located and that addresses the psychological resilience, vulnerabilities, and attitudes toward lesbians primarily focuses on White, middle-class to upper-middle-class, American population (B. Greene, 1994a, 1997; B. Greene & Boyd-Franklin, 1996). Similarly, literature regarding ethnic minority populations primarily focuses on heterosexual populations, rarely acknowledging other sexual orientations (B. Greene, 1994b, 1997). This failure to pair sexual orientation with racial identity supports the myth that African Americans and homosexuality are mutually exclusive (B. Jones, 1996). As a result, the African American lesbian population is socially invisible (B. Greene, 1994a). The lack of generalizability of studies from these two areas of literature (those including both majority and ethnic minority populations) not only leaves a void in understanding diversity within groups, but also prevents awareness of the repercussions of that void (B. Jones, 1996).

It is recognizable by the government that firing and refusing to hire or promote employees for an improper reason may be instances of discrimination (Vaid, 1996). However, whether the law considers such situations instances of discrimination is another matter. In most states, staffing is at will and the employer can fire an employee for any reason (Vaid, 1996). Reasons that prevent at will termination include those barred by federal, state, local law, or an employee–employer contract (Vaid, 1996). The attempts by the National Commission on Employment Policy to quantify the costs of discrimination suggest that taxpayers and corporations ultimately bear the cost for discrimination. Approximately 42,000 workers are dismissed each year due to their sexual orientation (Vaid, 1996). Most recently, the U.S. Department of Labor (2005) estimated that American business loses about $1 billion annually in absenteeism, low morale, and new employee training and replacement costs because of sexual orientation harassment. In terms of a current national context, coupled with there being no federal law that expressly forbids workplace discrimination against the LGBT community, less than half of all states specifically ban workplace discrimination in the private sector based on sexual orientation (Lambda Legal, 2008). According to Lambda Legal (2008), an increasing number of employers and city and local governments have enacted policies and laws to address sexual orientation discrimination, many people across the country, even where laws and policies exist, still have little recourse when they are fired or their benefits are attacked.

Legal and social discrimination against lesbians have been prevalent in America since the 1890s (Renzetti & Curran, 1992). Renzetti and Curran (1992) pointed out that "because of the stigma associated with homosexuality, gay men and lesbian women have been forced to be silent about their sexuality or suffer consequences such as imprisonment, violence, and loss of jobs" (p. 377). Researchers know little about the processes underlying the disclosure of a gay identity at work (Ragins, Singh, & Cornwell, 2007). In part, this is because research on sexual orientation in the workplace is a very new area of scholarship that needs theoretical guidance (Creed, 2006). In the United States, there is currently no federal protection or federal antidiscrimination legislation barring lesbian and gay employment discrimination (Human Rights Campaign Foundation, 2007), and sexual orientation is still not covered under Title VII of the Civil Rights Act (Human Rights Campaign Foundation, 2007).

The Glass Ceiling Commission (U.S. Department of Labor, 1991) pointed out that glass ceiling levels include employment barriers related to educational opportunities and the level of job attainment.

People who do the hiring within organizations feel most comfortable offering positions to those who look like them (Redwood, 1996), which can create a barrier manifested through conscious and unconscious stereotyping and bias. Redwood (1996) noted that stereotypes must be met with hard data because, if not discussed and then eliminated, they become factual in the popular mind and reinforce the glass ceiling barriers.

Disaggregation of hard data involves dismantling, or separating, the aggregate information and looking at the performances of specific subgroups by variables such as ethnicity or gender (Technology Alliance, 2005). Analysis of this separate data may allow researchers to focus on specific needs of the subgroup. Governmental barriers such as non-federal LGBT workplace discrimination protection and the lack of inclusion of the collection and disaggregation of employment-related data makes it difficult to ascertain the status of various groups at the managerial level (Redwood, 1996). This is often difficult given inadequate reporting and dissemination of information relevant to glass ceiling issues (Redwood, 1996). The relative absence of women and minorities in leadership positions is often attributed to organizational boundaries

(Catalyst, 2000). These are boundaries for those that can see, but not reach, the peak of corporate power, and this is the focus of the term *glass ceiling* (Cox, 1994; Morrison, White, & Van Velsor, 1987). Current research shows despite significant gains in the past 10 years, women still face an uphill battle to achieve workplace equality, a study by consultancy Accenture (2008) shows. "There actually has been tremendous progress and women are so much more visible, yet we see discrimination continuing," says Vicky Lovell of the Institute for Women's Policy Research, a nonpartisan research group in Washington (as cited in Trumbull, 2007, p.1). According to Trumbull (2007), the issue matters not just for women but the whole economy, because the underlying question is whether businesses are making the most productive use of the talent available and gender discrimination represents a failure involving nearly half the workforce.

The glass ceiling exists at the middle levels of management (U.S. Department of Labor, 1991). The result is that women are prevented from advancing beyond middle management levels in organizations on the basis of their gender rather than of any lack of ability to perform at higher levels (Fagenson, 1993; Powell & Butterfield, 1994). Although some women attain top management positions, these rare occurrences may be attributed to tokenism (Kanter, 1997). Tokenism, or the practice of hiring or appointing a select number of people from underrepresented groups in order to deflect criticism or comply with rules, enables organizations to present an illusion of fairness and access to equal promotional opportunities for their important constituencies (Cox, 1994; Kanter, 1997). Specifically, a token is defined as a member of a subgroup that makes up less than 15% of the majority group (Kanter, 2000). As tokens, women often become trapped in stereotypical roles, limiting their chances for successful performance or promotion (Kanter, 1997). Lesbians also may be seen as token employees, and thus may face greater visibility and also concerns that majority employees are spared from and that can create internal stress (Kanter, 2000). For example, they may feel isolated from other employees, left out of informal communication and support networks, or measured against other token group members, and they may fear being negatively singled out by the majority employees for being different (Kanter, 2000).

In addition, given that very little research was located on the pink ceiling (Slobodzian, 2006), this research study is designed to help discover what barriers an openly gay woman might experience when trying to penetrate the next level of career advancement in an organization. The study looks at the workplace experiences of African American lesbians and the possible perceived discrimination they have experienced in their attempts to reach higher levels of responsibilities in their organizations.

## Statement of the Problem

In reviewing studies on adult development in women, Wheeler-Scruggs (2008) found only one study that mentioned lesbian participants and as a result, very little is known about lesbian adult development, which is inclusive of career development (Wheeler-Scruggs, 2008). Lesbians face many issues that heterosexual women do not encounter, such as possible heterosexist employment discrimination while being an out lesbian at work. How these issues affect adult development in lesbians and how lesbians fit into adult development models need to be addressed. Individuals in the LGBT community often share similar experiences of prejudice and discrimination in the workplace; however, each group does face unique challenges in its identity management (Pepper & Lorah, 2008). Gomez (2005) refers to this as the continued invisibility of African American lesbians in academic and literary texts and its detriment to African American lesbian identity, professional advancement, and community.

Workforce discriminatory practices are also topic areas in literature that focus specifically on LGBT job development issues (Croteau, 1996; Croteau & Hedstrom, 1993; Driscoll, Kelley, &

Fassinger, 1996). Employment discrimination significantly influences career development and advancement decisions of LGBT populations. Although literature exists on the overall topic of employment discrimination, little research has been found examining its effects. This research was an important expansion in the literature, given the lack of research on employment discrimination and career-development paths of African American lesbians.

Purpose of the Study

The purpose of this study is to describe how the participants perceive their career development experiences. The research explored their lived experiences as out African Americans managers in the workforce or those identifying publicly as a lesbian. Research has supported the claim that career counseling is most effective when personal issues are addressed as well (Swanson, 2002). This study may lead to further research in the area of vocational counseling relative to African American lesbians and expand on the social, cultural, and psychological literature in the field. In addition, clinical, policy, and service areas may be advanced with the results of this study. It may also be useful for federal policy protection data in cases of employment discrimination. And finally, it may provide insight to African American lesbians who encountering their own career hindrances, including employment discrimination, denial of promotions, and lack of role models and mentors.

## Rationale

Although a growing body of research on career barriers exists, minimal studies to date have focused on the LGBT population. Despite recent shifts in attitudes about sexual orientation and the expansion of literature on LGBT populations, large gaps still remain (Zea, Jernewall, & Toro-Alfonso, 2003). Generally, empirical research on issues affecting LGBT people has been hampered by sampling and other methodological difficulties (Meyer, 2001). The research is also impacted by limited funding, and heterosexist norms and polices that promote the exclusion of LGBT people from mainstream research and publications (Meyer, 2001).

Relevant vocational career counseling research is usually published in psychological journals and when focusing exclusively on that research, it is apparent that there is scant empirical research on

LGBT people of color, including African Americans. An examination of this literature on LGBT people of color over a 10-year period (1992 to 2002) indicated that less than 10% of the 14,482 empirical articles published in American Psychological Association journals included LGBT samples (Jernewall & Zea, 2004). In fact, during that 10-year period there were only 124 LGBT-specific articles published in all of the American Psychological Association journals, and only six, or 0.04%, focused on people of color in general (Harper, Jernewall, & Zea, 2004). In 2004, Bowleg, Craig, and Burkholder pointed out that specific psychology theory and research on African American lesbians only included eight empirical studies that they were aware of (Battle, Cohen, Warren, Fergerson, & Audam, 2002; Bowleg et al., 2003; Cochran & Mays, 1988a; Cochran & Mays, 1994; R. Hall & Greene, 2002; Mays & Cochran, 1988; Mays, Cochran, & Rhue, 1993; Peplau, Cochran, & Mays, 1997).

Recently, there has been a call from career counseling professionals to move LGBT issues away from the margins, in an effort to counteract the dominant heterosexist discourse in the field (Croteau, Lark, Lidderdale, & Chung, 2005), which extends to career research, theory, and counseling. Although the career development of

LGBT individuals has received increased attention from researchers and theorists in recent years (Chung, 2003; Phillips, Ingram, Grant Smith, & Mindes, 2003), this area of research is still considered to be in its infancy (Croteau, Anderson, Distefano, & Kampa-Kokesch, 2000; Croteau, Lark, & Lance, 2005), and even fewer studies have focused on LGBT career development (Pope, 2000).

The fact that there has not been adequate investigation of these issues in the past may suggest the existence of a human resources development problem. Here exists a need to expand the boundaries of research orientation, research models and theories, and research foci. From an organization's perspective, this research study will be useful for two reasons. First, it will provide greater insights into the career development process of African American women and their perceptions of an organization's approaches to career development. Second, this information will help human resources programs and career counseling development. The research, in turn, would also benefit African American women in terms of providing data on a segment of an increasingly diverse workforce given women and people of color are growing in the labor market projections (Bureau of Labor Statistics, 2008).

African American women may face unsupportive environments as they progress through their career development. Research has indicated that a lack of both encouragement and discouragement may lead to a null environment (Betz, 1989). A null environment is one with little or no support, which leaves an individual with only the environmental or personal resources he or she can access (Betz, 1989). A null environment may be particularly damaging for African American women, who may find barriers in their career development. The environment may be unsupportive or hostile to their career aspirations and goals, which would weaken efficacy beliefs and outcome expectations (Betz, 1989). Even recently, it is critical to create a supportive environment where differences in background are not only recognized and accepted but also valued and where performance measures focus on productivity and skill (Catalyst, 2003b; USBE Diversity Watch, 2007).

Although generally satisfied with their career progress, African American study participants from the Catalyst research are now less hopeful than they were a few years ago about opportunities to advance (Catalyst, 2003b). The participants also feel that opportunities for African American women are declining rather than improving

(Catalyst, 2003b). Companies interested in retaining the talent of these women might consider creating open, less hierarchical work environments where differences in behavioral style are encouraged. Including these employees in decision-making, and employees initiate discussions with higher ranking employees can be vital (Catalyst, 2003b).

This research examined (a) this failure to identify and understand the problems of African American women in management and (b) the fact that African American women are seen as incapable of playing useful roles in management (Catalyst, 2003). This kind of myth may discourage the development of attitudinal aspiration among African American women that might lead to their incorporation into the professional workforce in a substantial manner. This problem also highlights the structural barriers that might impede the recruitment and development, by human resources practitioners, of substantial numbers of African American women into managerial ranks.

The research results may allow human resources practitioners to address the potential differences in how African American lesbian women approach career development. Thus, examining the specific career development experiences of African American lesbian managers would be an important contribution to the development theory by further illuminating the career process undertaken by this group as they attempt to progress in their careers. The research deliberately seeks African American lesbians who are relatively well-established in their career for the sample. The rationale for using managers in this sampling method is to explore those dynamics that contribute to the career success of African American lesbian women. It is hoped that by gaining further understanding of these phenomena, one might be able to help younger lesbian African American women and girls achieve career success.

This dissertation research study focused specifically on African American lesbians because there is currently little to no comparable research in the psychological literature. Empirical research that focuses on women has generally given minimal attention to the specific issues of importance to African American women and the ways that ethnicity and racism interact with the experience of sexism (R. Hall & Greene, 1996; C. Williams, 1999). Women of all races may be subjugated and victimized by race, class, and gender oppression (Collins, 1990). According to newer research, Deutsch (2006), oppression exists as the experience of repeated, widespread, systemic injustice and it need not be extreme. We cannot eliminate this structural oppression by getting rid of the rulers or by making some new laws, because oppressions are systematically reproduced in the major economic, political, and cultural institutions (Deutsch, 2006). However, there is little research that specifically addresses the interaction of lesbian sexual orientation with racism, sexism, homophobia, and the management of multiple identities (B. Greene, 2000) in career development. Even though the research study focused on African American women, all women of color face these vocational and career linked issues in many ways (Comas-Diaz & Greene, 1994). The research based on the psychology of women is marginally inclusive, but lesbians of color are mostly unrepresented in the scholarly literature (B. Greene, 2000) and empirical research on lesbians has focused heavily on White and middle class populations (D'Augelli & Patterson, 1995).

  This research explored the intersecting of race, gender, and sexual orientation in the lives of African American lesbians and its effects on the development of career and professional identity. This study explored the influence of sexual orientation on the career paths of lesbian managers. Results of this study may have viable implications for employers, vocational counselors, and human resources professionals. The research results may add evidence to support the importance of using effective career-development theory and techniques with African American lesbian clients.

The prevailing reality of social inequality and power imbalances can implicate internalized racism and homophobia. The effect this has on individuals' opportunities to develop their talents is important to understand as well (B. Greene, 2004). Understanding the bearing these social inequities has on one's conceptualization of who he or she is, what that person may or may not do, and what one can become is important. Systematic barriers experienced in the workplace can include gender, sexism, racism, organizational culture, and lack of diversity. This study (a) examined the possible systematic barriers that might affect the career development and professional advancement of African American lesbians and (b) increased the knowledge of lesbian vocational issues through an exploration of career barriers.

Furthermore, most of the empirical work on vocational barriers has focused on personal factors, to the exclusion of contextual factors (Lent, Brown, & Hackett, 2000). Because lesbians face both internal and external barriers, this study assessed both possible personal factors, such as lack of confidence, and contextual factors, such as sexual-orientation discrimination. This study also looked to advance the relevant research examining the effect of barriers by assessing both past and anticipated barriers such as employment discrimination as by Lent et al. (2000).

## Research Question

This research explored the meaning of the career advancement experiences of African American lesbian managers. The research question is, "How does employment discrimination, or the fear of such discrimination, affect African American lesbian managers' perceptions of their career advancement?" The study looked at the possible underlying themes and contexts accounting for the work experiences of African American lesbian managers and the effect of corporate and government policy development on African American lesbian career advancement. The research analyzed (a) how African American lesbian managers cognitively and emotionally synthesize their experiences at the workplace with preexisting thoughts and feelings about their sexuality and external perceptions and (b) how sexual-orientation disclosure might affect their career advancement and professional development.

Discriminatory practices related to career advancement for African American lesbian managers may have influenced work experiences, as well as other formative experiences, such as sexuality, gender socialization, and early work roles. Probing research interview questions (Appendix B) will include items that focus on the experience of the participants being out at work. The questions were used as a guide and are not a rigid tool that mandates that each question in the guide has to be asked or asked in the exact order listed.

## Significance of the Study

Based on the research, heterosexism, or discrimination against gay men and lesbian women, can result in harassment, loss, lack of promotion and advancement, lack of same-sex domestic partner benefits, social isolation, and other factors (Croteau, 1996). Given that in the United States, there is no federal legal protection from these antigay discriminatory practices in employment (Fassinger, 1995; House, 2004); heterosexism can influence work environments and policies, as well as interpersonal work relationships (Croteau, 1996; Waldo, 1999). Heterosexism describes an ideological discriminatory system that denies, denigrates, and stigmatizes homosexual forms of behavior, identity, relationship, or community (Herek, 1990).

This discriminatory system has significance for an estimated 1.8 million African American women in the United States who are lesbian and/or bisexual (Jackson & Greene, 2000) and thus possible victims of heterosexism. Of the 594,391 same-sex couples counted in the 2000 United States census, 34.3% of female partner households and 85,000 households are made up of African American same-sex couples or approximately 14% of all same-sex couples in the United States (National Gay and Lesbian Task Force, 2005).
Sound numbers on African American lesbians are difficult to determine, partly because of the lack of published empirical studies including this group, this may raise questions about the accuracy of the racist, sexist, and heterosexist assumptions made about this population. B. Greene (2003) referred to the need to analyze the history of discrimination of any ethnic group and to incorporate group members' own understandings of their history, oppression, and coping strategies. It is hoped that this research will help to increase the understanding of

the career advancement of African Americans lesbians in comparison with dominant cultural analyses. Those cultural analyses usually reflect White, heterosexual men and may reinforce any existing racist, heterosexist, and sexist biases. In addition, this research is significant, given that it is phenomenological in nature, which will allow the participants to reflect on and express their lived experiences.

The findings of this study may also have implications for career development research. Researchers who study the career advancement of women see a need for the development of a comprehensive career advancement theory that takes into account the gender, sex role socialization, career experiences, and learning of women (Bierema, 1994; Johnson-Faniel-Bailey & Tisdell, 1998; Schreiber, 1998). The findings from this study may lead to further research that will contribute to the development of a comprehensive theory on the career development of women, including African American lesbians. The opportunities given to women to advance in management positions are important for both individuals and organizations. Those organizations that invest in promoting women equitably are primed to be rewarded with increased productivity, improved employee attitudes, greater worker satisfaction, and greater loyalty among employees (Gilley & Eggland, 1989).

More research surrounding the career development of lesbian women is needed. Despite the large number of empirical studies conducted on the career development of minorities and women, literature on the career development of African American lesbian women was not located given its rarity. It is hoped that results of this study will enhance the research that counselors need in order to offer appropriate career counseling assistance with lesbian clients. This study can contribute to the research that can lead to even more successful career counseling to help lesbians explore their career beliefs.

Without information on the unique experiences and career needs of African American lesbians, efforts to support and enhance the psychological well-being of this population will be limited. This research can be part of a potential movement to increase the collective voice and presence of LGBT people of color through empirical research. This development of research will require the concerted effort of allies from various backgrounds, and is not only a responsibility for LGBT or ethnic minority researchers to explore separately (Harper et al., 2004).

## Definition of Terms

The following terms appear throughout the dissertation research study and are defined to ensure consistency of meaning.

*African American.* An American person who is of African or Black descent ("African American," n.d.).

*Career advancement.* Progress, growth, or acceptance in one's field of employment ("Career advancement," n.d.).

*Career development.* "An on-going process of planning and directed action toward personal work and life goals. Growth, continuous acquisition and application of one's skills. Tthe outcome of the individual's career planning and the organization's provision of support and opportunities, ideally a collaborative process" (Simonsen, 1997, p. 6).

*Career path.* "A sequence of job positions involving similar types of work and skills that employees move through in the company" (Noe, Hollenbeck, Gerhart, & Wright, 1994, p. 517).

*Discrimination.* Unfair treatment of a person or group based on prejudice ("Discrimination," n.d.).

*Employment discrimination.* Not being hired, receiving unfavorable performance evaluations, being denied promotions and wages, or losing a job due to bias based on gender, race, sexual orientation, or social-group belonging; unfair and negative treatment of workers or job applicants based on personal attributes that do not influence work performance (Pope, 1995).

*Glass ceiling.* A subtle barrier of prejudices that prevents women and minorities from moving beyond a certain level in the corporate hierarchy. The result of which can be missed promotions, working for a lower wage, and in some cases, harassment (Crampton & Mishra, 1999).

*Heterosexual.* A person whose affection and sexual orientation is for a member of the opposite sex (Alliance for Full Acceptance, 2003).

*Homophobia.* The fear, dislike, or hatred of gay men or lesbians. The Greek word *phobia* denotes an irrational fear. The word *homo* literally means the same, but the word is frequently used as a shortened form of *homosexual*. Engaging in behavior aimed at restricting the human rights of a person who has a homosexual orientation and/or who engages in homosexual behavior and having a fear, hatred, or intolerance of persons with LGBT sexual identities (Zunker, 2001).

*Homosexual.* An individual who is sexually and/or affectionately attracted to same-sex individuals (American Psychological Association, 1997).

*"In the closet".* Having a hidden sexual orientation or one differing from what others might assume. A termed used to define a person whose sexual orientation is not known to others and who identifies as gay, but is not out with his or her family, close friends, and/or coworkers (Alliance for Full Acceptance, 2003).

*LGBT.* Lesbian, gay, bisexual, and transgender (Alliance for Full Acceptance, 2003).

*Lesbian.* A woman who is a homosexual ("Lesbian," n.d.). A woman who loves another woman in an intimate manner and her sexual preference is for other women (Alliance for Full Acceptance, 2003).

*Manager.* Person in a management position who coordinates the operations of companies. Duties include formulating policies, overseeing, and planning to include supervisory responsibility and directing the work of others and taking corrective action. Typical titles include Manager, Director, and Supervisor, (Bureau of Labor Statistics, 2001).

*Organization.* A collection of parts that are highly integrated in order to accomplish an overall goal. Generally comprised of people intentionally focused on accomplishing an overall, common goal or set of goals. Business organizations can range in size from two people to tens of thousands and this includes the administrative and functional structures of the system ("Organization," n.d.).

*Out.* Identifying publicly as a gay man or a lesbian and allowing this to become publicly known. out also refers to a person's sexual orientation being known by other employees within one's company, such as the employees one supervises and one's own supervisor. Being out is a process between the person and his or her social environment and one of establishing self-image. It is a form of self-disclosure and identification sexual identity ("Out," n.d.).

*Pink ceiling.* The intangible barrier that keeps LGBT professionals out of the executive offices and boardrooms of corporate

America. *Pink* often refers to the traditional idea that "pink is for girls and blue is for boys."

*Sexual orientation.* Implies that a person has a predisposition sexually and/or affectionately toward members of the same sex. A longer lasting feeling of emotional, romantic, sexual, or affectionate type of attraction to another person that ranges from heterosexuality to bisexuality to homosexuality (American Psychological Association, 1997).

*Tokenism.* A policy or practice of limited inclusion of members of a minority group, usually creating a false appearance of inclusive practices, intentional or not ("Tokenism," n.d.). A typical example is purposely selecting a member of a minority race for a group specifically because of that person's race.

Assumptions and Limitations

Because this study used a qualitative methodology, it carries with it the limitations shared with other qualitative methodologies.

First, there were potential limitations based on the biases of the researcher. Although the researcher explicitly stated and attempted to set aside biases and expectations for this study's findings, the results of the study may reflect in part the perspectives of the researcher. Second, because of the in-depth nature of qualitative research, the sample size of this study was relatively small when compared with the larger population. This limits the extent to which the findings of the study can be applied to all African American lesbians. Further, the sample was also unique because it might be composed of women living in the same geographic area. Most important, the sample used in this study was composed of managers which might be perceived as high-achieving African American women as the researcher is attempting to ascertain a retrospective perspective of the variables that influence participants' career trajectories.

Phenomenology was important to this study because of its emphasis on understanding the interpretations of the world. A phenomenological approach attempts to construct a full interpretive description of some aspect of life and yet remain aware that lived life is always more complex than any explication of meaning can reveal. Phenomenology equates two ideas (complete reduction not being possible and full descriptions not being attainable) because a researcher must bracket past experiences and professional and theoretical assumptions in order to set aside any assumptions about life in the workplace.

The researcher acknowledged a belief that African American women face challenges in the workforce as they attempt to advance in their careers. Models of career development usually are based on the studies conducted on White men (Fassinger, 1996b). More recently, the career development of White women has been a focal point of research, but research on the career development of African American women has not. African American women are forced to choose different and more complex career paths to achieve management status (Catalyst, 2003a). The researcher's background and values influenced the decision to select the participant type. It is hoped that, as a result of this study, human resources practitioners were better able to understand the dynamics of this minority population and assist them to plan effective career development programs which can propel and equalize the career advancement of African American lesbians to their peers.

The study utilized interviews as the primary means of collecting data for a variety of reasons. Interviewing, a basic mode of qualitative inquiry, provides access to the context of experience and a way to understand the meaning of experience as constructed by the participant (Marshall & Rossman, 1995). During the interviews, it was assumed (a) that the participants were honest about their interactions with their supervisors and with those who report to them and (b) that the experiences they share will reflect the true nature of their supervisor and employee relationship.

General disadvantages of qualitative research include the following: long data-collection period; researcher bias; labor intensity; data overload; adequacy of sampling; credibility and quality of conclusions; reliability, or the consistency of a set of measurements; validity, or the study measuring what it claims to measure; and generalizability of findings (Miles & Huberman, 1994). Again, a major limitation of this study was the lack of generalizability comparison to other groups of lesbian women of differing ages, nationalities, ethnicities, and job levels, but generalizability is not a true factor within qualitative research. A sample drawn from a limited group may adversely affect external validity, thus the sample of eight African

American lesbians for this study will not be representative of the entire lesbian population, which includes women diverse cultural backgrounds. It is noted that researcher bias in given possible participant commonalties and the retrospective life review type of the study may also be a study limitation because of possible personal identification with the participants. In the interview, the researcher avoided speaking from the "I" and colluding with the participants, given the researcher's personal group identity.

This research might also included interviews from individuals in a particular geographic region, occupation, and population group, given the use of convenience samples, as opposed to random or probability samples. Individuals who have been subject to sexual-orientation discrimination may be more likely to participate in the research, which would skew the rate of discrimination reported. Therefore, the study did not necessarily apply findings to all LGBT individuals or to all African American lesbian managers.

Another limitation related to the research's reliance on perceptions of discrimination is worth noting because people's perceptions may not be accurate measures of actual discrimination. For example, individuals may misperceive employers' motivations behind hiring and promotion decisions, ascribing discriminatory motives to employers when none exist. Alternatively, employers may conceal their discriminatory motives so that LGBT individuals perceive less discrimination than actually exists. The study may also be limited by the participation criteria (e.g., the fact that participants must to be out at the workplace). Participants may not be willing to discuss their life experiences and/or work interactions relative to career advancement if there is a fear of job loss or repercussions from study participation.

The overall advantage of this qualitative method is the ability to learn from the participants' lived experiences, and participant feedback is a method of increasing interpretive validity within the study. Other advantages to the qualitative method include its allowing the researcher to explore this new area of research and build upon theory. The overall purpose of qualitative research is to explore and describe socially constructed realities (Denzen & Lincoln, 1994). Validity within this qualitative constructivist paradigm is one of meaning (Moustakas, 1990). Guba and Lincoln (1994) provided two criteria for validity, "trustworthiness and authenticity" (p. 114). According to these authors, trustworthiness, or credibility, as an indication of validation in the constructivist paradigm, is an internal process in which the researcher creates legitimacy through credibility. A researcher can require validation, objectivity, and reliability. They further state that authenticity, defined as fairness, addresses the question of validity. Authenticity also leads to improved understanding of constructions of others and was relevant to this phenomenological study, given that it examined the lived experiences of the participants.

## Nature of the Study

This study explored the challenges that African American lesbian managers may experience in terms of career advancement and the strategies, if any, they employ to cope with the resulting conflicts. This study was accomplished through the use of a qualitative, phenomenological approach with multiple in-depth, semi-structured participant interviews (Appendix A) to search for meaning units. All interviews were audio taped and transcribed verbatim. Themes were then extracted from the transcripts by following the procedure of content analysis modeled after Wong and Watt (1991). ATLAS.ti software was utilized during the research (ATLAS Computer Software, Berlin, Germany: Student Version). During the initial step, all statements were grouped into themes to ensure that each one has a coherent and complete meaning. The second step was to identify all themes relevant to the research question. The third step was to code all statements relevant to the research question; the label attributed to each statement will need to accurately reflect its meaning. The fourth step includedwere grouping similar labels into themes. This fourth step involved a series of revisions and was guided by both the content of the oral data as well as the literature and use of software.

According to Moustakas (1994), qualitative research uncovers human experiences, engages the participant, and creates a comprehensive rendering of the experience. The research will use prepared interview questions; however, according to Pollio (1997), questions can also flow from dialogue, rather than being predetermined, to help show the essence of the participant's experiences. The research interview used open-ended, semi-structured questions, with these probing questions available as a guide, to explore the life experiences of African American lesbians in the workforce and will also allow for free-flow interactions.

The phenomenological approach was used in this study with multiple-participant research, which allowed for the strength of inference to be made once factors recurred with more than one of the eight participants. Interviews were conducted with managers who are currently employed or who retired within two years prior to the interview date. These African American women were asked to talk about their challenges and experiences related to their personal and professional experiences as lesbians in the workforce. Themes emerged from the research data on the basis of the participants' challenges and experiences. This information, in turn, will add to the literature so that institutions may become increasingly supportive, reducing the challenges that hinder the career advancement of African American lesbians.

A phenomenological approach was appropriate, given that there is little known about the topic. Phenomenological studies allow the researcher to understand an experience from the participant's point of view, given that it explored lived social realities of those who experience, perceive, and construct those realities (Creswell, 1994). The research was set to use a minimum of 8 and a maximum of 12 participants. Requirements for participation in this study were for each woman to (a) define herself as African American; (b) define herself as an out lesbian, not bisexual or transgender; (c) be currently or previously employed as a manager; and (d) be between the ages of 32 and 72 years old, to allow for progressive work experience and managerial level growth and progression.

# CHAPTER 2. LITERATURE REVIEW

## Introduction to Employment Discrimination Based on Sexual Orientation

According to major studies, the number of LGBT people in the United States is estimated to be between 13 million and 17 million (U.S. Census, 2004). The percentage of LGBT people in the United States ranges from 3% to 10% of the total population (U.S. Census, 2004). According to the 2004 U.S. Census data, both market and social science researchers concede that the number is an estimate of the actual LGBT population. There is no way to derive a true count given the challenge of relying on self-identification to extrapolate a figure; however, 7% of various study respondents consistently self-identify as LGBT individuals (U.S. Census, 2004). In the past, the percentage of gay and lesbian people was believed to be 10% of the general U.S. population. That figure was originally derived from various studies conducted by sexual behavior researcher Alfred Kinsey in the 1930s and 1940s (U.S. Census, 2004), which found 10% of research subjects to be exclusively gay. In a follow-up study conducted by Kinsey in the 1950s, 2% to 6% of women were found to be exclusively lesbian

(U.S. Census, 2004). According to 2004 U.S. Census data the percentages of gay men and lesbians presented by Kinsey's research were proven unreliable because of the researcher's sampling methods; however, according to data from *Advertising Age Magazine* (Gardyn, 2001), up to 10% of the population in urban markets, where large populations of LGBT people reside, identify themselves as gay (U.S. Census, 2004).

One of the most important career decisions faced by gay men and lesbians is whether to disclose their sexual orientation to others in the workplace. Most gay men and lesbians limit the disclosure of their sexual identity at work, and up to one third do not disclose their sexual orientation to anyone at work (Croteau, 1996). Eighty-one percent of lesbian women fear they would be the victims of employment discrimination if they came out at work (Carr-Ruffino, 2002). This appears to be a valid concern, as one third of gay men and lesbians who have come out say that they have experienced some form of employment discrimination (Carr-Ruffino, 2002).

According to Snyder (2003), there are five specific types of discrimination against gay men and lesbians that occur in the workplace. These are (a) offensive language, or the or occasional instances of verbal antigay references in the form of innuendo, jokes, or personal opinion statements that demean any member because of their sexual orientation; (b) offensive materials, including single or occasional instances of posting antigay notes, newspaper articles, flyers, or religious slogans in public or private workplace spaces; (c) persistent harassment, or continual acts of antigay behavior, including offensive jokes, language, or posting antigay literature or materials, that seek to demean a member of the gay community; (d) overt hostility and acts or events that threaten, intimidate, or discriminate against a person because of his or her sexual orientation; and (e) severe aggression or any act or event that jeopardizes the physical or mental well-being of an employee because of his or her sexual orientation.

## General Overview of Employment Discrimination and the LGBT Community

Irwin (1999) demonstrated the prevalence of workplace discrimination and prejudicial treatment of LGBT people on the basis of their sexual orientation. In Irwin's study based on workforce discrimination and homophonic harassment, 59% (532) of the 900 LGBT participants reported behaviors including sexual and physical assault, verbal harassment and abuse, destruction of property, ridicule, and homophobic jokes. Participants had experienced some form of discrimination or prejudicial treatment at some time in their working life, and for 52%, this discrimination was in their current employment situation. For many, it was not a single incident but continuous, and it affected the way they felt not only about their colleagues and employers but also about themselves (Irwin, 1999). The study found that prejudicial treatment in the workplace included unfair rosters of shift work preference, unreasonable work expectations, undermining of work, and limitations on career advancement (Irwin, 1999).

According to several national public polls (National Defense Research Institute, 1993) a majority of heterosexual American workers also reported being uncomfortable with the idea of working with gay men and/or lesbians, and similarly, according to a *Wall Street Journal* survey, 66% of surveyed CEOs reported being reluctant to include a gay man or a lesbian on a management committee (Neely-Martinez, 1993). When respondents were confronted with the issue of working with gay men or lesbians, one study found that 27% said they would "prefer not to," and 25% said they would "strongly object" (National Defense Research Institute, 1993). Recently, in 2006, 24% of heterosexuals surveyed by Harris Interactive said that they would feel uncomfortable if any of their coworkers were openly LGBT (Out & Equal Workplace Advocates, 2006), indicating little change in those 14 years. The study shows that only half (51%) of heterosexuals feel that LGBT people are treated fairly and equally in their workplace (Out & Equal Workplace Advocates, 2006). Given the fact that 25% to 66% of gay men and lesbians experience workplace discrimination based on their sexual orientation (Croteau, 1996), the decision to be out at work is not an easy decision and is often preceded by anxiety and fears of rejection and discrimination (Friskopp & Silverstein, 1996; Woods, 1994). The fear of negative consequences of disclosure may have a greater effect on the psychological health and well-being of gay men and lesbians than does the decision of disclosing sexual orientation, which often brings them a sense of relief (Friskopp & Silverstein, 1996; Woods, 1994). Gay men and lesbians constitute between 4% and 17% of the workforce (Gonsiorek & Weinrich, 1991), a larger proportion than many other minority groups, and a Society for Human Resource Management (2001) survey found at least 10% of the workforce is gay or lesbian, a consistent pattern with older research data.

According to Out and Equal (2007), an overwhelming majority, 79%, of heterosexuals feel that how an employee does his or her job, and not their sexual orientation, should be the standard for judging an employee. Recently, 51% of gay men and lesbian employees say they hear homophobic comments at work and 15% say they were harassed on the job by co-workers (Out and Equal, 2007).

## African American Lesbians in the Workforce

*Gender and Racial Inequity*

This section addresses gender and racial identity, the second addresses sexual identity for African American women, and the third addresses factors specific to their workforce experiences. It is important to gain insights into one of the most important career decisions faced by this under-studied population.

African American lesbians represent both a sexual and an ethnic minority and are thus at risk of experiencing discrimination and oppression (S. White & Shoffner, 2002). According to research this oppression can lead to limited access to resources, risk of employment discrimination, risk of heterosexism and/or gender oppression, and because of their triple stigmatization, a higher risk of psychological distress than other groups (Cochran & Mays, 1994). Equitable pay, positive working relationships, and professional advancement opportunities are a few of the needs that may go unsatisfied for women who are openly lesbian at the workplace (S. White & Shoffner, 2002).

Recent employment discrimination literature points to more progress being made for women, but most women continue to work in jobs stereotyped as female jobs, and women in nearly all job categories receive less pay than comparable males (*Hidden barriers*, 2008). Women face limits on promotion to high level management positions because of bias, and continue to experience sexual harassment on the job despite increased employer awareness of their obligation to take preventive and corrective action (*Hidden barriers*, 2008). According to *Hidden barriers* (2008), pregnant women suffer from discrimination in hiring, promotion, and job performance evaluation because of false assumptions about their ability to work, and women with family care giving responsibilities are disadvantaged by employer insensitivity to the family responsibilities of their employees. White men are also twice as likely to get management jobs as equally qualified African

American men; three times as likely as African American women (Ryan & Elliot, 2004). Women of color are particularly vulnerable to discrimination in the workplace because they face a combination of racial and sexual barriers (*Hidden barriers*, 2008). Research has noted that African American women are more likely than White women to share a number of socioeconomic conditions that place them at greater risk for depression, such as discrimination, lower educational and income levels, high-stress jobs, unemployment, poor health, larger family sizes, and more (Abu-Bader and Crewe, 2006).

A review of literature suggested that employment discrimination affects many groups of people, specifically African Americans ("Workplace barriers," 2008). According to a Kelly HR Services study, 30% of African American employees in the Diversity in the Workplace Study report experienced discriminatory treatment at work (USBE Diversity Watch, 2007). The study focused on many diverse segments also including African Americans, women, and LGBT workers and 45% of African American workers reported dissatisfaction with career progress. LGBT employees reported the highest incidence with 60% having experienced discrimination or unfair treatment in the workplace at least once a month, the highest incidents of all diverse segments surveyed (USBE Diversity Watch, 2007). "While employers have come a considerable way in implementing fair and equal workplace practices, this study indicated that there is still much room for improvement and it is critical that policies and programs be championed by senior management and communicated to all employees." said Rosemary Haefner, VP, HR for CareerBuilder.com (USBE Diversity Watch, 2007).

Lesbians can potentially encounter job discrimination related to both sexism and heterosexism. Lesbians face at least a double minority status, or more, if they also belong to other devalued groups (Laird, 1994), such as being a member of racial minority group. A review of the literature revealed that women and ethnic minorities have consistently been found to perceive either more barriers or different types of barriers than do men and Whites (Luzzo, 1996a, 1996b; McWhirter, 1997). Along this line, studies examining one's perceived ability to overcome barriers have revealed lower self-esteem for ethnic minorities (Luzzo, 1996a, 1996b; McWhirter, 1997).

African American lesbians are racial minorities and have multiple stigmatized identities. They are affected by institutional or public organizational patterns of prejudice such as racism and sexism, joined with homophobia, in the workforce (Ragins & Cornwell, 2001). Ethical practices, diversity initiatives, and management support are important aspects to the elimination of negative employment-related issues of African American lesbians. Even though literature on the topic of employment discrimination exists (Unity First, 2002), little work has been found that examined the effect of employment discrimination and the career development paths of African American lesbians.

Homophobia in ethnic populations exists for several reasons: (a) A homosexual orientation is often viewed as a preference or a choice; (b) homosexuality is considered a product or a defect of the dominant culture (B. Jones, 1996); (c) there is a fear that gay men and lesbians will reflect negatively on the culture of the given ethnic group; and (d) there is a perceived threat that homosexuality will contribute to the extinction one's race or ethnicity (Leslie, 1995).

In regards to sexual identity homophobic-based discrimination, or heterosexism, in the workplace can involve job loss, lack of promotion and advancement, harassment, lack of partner benefits, and social isolation (Fassinger, 1995; House, 2004). Neisen (1990) described heterosexism as "a form of oppression" and the "subordination of all non-heterosexual lifestyles" (p. 37). Homophobia can influence work environments, work policies, and interpersonal relationships at work (Croteau, 1996) and is a significant career issue for lesbians (Herek, 1991). Lesbians have recognized that being out at work can have any number of negative personal or professional consequences (Herek, 1991). Such heterosexism in the workplace has implications for women's mental health (Croteau, 1996); physical health and safety from violence at work (Comstock, 1991); financial losses, such as ineligibility for certain benefits; and loss of job and career opportunities (Dunne, 1997; Fassinger, 1995).

According to the *Survey of the African American Community* (Gay and Lesbian Victory Foundation, 2001), for women, the three most important issues facing LGBT African Americans were (a) HIV/AIDS, (b) hate crime violence, and (c) marriage and domestic partnership. For gay and bisexual men, the three issues were (a) HIV/AIDS, (b) hate crime violence, and (c) health care. For transgendered respondents, both male and female, the three issues were (a) a tie between HIV/AIDS and job discrimination and/or lack of jobs, (b) hate crime violence, and (c) drugs. Political issues, including employment discrimination, affect all groups. Fear of hate crime and job discrimination reinforce the need for effective diversity initiatives in the workplace, especially given that the United States does not offer federal protection for discrimination based on sexual orientation (Gay and Lesbian Victory Foundation, 2001). There have also been several significant racial discrimination class action suits including those against Texaco, which paid $176.1 million, and Coca-Cola, which paid $192.5 million, to settle racial discrimination litigation race imposes billions of dollars in macroeconomic costs annually in the United States (Sarra, 2005). 2004 marked a year filled with numerous sizable settlements for racial discrimination claims, some involving high-profile companies. For example, Abercrombie & Fitch Stores, Inc. settled three lawsuits for some $50 million alleging that the company had discriminated against minorities and females in its hiring practices (Ethics & Legal Compliance, 2008). Similarly, in October, a federal judge in Illinois gave preliminary approval to a $15 million settlement between R.R. Donnelley & Sons and a group of former employees who had alleged race discrimination (Ethics & Legal Compliance, 2008). The latter suit had previously made its way to the United States Supreme Court, where the Court ruled that the federal four-year statute of limitations should be applied to claims

(Ethics & Legal Compliance, 2008). In the public sector, a New York district court approved a settlement establishing a $20 million compensation fund for New York City Police Department Latino and African American police officers who had alleged racial discrimination by the NYPD (Ethics & Legal Compliance, 2008). The ConocoPhillips Company removed sexual orientation from Conoco's nondiscrimination statement after merging with Phillips Petroleum Company in 2002, but then moved to restore the category a few months later. The change of heart came just days after HRC issued a press release condemning the corporation (Raeburn, 2004).

Swim, Hyers, Fitzgerald, and Bylsma (2003) found that African Americans experience small daily racial hassles more frequently than egregious racial events, but, nonetheless, these daily events are stressful. Racism has had emotional, political, and economic impacts on African Americans. In much the same way, there are long-term effects on adults who as children realized they were attracted to same-sex friends or their sexual orientation was not what was discussed as normal in their families, a phenomenon that stigmatizes them and limits their career and life options. Statewide protections against workplace discrimination exist in less than half of the United

States; in the rest of the country, employees fired for being gay have no legal recourse unless they work in a locality with its own anti-discrimination ordinance (Lambda Legal, 2008. A worker who lives in constant fear that someone will find out that he or she is a sexual minority faces institutionalized forms of discrimination also have economic consequences for the victims and society (Alfred, 2007). The victims earn less and therefore make reduced contributions to the tax base than they might have otherwise (Alfred, 2007).

African American women have seen many advances in their economic status, and as a group, they have increased their educational attainment more quickly than White women (Alfred, 2007). Yet, they continue to earn considerably less than White and Asian women in the United States, and they have the lowest rate of employment in professional and managerial occupations of any group besides Hispanics (Ciazza, Shaw, & Werschkul, 2004). Moreover, Ciazza et al. (2004) found African American women to experience some of the highest poverty rates in the United States. Several reasons have been cited for their economic conditions. These include discrimination in hiring and promotion, occupational segregation by race and gender, and differences in access to higher education (Neubeck & Cazenave, 2002).

Specific barriers facing African American women in business include negative, race-based stereotypes; more frequent questioning of their credibility and authority; and a lack of institutional support (Catalyst, 2003a). African American women experience a "double outsider" status, unlike White women or African American men, who share gender or race in common with most colleagues or managers. African American women report (a) exclusion from informal networks and (b) conflicted relationships with White women among the challenges they face (Catalyst, 2004a). Women constitute nearly half of the Unites States workforce, yet they experience discrimination that influences their position, pay, and promotions. White women, however, do fare better than women of color, who often receive lesser wages, fewer jobs, and less frequent promotions (Hackett & Byars, 1996). For example, Lach (1999) reported, on a Catalyst study of more than 1,700 professional women of color, that only 47% feel their advancement opportunities have improved over the past five years, compared with 60% of White women. Moreover, only 22% felt their boss was trained to manage a diverse workforce.

Although approximately 75% of Fortune 500 companies have formally stated diversity programs, only 33% of the African American women surveyed believe that these programs effectively create supportive environments (Catalyst, 2003a). Catalyst (2003a), tracked a group of managers who were women of color, over 3 years after the initial Catalyst study to chart their career movement and outline their steps to success. Although current job and career satisfaction was high, these women do perceive a decline in opportunities to advance to senior leadership and were less satisfied with their prospects for further advancement with their current employer (Catalyst, 2003a).

The expected increase of African American women in the labor force between 1994 and 2014 is 39%, (Catalyst, 2002) and will affect the number of African American lesbians entering the workforce. African American women represent an important and growing source of talent (Catalyst, 2002), yet they currently represent only 1.1% of corporate officers in Fortune 500 companies, a mere 106 African American women out of a group of over 2,140 female corporate officers consisting of CEOs, CFOs, and Counsels (Catalyst, 2002)

Although the percentage of women among the highest-paid corporate officers has increased in small increments over the last five years, the number of women of color among that group remains stagnant (Scott, 2001).

Employment discrimination, or the fear of such discrimination, has limited the career advancement of African American lesbian women (B. Greene, 1997, 2004). Catalyst (1999) reported that the percentage of women in top corporate jobs had increased only 4% in five years, an increase below most expectations, with the small increase due to only a few women being prepared for top leadership positions and a minimal amount of them being African American women (Catalyst, 1999).

Although African American women are advancing, there remains a significant income gap for the majority of African American women, whose average annual earnings are lower than those of African American men, White men, or White women (Catalyst, 2002). African American women are behind on many indicators of American success, including economic and wage parity; and whereas women in general earn 72% of men's salaries, even after controlling for work experience, education, and merit, African American women earn even less—only 60% of men's salaries (Catalyst, 2002). According to Browne (1999), analyses by the Lawyers Committee for Civil Rights, White women and African American men must work about eight months to earn a salary equal to what White men earn in six months, and African American women must work 10 months to earn a comparable salary (Browne, 1999).

*Striving for Managerial Status*

In regards to workforce experiences women of color have made great strides in terms of gaining access to management positions in municipal governments, and that is a major source of economic progress for members of traditionally disadvantaged groups (Kerr, Miller, & Reid, 2002). Unfortunately, this progress may not equate greater federal responsiveness to the policy concerns of the traditionally disadvantaged or descriptive representation (V. Greene, Selden, & Brewer, 2001). Focusing on municipal bureaucracies is especially relevant because city governments are more directly involved in the daily lives of traditionally disadvantaged residents than are most state and federal agencies (G. Hall & Saltzstein, 1975). One indicator of the assimilation of traditionally disadvantaged groups into society as a whole is widespread access to attractive employment opportunities (Welch & Seigelman, 2000), but according to the research, women of color tend to be disproportionately represented on welfare rolls and in low-paying occupations (Kerr et al., 2002).

African American women may often deal with attitudes in the workplace that White women will not encounter, such as ethnic stereotyping and racial prejudice (Browne, 1999). Hunter (1991) argued that minority women are subjected to both gender and racial inequalities and discrimination, and that discriminatory burdens are heavier for minority women than for any other group, including minority men. This claim is supported by empirical findings in the literature (Dometrius & Sigelman, 1984; V. Greene et al., 2001; Naff, 2001; Welch, Karnig, & Eribes, 1983). According to *Women of Color in Corporate Management: Opportunities and Barriers* (Catalyst, 1999), 40% cite the lack of informal networking with influential colleagues, 29% note the lack of company role models who are members of their racial or ethnic group, and 28% speak of the lack of high-visibility assignments.

Even though African American professionals indicate greater achievement of success with the presence of mentoring (Palmer &

Johnson-Faniel-Bailey, 2005), African American mentoring relationships have remained largely undefined, and there is an absence of a theory-based African American mentoring success model framework. In a survey (Catalyst, 2003b) of over 1,700 women of color and African American women from 30 leading U.S. companies, 47% of respondents cited the difficulty of not having an influential mentor or sponsor as a barrier. Fifty-eight percent reported having a mentor, and that figure is up from 38% in 1998. Seven out of 10 women of color who had a mentor in 1998 have since had a promotion and moreover, Catalyst (2003b) found that the more mentors a woman has, the faster she moves up the corporate ladder into managerial positions. Obtaining a larger share of these managerial positions may lead to greater responsiveness on the part of policy makers to the policy concerns of the traditionally disadvantaged and those groups that may fall victim to employment discrimination (Herbert, 1974). The current literature on career development consistently reflects the lack of role models as negatively affecting career development, particularly of lesbians and because lesbians generally remain closeted at work, they cannot serve as role models for other lesbians (Gedro, 2006). The lack of role models reinforces the trial-and-error learning identified and discussed by Gedro, Cervero, and Johnson-Faniel-Bailey (2004).

In a study of hiring preferences, Crow, Fok, and Hartman (1998) asked 548 full-time employees in a variety of occupations, in both the public and private sectors, to rank six out of eight equivalent hypothetical candidates for a job opening. Participants were told that they were free to select any of the candidates, as consideration of hiring quotas was unnecessary. The eight hypothetical candidates were each described only as male or female, Black or White, homosexual, or heterosexual. Those candidates most likely to not be selected were the gay or lesbian candidates, as the four heterosexual candidates were always selected before the gay or lesbian candidates. The candidates least often selected were the African American gay men and women.

The results of this study suggest that heterosexism, as well as racism, continue to have a strong effect on hiring practices of African American lesbians in the workplace. Sexism and racism are linked to unemployment, underemployment, and poverty (Kerr et al., 2002). They are reciprocal, feed on each other, and perpetuate a cycle of unfulfilled aspirations among women and people of color (Kerr et al., 2002).

One area central to the career assessment of lesbians is an investigation of the heterosexist influences and barriers in environments outside of work that would discourage, inhibit, or otherwise negatively affect one's freely choosing a desired career path (Prince, 1997). Research has found that African American lesbians, compared with their White counterparts, are more likely to maintain a strong involvement with their families of origin, have children, continue contact with heterosexual peers (both women and men), and have an increased sense of "conflicting loyalties" between their ethnic culture and sexual orientation (B. Greene, 1997). In the lesbian community, however, Whiteness often manifests itself as unconscious exclusion of other races. When African American lesbians are not visible in social and political functions, the predominance of White Americans seems unremarkable, tokenism is visible, and there is an assumption that the needs and feelings of the White American lesbian community are the same for all lesbians (Leslie, 1995). A sense of tension and estrangement by African American lesbians may be reduced with diversity training and policy development (B. Greene, 1997).

*Managing Diversity in the Workplace*

Diversity, including sexual orientation, is a socially constructed concept that simply acknowledges the presence of differences (B. Greene, 2005). The more congruent a woman is with her sexual orientation, the less likely she is to express high levels of internalized shame and irrational career beliefs (Wells & Hansen, 2003).

Carr-Ruffino (2002) cited the benefits of managing diversity in the workplace, including attracting and retaining the best available human talent, increasing organizational flexibility, and increasing productivity. Gaining and keeping market share, reducing costs, improving the quality of management, and creating and innovating more powerfully were other listed benefits. Additional benefits linked to diversity management in the workplace were solving problems more effectively, contributing to social responsibility, and increasing profits. Ethical practices, diversity initiatives, and support from management are important aspects of the elimination of employment and sexual orientation discrimination issues of gay men and lesbians. With careful planning, clarity about goals, and appropriate techniques, organizations can also realize the benefits that come from valuing a diverse workforce (Day, 1995). Diversity initiatives can improve the quality of an organization's workforce and be the catalyst for a better return on investment in human capital. According to the Society for Human Resource Management (2001) diversity enhances connections with stakeholders and increases employee motivation and innovation. Moreover, a workplace that emphasizes interest and concern for its employees as people is able to attract a higher quality workforce (Society for Human Resource Management, 2001).

There is some evidence that human resources departments are not fully supporting this growing need for support of workforce diversity. For example, a sample of human resources professionals found that, even though most believed that sexual orientation should be addressed in the workplace and antigay acts spoken against, only 20% of their companies had diversity programs that specifically addressed gay and lesbian issues (Rynes & Rosen, 1995). Because sexual orientation is not a protected class at the federal legislative level, African American lesbians face additional barriers, such as the issue of the invisible minority, which many diversity management programs do not address.

The Role of Heterosexism in Employment Discrimination

A major political factor that influences employee discrimination is the fact that, in the United States, there is no federal protection or antidiscrimination legislation barring lesbian and gay employment discrimination. Heterosexism in the workplace may affect a lesbian woman's career decision making if there is perceived discrimination and this may lead one to consider a different career choice.

Racial discrimination and sexual harassment are commonplace even with diversity programs (Chapman, 2008), and employment discrimination has been a major topic in the literature concerning vocational issues of LGBT persons as well (Croteau, 1996; Croteau & Hedstrom, 1993; Driscoll et al., 1996). Employment discrimination significantly influences career development, and advancement decisions of LGBT populations, especially African American women who are often victims of additional discrimination based on race and gender (B. Greene, 1997). Sexual harassment became a major legal issue in the workplace during Judge Clarence Thomas's senate confirmation for the Supreme Court appointment, in which Anita Hill accused Judge Thomas had sexually harassed her while she was working for him (Troung & Kleiner, 2001). Since then the issue of sexual harassment has been one of the most widely discussed legal topics and over the past several years, sexual harassment discussions have encouraged people to re-examine the issue of gay rights, especially in the area of employment. The concern of equal rights for homosexuals in this area is not a new issue. Over the past several years, sexual harassment discussions have encouraged people to re-examine the issue of gay rights, especially in the area of employment. Recent developments concerning sexual orientation harassment in the workplace and highlight the current trends and attitudes toward the employment of the LGBT community. Court rulings from early sexual harassment cases, involving gay men and lesbians as plaintiffs, suggest that the law is not written to protect workers on the basis of sexual orientation but solely on the premise of gender (Troung & Kleiner, 2001).

Ragins (1997) suggested that formal heterosexism, defined as the presence of discriminatory policies and hiring and promotion procedures (Levine & Leonard, 1984), marginalizes the LGBT community, even though gay employees constitute a larger proportion of the workforce than many other minority groups (Croteau, 1996). Croteau and Lark (1995) pointed out that the lack of recognition of LGBT aspects of life by heterosexual individuals, including (a) avoiding LGBT people and issues, (b) using noninclusive language, and (c) assuming that everyone is heterosexual, is a part of informal heterosexism. Informal workplace heterosexism experiences of LGBT employees are linked to lower levels of job satisfaction (Lyons, Brenner, Bradley, & Fassinger, 2005). Research has indicated that many LGBT persons have experienced heterosexist events, including prejudice, harassment, discrimination, and violence, and that these experiences are related to adverse psychological, health, and job-related outcomes (Herek, Gillis, & Cogan, 1999; R. J. Lewis, Derlega, Berndt, Morris, & Rose, 2001; Mays, Chatters, Cochran, & Mackness, 1998).

As Garnets and D'Augelli (1994) pointed out, heterosexism fuels the disenfranchisement of lesbians and gay men by perpetuating the view that their sexual orientation is inherently flawed. Garnets and D'Augelli cited historical marginalization of lesbians and gay men, and note that it is still prevalent in many areas of the United States and has disempowered this group.

## Early Attempts at Federal Legislation

United States citizens have the right to work and not face discriminatory practices, and equality in the workplace is a right that can be protected under federal law (Human Rights Campaign Foundation, 2007). To date, there is a federal law (the Civil Rights Act) providing basic legal protection against employment discrimination based on race, age, gender, religion, national origin, or disability but no such law for sexual orientation or gender identity and gender expression (Task Force on Sexual Orientation and the Legal Workplace, 1999).

The policy of the government in the 1950s pronounced gay men and lesbians unsuitable for government employment (Peiss, 2002). Lesbians and gay men have been deemed unfit for military service in the United States and, if formally discovered, historically have been discharged (Cammermeyer, 1994). According to the Service Members Legal Defense Network, 997 service members were discharged as unfit for service under this policy in 1997 (Sobel, Westcott, Benecke, & Osburn, 2000). The United States military's current policy of "don't ask, don't tell," initiated during President

William Clinton's term in office (Halley, 1999), perpetuates inequality in the armed forces. With the military being the largest employer in the United States (American Civil Liberties Union, 2003), gay men and lesbians remain disadvantaged and in the closet, as they do in many organizations.

"The closet" has many levels, depending on how many people one has told about one's sexuality and who those people are (Signorile, 2003). Examples of being out of the closet include not caring if a straight friend sees one as an LGBT person holding hands with a lover; not hiding letters, cards, and magazines, either at home or in the office; not devising fake plans for the weekend; or not labeling a significant other as simply a friend at a company picnic. Being out of the closet allows a person to be less aware of how his or her sexuality is being perceived by others (Signorile, 2003).

American laws continue to perpetuate the inferiority and presumed criminality of gay men and lesbians according to the American Civil Liberties Union (2003) and no federal antidiscriminatory protection exists for those with a minority sexual orientation. This makes certain careers, such as teaching, even more risky for members of the gay community, as homophobic myths compound the possibility of firing based on discriminatory beliefs alone. This means that even in the absence of criminal behavior, lesbians and gay men can be fired simply for being gay, even in a nonprofit, social service, or public working setting that is not a private corporate employer. Nonprofit employers are increasingly held liable for damages stemming from employment policy negligence. They also face legal problems if they do not follow the guidelines set out in an increasingly long list of state and federal employee legislation (Thiagarajan, Hou, Cain, & Perry, 2002).

"Title VII of the Civil Rights Act of 1964 prohibits employment discrimination by private employers on the basis of race, color, religion, sex, and national origin" (U.S. Department of Labor, 1991). Since then, provisions for the prohibition of age and disability discrimination have been added. These antidiscrimination laws apply to all aspects of the employment process, including job descriptions, employment advertisements, interviews, job applications, salaries and benefits, promotions, and all decisions related to hiring and firing personnel (U.S. Department of Labor, 1991). House of Representatives Bill 14752 was introduced into the U.S. Congress in 1974. This "Gay Rights Bill," which would have added sexual orientation to the 1964

United States Civil Rights Act, would have done for gay men and lesbians what various civil rights bills such as the Americans Disabilities Act and the Voting Rights Act, did for African Americans, women, disabled, and others, but it did not pass. For the next 20 years, legislation was introduced in Congress to provide a similar prohibition on discrimination based on sexual orientation, but these efforts have failed (Human Rights Campaign Foundation, 2003). Each year the number of sponsors in both the House and Senate has grown, but until 1995, the bill had not been the subject of hearings, let alone a vote.

Equal Employment Non-Discrimination ACT (ENDA; H.R. 2015, 2007)

A civil rights victory for the LGBT community is one that will have to be won at the federal level. According to Out and Equal (2007), a Harris Interactive 2007 study among 2,868 adults, of whom 2,518 indicated they are heterosexual and 350 self-identified as LGBT, nearly 64% believe it is unfair that federal law currently allows for an employer to fire someone because they are gay or lesbian and 60% of heterosexual adults were not even aware that federal law does not provide protections for employees on the basis of sexual orientation

(Out and Equal, 2007). Despite this continued rejection of efforts to extend Title VII to sexual orientation, the stage may be finally set for addressing discrimination against lesbians and gay men in employment. This development comes in the form of the ENDA bill, first introduced to the U.S. Congress in 1994 (Human Rights Campaign Foundation, 2003). In 1995, former President Clinton guaranteed that all Americans, regardless of their sexual orientation, would be able to find and keep jobs based on their ability and supported the bill. According to the Human Rights Campaign Foundation (2003), when the bill was not enacted, it was reintroduced in 1996 as an amendment to the Defense of Marriage Act. ENDA gained a record number of 30 sponsors for a Senate bill addressing sexual-orientation discrimination (Human Rights Campaign Foundation, 2003). In the House of Representatives, Congressmen Frank and Studds introduced it with the support of over 120 sponsors (Human Rights Campaign Foundation, 2003).

ENDA would prohibit discrimination on the basis of sexual orientation, providing basic protection to ensure fairness in the workplace for Americans who are currently denied equal protection under the law (Herrscaft & Mills, 2003. ENDA would extend federal protection against employment discrimination based on sexual orientation from the protection currently provided regarding race, religion, sex, national origin, age, and disability. Thus ENDA would provide fair employment practices, but not special rights, to LGBT individuals.

ENDA, reintroduced in April 2007 as House of Representatives Bill 2015, would prohibit public and private employers, employment agencies, and unions from using a person's sexual orientation as the basis for employment decisions, such as hiring, firing, promotion, or compensation (Neuman, 2007). It would provide for the same procedures, and similar, but somewhat more limited, remedies as are permitted under both Title VII of the Civil Rights Act and the Americans With Disabilities Act. ENDA does not cover businesses with fewer than 15 employees, nor does it cover religious organizations, which include educational institutions substantially controlled or supported by religious organizations. An exception is that it covers employees whose duties pertain solely to religious organizations' activities that generate profits that are deemed taxable by the Internal Revenue Service. ENDA also does not apply to the uniformed members of the armed forces, and thus does not affect current law on lesbians and gay men in the military. ENDA does not allow for quotas or preferential treatment based on the sexual orientation of an individual, and it does not allow a disparate effect claim, as is available under Title VII of the Civil Rights Act of 1964 (Bailey, 2000).

ENDA was recenlty scheduled to move for approval by the 110th Congress to the Senate, where Senator Edward Kennedy, a Massachusetts Democrat and longtime supporter of gay-rights legislation, l introduced the same bill (Herszenhorn, 2007). The concept is of no American facing workplace discrimination because of sexual orientation, and it is a sentiment that should appeal across the political lines, but President George Bush threateneda veto (Herszenhorn, 2007). The reasons the federal government had given for opposition include it being too burdensome on organizations and it leading to a much higher rate of legal action. These reasons seem to resemble the prejudice rationale given by opponents of other civil rights legislation to pass Congress in the last 50 years (Herszenhorn, 2007). The Bush administration also pointed out the bill might weaken the Defense of Marriage Act, which defines marriage as the legal union between a man and a woman (Neuman, 2007).

A total of 19 states and the District of Columbia have laws barring discrimination based on sexual orientation, and 35 Republicans joined 200 Democrats voting for the ENDA bill, which was approved, 235 to 84 (Herszenhorn, 2007) in late 2007. Voting against the bill were 25 Democrats and 159 Republicans and Democrats, thus it fell far short of the 280 votes that would be needed to override a presidential veto (Herszenhorn, 2007). The bill's future is uncertain; according to Neuman (2007), the Senate came within 1 vote of passing similar legislation in 1996, and although sponsors say they have at least 51 votes in the Senate, 60 votes would be needed to override a threatened Republican filibuster. ENDA is currently scheduled for review under the Obama administration and with or without passage; the struggle for women of color and career advancement is real.

According to Kirby (2006), organizations and government should look to their own policies and actions to see why there is both a perception of discrimination and actual discrimination in legal protection. Additional research needs to determine how much employment discrimination is actually occurring, where it is originating and how it can be eliminated (Kirby, 2006). There are 8,276 public and private sector employers, including 130 city and county governments and 290 colleges and universities, that offer health insurance benefits for domestic partners of their employees, compared to 21 in 1989 (Hornsby, 2006), but the failure of the United States Congress to pass the Employment Discrimination Act attests to the continued lack of acceptance for the needs of gay men and lesbian women in the workplace (Rocco & Gallagher, 2006). Anxiety, fear, and tension lead to a loss of employee productivity and victims do have recourse under sexual orientation through the Equal Employment Opportunity Commission. Opponents of ENDA have argued that this bill would extend protection normally reserved for characteristics that a person cannot change, such as race, gender, and skin color (Bauer & Kleiner, (2001). This argument assumes that sexual orientation is a chosen behavior, not something you are born with. Yet legal protection has been extended to cover religious affiliations, and religion is a chosen activity (Bauer & Kleiner, 2001). Opponents also argue that ENDA is seeking special treatment for gays and lesbians, but ENDA does not include hiring quotas and it covers all sexual orientations (Bauer & Kleiner, 2001). ENDA could also lead to the reduction of sexual orientation related lawsuits (Human Rights Campaign Foundation, 2007).

Corporate Equality

In spite of the federal government's lack of action regarding antidiscrimination policies for the LGBT constituency, large Fortune 500 companies are taking on the challenge of equality. The Human Rights Campaign Foundation's Corporate Equality Index is a tool to rate large American businesses on how they are treating LGBT employees, consumers, and investors. The Equality Project, a group based in New York that monitors corporate policies and practices surrounding sexual orientation and gender identity and expression, developed the index in 1992. The index is guided by benchmarks for companies seeking to demonstrate a commitment to equal treatment of LGBT employees, consumers, and investors. The group's Corporate Equality Index ranked 319 survey respondent companies from 100% to 0% on the basis of whether they have written nondiscrimination policies. These policies cover sexual orientation and gender identity and/or expression, offer health insurance coverage to employees' same-sex domestic partners, and officially recognize and support an LGBT employee resource group or council. The policies give employee groups equal standing regardless of sexual orientation and gender identity and offer diversity training that includes sexual orientation and/or gender expression in the workplace. The policies also engage in respectful, appropriate marketing to the LGBT community and/or provide support through a corporate foundation or otherwise to LGBT or AIDS-related organizations or events and refrain from corporate actions that would undermine the goal of equal rights for LGBT people (Agrast, 2003). Recently 33% of a national sample of members of the National Gay and Lesbian Task Force, the National Latino/a Lesbian, Gay, Bisexual and Transgender Organization, and the National Black Lesbian and Gay Leadership Forum reported employment discrimination (University of California Los Angeles, 2006). A more recent Los Angeles Times poll found similar levels of support nationwide, with 72% of Americans favoring a law that would protect gay and lesbian people from job discrimination, an increase from 52% in 1993 (University of California Los Angeles, 2006). Although the gay and lesbian rights supporters encounter many difficulties while trying to improve and bring equality to their lives, it is unquestionable the progress made (Hirata & Kleiner, 2001). Many are the indications that private and public employers continue to institute policies and domestic partner benefits and more employers become aware of issues surrounding equality for gender-different employees, it is expected they will institute policies to protect these workers as well (Hirata & Kleiner, 2001). While many companies strive to promote a work environment of understanding and productivity, ignorance, prejudice and homophobia are still present and often are manifested in the form of discrimination and harassment (Hirata & Kleiner, 2001). Around the country, many employers have included, in their non-discriminating policies, specific items addressed to LGBT workers' civil rights. There are significant reasons for employers to embrace such policies and benefits. According to Hirata & Kleiner, (2001), they include competitive advantage and increased productivity. Literature which states that people are more likely to be stigmatized in organizations, industries, and jobs where passing for normal is implicitly or explicitly encouraged (Clair, Beatty, & MacLean, 2005). Individuals, universities, researchers, and governments need to continue to address stigma-based discrimination as it is evident from the findings that there is much perceived discrimination facing the LGBT community (Kirby, 2006).

Given that federal law does not currently prohibit employment discrimination based on sexual orientation or gender identity or expression, some employers have started to acknowledge that the recognition of committed same-sex relationships across the United States is better for business. Companies are now designing benefits packages that appeal to a diverse workforce, enabling them to maintain a recruitment edge and demonstrating that they value diversity.

Since at least 1995, large counts of *Fortune* 500 companies have included sexual orientation in their antidiscrimination policies (Phelps, 2003). More recently, 90% of *Fortune* 500 companies have those policies (Human Rights Campaign Foundation, 2007). The Human Rights Campaign Corporate Equality Index revealed that many of those companies have gone further in defining their actions around LGBT diversity in the workplace. The majority of companies are offering diversity training and domestic partner benefits, and companies are moving forward rapidly on these issues (Herrscaft & Mills, 2003).

In 2002, more U.S. cities and counties enacted laws to protect gay men, lesbians, and bisexual workers from discrimination than in any other year, with a total of 15 jurisdictions adding protections that extend to private sector employers (Herrscaft & Mills, 2003). As of December 31, 2002, a total of 119 U.S. cities and 23 U.S. counties prohibited discrimination based on sexual orientation in private workplaces. The number of private sector employers addressing gender identity and expression also grew at an impressive rate, with a total of 15 *Fortune* 500 companies including gender identity and/or expression in their nondiscrimination policies in 2002. This was a threefold increase from 2001, when only five companies did so (Herrscaft & Mills, 2003). In 2005, a total of 167 cities and counties prohibited discrimination based on sexual orientation in public and private employment. Nine of those jurisdictions have enacted laws since January 1, 2005, a 6% increase from 2003 (Human Rights Campaign, 2006). A total of 82 cities and counties prohibit workplace discrimination based on gender identity and/or expression, with 15 of those adding the protections since January 1, 2005, a 22% increase (Human Rights Campaign, 2006).

According to the Human Rights Campaign (2006), 254 of the *Fortune* 500 companies now provide equal benefits to same-sex couples. At the end of 2005, 430 companies in the *Fortune* 500 (86.0%) included sexual orientation in their nondiscrimination policies. Ninety-eight percent of the *Fortune* 50 (49 companies) include sexual orientation in their nondiscrimination policies (Human Rights Campaign, 2006).

Further, 10 times the number of *Fortune* 500 companies cover gender identity today as compared to 2001 (Human Rights Campaign, 2006). Seven states and the District of Columbia prohibit discrimination in private sector employment on the basis of sexual orientation and gender identity and/or expression, and three states, Illinois, Maine, and Washington, joined the list after January 1, 2005 (Human Rights Campaign, 2006). More than 11 additional states ban workplace discrimination based exclusively on sexual orientation or implemented a ban on antigay discrimination in public employment after January 1, 2005 (Human Rights Campaign, 2006).

The following states prohibit discrimination based on sexual orientation and gender identity (seven states and the District of Columbia): California (prohibited discrimination based on gender identity in 2003 and sexual orientation in 1992), Illinois (2005), Maine (2005), Minnesota (1993), New Mexico (2003), Rhode Island (gender identity, 2001; sexual orientation 1995), Washington (2006), and the District of Columbia (gender identity, 2006, sexual orientation, 1973). The following states prohibit discrimination based on sexual orientation (10 states): Connecticut (1991), Hawaii (1991), Maryland (2001), Massachusetts (1989), Nevada (1999), New Hampshire (1997), New Jersey (1992), New York (2002), Vermont (1992), and Wisconsin (1982; Human Rights Campaign, 2006). The following states have an executive order, administrative order, or personnel regulation prohibiting discrimination against public employees based on sexual orientation (8 states): Alaska (2002), Arizona (2003), Colorado (2002), Delaware (2001), Louisiana (2004), Michigan (2003), Montana (2000), and Virginia (2006). The following states have an executive order prohibiting discrimination against public employees based on sexual orientation and gender identity (two states): Indiana (2004) and Pennsylvania (2003). In the following states, courts, commissions, agencies, or attorneys general have more recently interpreted the existing state law to include some protection against discrimination for transgender individuals (eight states): Connecticut, Florida, Hawaii, Illinois, Massachusetts, New Jersey, New York, and Vermont (Human Rights Campaign, 2006).

In summary, twenty-one states, the District of Columbia, and over 140 cities and counties have enacted bans on sexual orientation discrimination and according to the Human Rights Campaign (2010), the states specifically banning sexual orientation discrimination in private employment are California, Colorado, Connecticut, Delaware, Hawaii, Illinois, Iowa, Maine, Maryland, Massachusetts, Minnesota, Nevada, New Hampshire, New Jersey, New Mexico, New York, Oregon, Rhode Island, Vermont, Washington, and Wisconsin (the first state to do so, in 1982). In addition, four states have laws prohibiting sexual orientation discrimination in public workplaces only: Indiana, Michigan, Montana, and Pennsylvania and only a few states have laws prohibiting sexual orientation discrimination in public workplaces only (Human Rights Campaign). In 29 states, it is still legal to fire someone solely because they are gay (Human Rights Campaign, 2010). Even with the state and local government progress, no federal law that disallows workplace discrimination based on sexual orientation or gender identity and/or expression (Huamn Rights Campaign, 2010).

The number of companies that publicly endorsed ENDA dramatically increased in 2002, growing from 60 to 90 companies, and that number included 43 nationally none corporations (Herrscaft & Mills, 2003). Most recently, as of September 2009, 434, or 87%, of the Fortune 500 companies had implemented non-discrimination policies that include sexual orientation (Human Rights Campaign, 2010). In 2007, the U.S. Senate Health, Education, Labor and Pensions Committee voted to send ENDA to the full Senate, the second time the bill was reported out of committee since it was originally introduced in 1994. The bill was not scheduled for action before the full Senate prior to the end of the 107th Congress, and it was then reintroduced in the 108th Congress. The bill was not passed (Human Rights Campaign Foundation, 2007), and still has not been. ENDA was introduced in the 111th Congress by Representatives Barney Frank (D-Mass.) and Ileana Ros-Lehtinen (R-Fla.) in the House. The bill was introduced in the Senate by Senators Jeff Merkley (D-Ore.) and Susan Collins (R-Maine). On September 23, 2009, the House Education and Labor Committee held a full committee hearing in the House on the legislation. On November 5, 2009, the Senate Committee on Health, Education, Labor and Pensions also held a hearing on the bill. As of January 2011, the ENDA bill still has not passed (Human Rights Campaign, 2010).

Employers are recognizing that the American family is changing, and that workplace policy centered on the traditional definition of marriage is no longer "family-friendly" (Human Rights

Campaign Foundation, 2001). According to the 2000 census, same-sex coupled households were present in 99.3% of U.S. counties. This represents an apparent jump in the number of same-sex households nationwide, up 314% from 1990, and yet still amounts to an estimated 62% undercount of the actual number of gay or lesbian couples (Human Rights Campaign Foundation, 2001). This number does not include gay people in uncoupled households. It is possible that continuing prejudice and discrimination against gay people played a role in this undercount. Continuing prejudice and discrimination against gay people are present in workplaces, as well. Two fifths of adult gay men and lesbians reported facing some form of hostility or harassment on the job, according to a national study commissioned by Out & Equal Workplace Advocates, an LGBT employee advocacy group based in a San Francisco (Human Rights Campaign Foundation, 2001). Approximately two fifths (39%) of adult lesbians and gay men in America's workplaces reported facing some form of hostility or harassment on the job in 2005, and 11% reported having experienced very frequent or frequent harassment or discrimination (Lambda Legal & Deloitte Financial Advisory Services, 2006).

The United States Constitution is a primary source of legal rights for workers. The Constitution and its amendments apply to government action, whether federal, state, or local. The United States has not arrived at the time when everyone, as an expression of diversity and equality, applauds the presence of openly gay employees. However, even in those many places in which a gay presence is not welcomed, there is a legal bar to overt hostility from the government. The 14th Amendment to the Constitution guarantees due process before being deprived of life, liberty, or property, and equal protection of the laws. It has been found that the courts have had wide latitude in interpreting how these principles apply to the rights of gay men and lesbians (G. B. Lewis & Edelson, 2000).

In an opinion poll (Letellier, 2003), it was found that 66% of *Fortune* 500 executives would hesitate to give a management position to a gay man or lesbian. Nineteen percent of LGBT employees reported barriers in promotion due to their sexual orientation or gender identity (Lambda Legal & Deloitte Financial Advisory Services, 2006), and almost 1 in 10 adult lesbians and gay men stated that they were fired or dismissed unfairly from a previous job or pressured to quit a job because of their sexual orientation (Out & Equal Workplace

Advocates, 2002). According to Letellier (2003) studies tend to undercount and understate the problem and nearly 25% of lesbians surveyed reported that they have been discriminated against in the workforce. That 25% would probably rise if more of the 81% of lesbians who conceal their sexual orientation were to come out (Letellier, 2003).

Vaid (1996) reported that businesses are not immune to heterosexism. She asserted that violence and harassment against LGBT members is widely documented, and that nearly a dozen organizations nationwide revealed that lesbian employees reported high levels of workplace discrimination. Heterosexism adds another potential layer of discrimination to the work experiences of lesbians, who also face discrimination because of gender. Heterosexist bias can exist on the organizational level or at the individual level. Hence, a workplace where heterosexism is tolerated can place a toll on lesbian workers.

Overt discrimination is affected by the organizational culture, in which policies and benefits recognize and support heterosexuals while invalidating alternative sexual orientations. One example is that spouses of married employees receive health benefits under the policies of their respective employed partners, whereas partners of lesbian and gay employees remain uninsured. Because lesbians and gay men cannot marry or be partnered under the law in almost all states in the United States, the lack of legal protection affects their level of health protection and access to health care.

Informal harassment, such as verbal abuse or other actions from coworkers, may occur because the perceived independence of lesbians upsets the status quo of traditional gender role precepts (Van den Bergh, 1994). Van den Bergh (1994) stated that heterosexism of the organizational culture can generate informal workplace discrimination, such as a company's practice of not recognizing domestic partners when special events occur. Such practices may encourage an employees' heterosexist behavior toward gay men and lesbians.

Escoffier (1975) described lesbians as discredited because of the stigma of sexual orientation. This causes discrimination beyond that experienced by heterosexual women. He further asserted that as long as heterosexism could be used as an effective tool to discredit lesbians, a number of occupational hazards could occur. These hazards include (a) lower than average incomes and slower income growth over the course of one's career, (b) occupational segregation, and (c) high rates of job dissatisfaction. Thus, heterosexism presents a dilemma for a lesbian individual; that is, whether one is able to be oneself on the job without risking negative career and financial sabotage.

In a study by Croteau and Von Destinon (1994) 249 gay men, lesbians, and bisexuals who were members of an organization of student affairs professionals were surveyed about their work experiences as they related to their sexual orientation. The data showed that 26% of the respondents' perceived discrimination related to their sexual orientation during their job search. Those who disclosed their sexual orientation during the job search were more likely to have reported experiences of discrimination. 30% of LGBT workers feel they have less career advancement opportunities than heterosexual co-workers who have the same skills and experience (USBE Diversity Watch, 2007).

Although not limited to lesbians, this study has implications for lesbians and the full LGBT community seeking employment, as heterosexism may often be present not only in the workplace but before one is hired. It seems likely that heterosexism in the workplace may be a significant factor in many lesbians' career decision making, even with the minimal progress made in recent years

In a study of 203 lesbians and their experiences with discrimination at work in and around New York City, job discrimination was experienced by nearly one quarter of the participants, whereas three fifths of the sample anticipated discrimination if their sexual orientation was known (Levine & Leonard, 1984). Discrimination on the job came from both formal and informal sources. Formal types of discrimination included action to restrict advancement officially connected with the job, such as money, promotions, and increased job responsibilities. Informal discrimination included unofficial actions by coworkers and supervisors, including verbal harassment. Some who anticipated harassment had observed it occurring with coworkers previously. Respondents admitted that heterosexism in the workplace was a great concern. Furthermore, those working in public institutions anticipated more discrimination than did those in private settings, although at the end of the study, the latter group actually reported experiencing more discrimination. This finding suggested that prevalent discriminatory practices are an issue not just for those in public and nonprofit sectors but for those in private industries as well.

## Workplace Diversity Training Programs

A national Diversity and Employment Gallup survey of more than 1,250 employees, released December 8, 2005, focused on workplace discrimination. It included a seven-question section that attempted to assess the value of workplace diversity programs (Leonard & Levine, 2006). The results indicated that employee satisfaction and retention are linked closely with the way employers manage and promote their diversity programs (Leonard & Levine, 2006). The Equal Employment Opportunity Commission's preliminary charge data show that employment discrimination continues to be a significant problem in the 21st century workplace and 82.5% of the charges were brought by African Americans and the overall figures were higher for women (U.S. Department of Labor, 2005). Fifteen percent of Gallup survey respondents reported that they had experienced some form of discrimination in the workplace over the previous 18 months, and the results reflect a need for employers to provide education on workplace bias and to strive to improve awareness of workplace diversity issues (Leonard & Levine, 2006). Indeed, Gallup researchers have discovered that organizations with high levels of employee satisfaction and retention also tend to have strong and well-run diversity programs (Leonard & Levine, 2006). Thus, to be effective in making the case for diversity programs to senior management, one should use this type of compelling data, which relates to their worldview. Notably, diversity programs are not evaluated just in terms of return on investment but must also be accepted as an integral part of an organization's strategic plan (Leonard & Levine, 2006). According to Major and Sinclair (1994), to be fully integrated and plausible, diversity in all areas such as race, sexual orientation, gender, and disability, needs to be systemic, accessible, practiced, and recognized throughout the company for its benefits.

The first question a CEO typically asks when setting up a diversity management program is "What will be the return on this program, and how do we measure it?" according to Anita Rowe, partner in the management consulting firm of Gardenswartz & Rowe in Los Angeles (Rowe & Gardenswartz, 1999). Diversity can be a hard thing to quantify in terms that senior management wants to see, as they want to understand how it contributes to the bottom line. As Rowe pointed out, data and research into the value of workplace diversity programs is lacking and mostly anecdotal (Rowe & Gardenswartz, 1999).

Workplace diversity and fair employment practices have a strong focus upon risk management implications, more specifically the liability exposure created when a firm fails to meet its fair employment obligations to employees (Sandroff, 1988). Rather than focusing on the potential costs involved with wrongdoing, perhaps insight could be gained by examining the benefits accrued by firms that embrace diversity. According to Sandroff (1988), in today's litigious society, nearly all of a firm's relationships provide a potential source of legal liability; the organization's relationship to current, former, and potential employees is certainly no exception. An organization's employment practice liability is an area of tremendous concern for nearly every organization, as decisions regarding hiring, firing, pay, promotion, and layoffs are potential sources of employment practices claims (Sandroff, 1988). These claims typically involve one or more of the following charges: (a) discrimination, (b) harassment, or (c) wrongful termination (Sandroff, 1988). Shareholders of an organization involved in employment practices litigation can suffer a loss with respect to the direct costs associated with litigation (Sandroff, 1988).

Employment practice claims typically necessitate a costly legal defense, as employment law cases can frequently take many years to reach resolution. They are also more subtle than court judgments or out-of-court settlements. One study indicated that sexual harassment alone cost the typical Fortune 500 Company $6.7 million per year in absenteeism, employee turnover, low morale, and low productivity (Sandroff, 1988). Litigation regarding harassment affects all employees and reflects on their safety as well. Given that almost half (45%) of LGBT adults feel that they, as a group, are often discriminated against at work (Unity First, 2002), managers must focus on increasing morale, reducing the possibility of workplace violence, and promoting EAPs or employee assistance programs (Martinez, 1996). The level of sophistication of the human resources department may also affect the employment practices risk.

According to Martinez (1996), a large firm should enjoy a greater degree of expertise and sophistication within its human resources function, have more experience handling and resolving employment practices disputes, and be more likely to have written, formalized employment practices. Companies should look beyond immediate needs and identify trends, such as diversity, that can and will affect the business (Martinez, 1996). In contrast; smaller companies as well as some nonprofit employers are more likely to have employment practices that are much less sophisticated than that of a larger firm. An owner or manager for a smaller firm is very likely to possess a great deal of specialized knowledge regarding the firm's particular business area but may not have a great deal of expertise in handling employment practices issues. A higher degree of formalization and a promotion of ethical standards may create an employment environment where manager duties are more clearly defined and a greater awareness of employment practices and diversity issues is cultivated and risk is reduced (J. Jones, 1996).

Many LGBT Americans are denied job opportunities, discriminated against, and/or terminated for reasons that have nothing to do with their performance and abilities (National Conference for Community and Justice, 2002). Currently, no federal protection exists for those who have experienced this form of employment discrimination, as the Constitution has been interpreted by the courts to offer no civil rights protections for the LGBT community (American Civil Liberties Union, 2002). Although some states have antidiscrimination policies that protect lesbians, gay men, and bisexual individuals, many of these policies could be better (American Civil Liberties Union, 2002).

According to Willmott (2003), many employers do not treat people in a manner consistent with motivating them to contribute to business success. Thus, employers have a unique opportunity to shape government guidance aimed at helping organizations prove the link between their people-management policies and the bottom line (Willmott, 2003). According to Adams (1998), clear, effective communication in organizations is a critical, yet often overlooked, aspect of the diversity process. If well done, it can dispel myths, help avoid backlash, and position a company and its employees for success. On the other hand, poorly handled communication can mislead staff and the communities, create obstacles, and even doom efforts from the start. Some of the essential aspects of effective initial communication about diversity include (a) explaining the business case, (b) building on existing values and vision, (c) showing staff what is in it for them,

(d) spelling out an inclusive definition of diversity, (e) explaining the process, and (f) demonstrating commitment (Adams, 1998).

According to McMahon (2002), diversity practices are best delineated when an organization gathers data on its existing diversity activities; keeps an electronic log of achievements, including ad hoc diversity practices; and develops a list of programs already in place. The log can include ad hoc diversity practices; review key documents that give the organization identity and shape its image, internally and externally; review existing data and revenue, as cost and utilization reports often can be used to provide preliminary business effect information about current practices that have diversity relevance; and benchmark the organization's practices. These practices allow organizations to begin the formal process of connecting diversity assessment to the organizational mission and core values while keeping systematic records of organizational outcomes, performance trends, and personnel patterns. Once a plan is in place, diversity practices should be communicated to all stakeholders and the findings of even preliminary assessment steps made available (McMahon, 2002).

Diversity training consists of interaction with multiple types of individuals in a manner that acknowledges and appreciates all of the similarities and differences that they bring to the table. Affirmative action and equal employment opportunity are government mandated, but the achievement of diversity is not. Diversity itself requires a company's motivation to form more inclusive policies that will add to its strength in the marketplace (Carbado & Gulati, 2003). As delineated in Carbado and Gulati (2003), there are three key reasons why diversity matters in business: (a) companies can increase their market share, (b) customers place importance on ethical business behavior, and (c) recruiting and retaining the best talent from a diverse labor market contributes to better business performance.

When one tries to manage affirmative action and equal employment opportunity the same as diversity, the initiative violates the very thing one was trying to do—that is it excludes people rather than focusing on the role of leadership (Carbado & Gulati, 2003). According to Adams (1998) a company cannot establish awareness in one day. Rather, people have to make it a part of their daily lives, and workers will take their cues from managers. If managers allow or participate in behaviors that are not accepting of all people, then their team will follow suit. Management of diversity actions should not be confused with affirmative action (Adams, 1998), and it is important to understand the history of each and to use the terms accurately (Adams, 1998). Affirmative action, valuing diversity, and managing diversity are separate points on the continuum of interventions designed to stimulate the inclusion of people from different backgrounds in an organization, and they are all grounded in a moral and social responsibility to amend previous minority group wrongs (Business Training Media, 2004). These legal obligations are based on numerical measures and were designed to increase the representation of minorities and women in employment areas where they were previously underrepresented (Business Training Media, 2004).

*Diversity Initiatives*

Managing diversity has a focus on the business case for diversity and is different from affirmative action. Capitalizing on diversity is a strategic approach to business that contributes to organizational goals, such as profits and productivity, and it does not involve any legal requirements (Business Training Media, 2004). Diversity management is a pragmatic strategy that focuses on maximizing the productivity, creativity, and commitment of the workforce, while meeting the needs of diverse groups (Carbado & Gulati, 2003). These interventions build upon one another, when affirmative action is tied with valuing and/or managing diversity. Diversity often becomes tainted by negative perceptions of affirmative action and is therefore frequently misunderstood. This leads to backlash, resistance, and polarization when the concepts of diversity and affirmative action are combined (Business Training Media, 2004). Many companies still have the mentality that diversity is compliance, but those companies are not thinking of the maximum opportunity for the individual (Schramm, 2003).

Companies may consider the following questions when making the case for diversity in their organization, as there are some factors that make diversity initiatives important to businesses for reasons beyond social or moral responsibility (Cadrain, 2003): (a) What are the demographics (e.g., race, religion, age, sexual orientation, sex, class) of the stakeholder base? (b) How many languages are spoken by the stakeholders? and (c) Where does the company operate? Other questions include (a) How much does employee turnover cost the organization? (b) How much is spent yearly on hiring need/level of certain group turnover? (c) What has been the annual cost of discriminatory claims? and (d) How is conflict management handled? Many companies also consider (a) Are the benefits appealing to diverse candidates? (b) Is the company losing employees because they do not feel valued, included, heard, or rewarded? (c) Is career advancement possible, and are employees mentored? and (d) Is diversity reflected in the company's policies and among its suppliers, vendors, contractors, board, and/or staff? (Cadrain, 2003).

According to Catalyst (1999), examination of corporate diversity programs revealed that diversity initiatives are not as effective as they could have been, nor were they intended to be for women of color, including African-American women. In addition, 75% of women of color surveyed by Catalyst (1999) reported being aware of training in their corporation to address race and gender issues, but only 22% reported that their managers receive adequate training in managing a diverse workforce. Catalyst (1999) emphasized that 53% of women feel that their companies' diversity programs are ineffective in dealing with issues of subtle racism, 26% of women report that career development is an important part of their companies' diversity programs, and only 17% of women believe their managers are held accountable for advancing of women in their racial or ethnic group. Moreover, in evaluating their work environments, many women, particularly African American women, cite pervasive stereotypes (Catalyst, 1999). According to a study by Catalyst (1999), although 86% of women report being satisfied with their careers overall, nearly 30% report greater difficulty with career advancement and less access to options that facilitate advancement (e.g., mentoring, sponsorship from senior management, working in line positions). In contrast, more men, approximately 42%, indicate that finding mentors has been easy at their current job. Catalyst (1999) indicated that effective diversity programs in turn foster retention.

One would expect that, over time, the measurements used will become more behavioral; in other words, measurements will change from what the company thinks about diversity to what is being done about diversity. For example, Pitney Bowes, a Fortune 500 company, sees the success of its program resulting from the CEO's view that diversity is a business imperative; thus, Pitney Bowes constantly reviews its organizational goals and assess how well the company is doing regarding its focus on diversity initiatives (Majors & Sinclair, 1994). The Catalyst Award for innovative efforts to advance women was awarded to Pitney Bowes and they were one of three companies to receive the honor (Majors & Sinclair, 1994). The comprehensive diversity plan that Pitney Bowes has for business units formalizes the company's long-standing culture of fairness and equality (Majors & Sinclair, 1994). Pitney Bowes uses a combination of quantitative and qualitative measures to monitor diversity initiatives progress, and four specific areas are monitored in each business unit: (a) communications, (b) career development, (c) training, and (d) recruiting (Majors & Sinclair, 1994). Although they look at representative numbers of women and minorities, the company also assesses which units are doing a good job hiring and promoting diverse individuals; management analyzes these representation numbers monthly for certain job groups (Majors & Sinclair, 1994). In addition, the complaints that are centered around equal employer opportunity complaints and the numbers of employees trained in diversity are tracked within the company. Moreover, Pitney Bowes looks qualitatively at the working environment, asking questions like "How do people feel?" and "Are there work options for working parents?" (Majors & Sinclair, 1994).

Climate surveys are used as another measure to get a sense of the working environment, and in all cases, the organization looks at business unit goals to determine actual performance (Majors & Sinclair, 1994). In this manner, diversity becomes a part of doing business, rather than another set of goals for managers to fret over. Periodically, the best practices in the business units are recognized and publicized throughout the company. Top-down and bottom-up methods are not effective at integrating diversity into a culture, given the totem pole perception are the us versus them perception of management versus line staff. Across the board is a better description of what must happen, given that all staff are held accountable equally. All sizes of organizations, private, public, and nonprofit, would benefit from the implementation of a strategic diversity plan (Majors & Sinclair, 1994). Leadership commitment and business integration are critical to the success of diversity plans and measurements. It is vital for all company employees to embrace diversity efforts and own a stake in the results of a successful organization (Majors & Sinclair, 1994).

As Cromwell (2003) highlighted, it is not unusual to attend a diversity conference or meeting and hear relative silence on LGBT issues. Reasons for this lack of information on LGBT issues may include (a) a lack of awareness, (b) a concern for diluting the diversity agenda, and (c) personal or religious beliefs (Cromwell, 2003). The concerns of White gay men forming a company LGBT group may be different from those of African American lesbians in the same company, for example. How do the White gay men ensure that they appropriately reach out to the diverse group of individuals within the LGBT community? Beyond that, how do all LGBT people become informed and reliable allies to other (non-LGBT) individuals in their organization, such as individuals with disabilities or individuals of differing ethnic descent (Cromwell, 2003)?

Creating a welcoming environment can start small. Always utilizing inclusive language, even when one assumes one is talking with heterosexual crowds, sends a strong message. Where one used to say "Bring your husbands and wives to the holiday party," instead one should consider saying "Bring your partners and spouses." Crowell (2003) recommended (a) asking a trusted LGBT colleague to give feedback or make suggestions about ways to improve company practices, (b) respectfully challenging jokes or comments that are intended to deride LGBT people, and (c) making a point of supporting and attending events that are intended to educate and celebrate diversity with respect to sexual orientation and gender identity.

According to Suellen Roth, vice president of global policy and diversity at Avaya, a communications systems provider based in Basking Ridge, NJ, diversity training and nondiscrimination policies for LGBT workers offer morale benefits as well (Cadrain, 2003). People who are comfortable and who feel included are more effective as employees and are more creative and committed. That helps the company attract and retain top talent and reach more markets (Cadrain 2003). Organizations at the forefront in establishing LGBT nondiscrimination policies share several key characteristics: (a) commitment at the top, (b) advocacy from the bottom up, and (c) human resources in the middle, as well as recognition of not only sexual orientation but also gender identity, characteristics, and expressions (Cadrain, 2003). In companies with strong LGBT nondiscrimination policies, human resources managers typically have played a critical part, benchmarking, gathering pertinent information for formulating the policy, demonstrating how the policy would be consistent with the company's strategic purposes, and drafting and implementing the policy (Cadrain, 2003). The human resources department can also be a key source of help for employees seeking to come out at work (Cadrain, 2003).

According to Barrier (2001), diversity training and policy implementation can dramatically improve not only employee relations but also a company's bottom-line revenue. Consistent with a company's nondiscrimination policy, harassment in the workplace based on sexual orientation should be strictly prohibited. In this regard, the company should strictly prohibit any form of unlawful employee harassment, whether it is physical, verbal, visual, or written. Similarly, the use of company Internet or e-mail systems for the purpose of displaying or transmitting offensive material should not be tolerated (Barrier, 2001). In addition, improper interference with the ability of employees to perform their expected job duties should be forbidden, and employees who violate this policy should be subject to disciplinary action up to, and including, immediate termination from employment. Employees who believe that they are being harassed or discriminated against in any way should immediately report any discrimination practice or observation to their immediate supervisor as well as to the human resources department. Thereafter, the human resources department should conduct an investigation of any complaint of inappropriate discrimination or harassment and take prompt remedial action where necessary (Barrier, 2001).

Confidentiality should also be maintained throughout the investigation to the extent that is practical and appropriate given the circumstances. Companies must be clear that they will not retaliate against employees who make complaints or participate in investigations about workplace harassment or other discrimination (Barrier, 2001). Retaliation is a form of discrimination and is strictly prohibited and employers fare best when they have a single, clear policy, one that encompasses acceptance of sexual and gender diversity rather than offering it as separate policy along with companion policies against sexual harassment or workplace violence (Barrier, 2001). This policy should be distributed to all new staff members during the orientation process and periodically distributed thereafter; in addition, staff members should attend a mandatory annual training on diversity and LGBT issues.

An LGBT diversity training workshop program can break down the barriers between LGBT and non-LGBT employees and customers by opening up the lines of communication in order to achieve three goals: awareness, assessment, and action (French, 2003).

With respect to awareness, via interactive exercises, educational materials, and personal sharing, trainers can encourage participants to consider how common myths and stereotypes about LGBT individuals influence their views of this population. In addition, trainers can provide definitions and information about LGBT terminology, as well as share personal experiences (positive and negative) as a result of identifying as gay, lesbian, bisexual, or transgender. All of these components should be conducted within the context of workplace issues. In terms of assessment, trainers can lead participants through exercises designed to help them assess the current environment for LGBT employees or for employees with family members or friends who identify as LGBT. Specifically, trainers would aid participants with assessing how the current environment affects productivity and/or employee retention, how customers and clients experience the environment, and how the environment may positively or negatively affect the bottom-line revenue. Finally, with respect to action, the workshop could conclude with the development of a plan to make changes, or affirm positive steps already in place, in order to create a more comfortable, productive, and profitable environment for all employees (French, 2003).

According to Conklin (2000), by the end of an LGBT diversity workshop, participants should (a) understand the significance of LGBT issues in the context of broader diversity issues, (b) learn the truth behind the myths and stereotypes regarding LGBT individuals, (c) discover the effect of homophobia and heterosexism on workplace relationships, (d) be able to assess the environment from the perspective of LGBT employees and customers, and (e) develop a personal or organizational action plan to address problem areas. This "Out and Equal" type of training (Conklin, 2000) could offer refreshments and run from 9:00am to 1:00pm on a Friday in an effort to relax and attract more staff. Ground rules would include (a) respecting confidentiality, (b) listening with respect, (c) no individual sidebar discussions, (d) speaking from your own experience, and (e) respecting individual's experiences. A sample agenda could include an opening by a company senior leader followed by an overview of why the training is needed and taking place and then a discussion of the following topics: (a) stereotyping and homophobia; (b) an introduction to the LGBT community (c) personal sharing; (d) power relationships; (e) discrimination in the workforce; (f) local, state, and federal protection; (g) organizational costs; (h) internal organizational examination; and (i) personal or organizational action planning.

The organizational LGBT diversity training workshop can be conducted by either an internal or an external group. The target participant group for this training depends on the current needs and goals of the company and should include senior executives, managers, human resources and diversity professionals, customer service representatives, and the general employee population. Upon completion of this training, each participant should receive an evaluation form to track his or her success level and document future needs (Conklin, 2000).

It is acknowledged that training sometimes cannot change an organization, nor can it always change individuals. Similarly, training alone cannot change systems or remove organizational barriers (Day, 1995). It has limits in terms of what it can effectively accomplish. However, what training can do is create and raise awareness, impart knowledge, and teach skills. If one knows what one hopes to accomplish and selects an array of individuals who reflect the population of interest, one will increase the chances of being heard by attendees (Day, 1995). Moreover, if organizations continue to revisit goals and build in measurement and accountability, training efforts should improve over time (French, 2003).

Evaluation of diversity initiatives is vital to establishing the credibility of the workshop, as well as to benchmarking growth and developing future programming that positively affects the company's revenue (Society for Human Resources Management, 2001). Although challenging, when attempting to evaluate the results of a diversity initiative, it is best to take the same approach with as with other business objectives (Day, 1995). According to Society for Human Resources Management (1999), the following procedure outlines a comparative process for adequately evaluating an organization's diversity effort. Evaluating diversity can begin with gathering data about current conditions, by conducting a diversity survey and holding employee focus groups. Then one can create clear objectives that are measurable. Once interventions have been implemented, one should evaluate again and compare the new findings to the baseline data. Of note, it is most valid to utilize the same processes in the post assessment phase that you did in the preassessment (Society for Human Resources Management, 1999). Measurement needs to be an integral part of a diversity process, not just a check at the end of an initiative. Gathering data and setting criteria are critical aspects of early planning, and measurement is not complete when an organization conducts the post assessment (Society for Human Resources Management, 1999). Rather, each measurement check and evaluation tool should provide feedback that is used to shape plans, so that evaluation is integrated into an ongoing diversity process. In establishing or evaluating a training program, the organization should consider how it relates to internal and external standards (Society for Human Resources Management, 1999).

Diversity initiatives can take on many forms, including training, mentoring, and/or revamping promotional procedures. Managing diversity initiatives can improve cost structures of organizations and increase the quality of human resources. Diversity in workgroups can also be leveraged to increase marketing effectiveness, creativity, innovation, and problem-solving. Diversity also requires managerial attention because differences among employees make supervision and work coordination more complex and challenging (Cadrain, 2003). Organizations that excel at leveraging diversity, which includes the hiring and advancement of women and men of color into senior management jobs and providing a climate conducive to contributions from people of diverse backgrounds, will experience better financial performance than organizations that are not effective in managing diversity (Cadrain, 2003). Redirecting compliance reviews to focus on broader measures of the diversity climate, including ensuring that change is taking place (rather than just identifying problems and shortcomings), is vital (Cadrain, 2003).

Workplaces, families, churches, and local governments are heterosexism entrenched, and this is a pervasive and alarming phenomenon (B. Greene, 1994b) in a civilization that prides itself on being open, democratic, tolerant, and free. To date, few scholars have found the social, cultural, or ethical imperative for thoroughly researching heterosexism's intersection with race as a larger interconnected system of White, male, heterosexual power (B. Greene, 1994b). Increased efforts in destroying the barriers of racial, sexual, class, physical, cultural, religious, and educational difference is needed in an effort to promote equality (B. Greene, 1994b).

Many factors influence the level of ethical behavior in an organization. An individual's moral values and value-related attitudes influence his or her business behavior. According to Vaid (1996), certain policies and procedures reduce the opportunity to be unethical, when management places importance on the company's code of ethics, and are perhaps the most effective way to encourage ethical behavior.

A written guide to acceptable behavior, as defined by the company, should outline uniform policies, procedures, and punishment for violations. Companies must also create an environment in which employees recognize the importance of complying with the written code. Managers must provide direction by fostering communication, actively modeling and encouraging ethical decision making, and training employees to make ethical decisions. With such direction, openness and communication will build trust and strengthen business relationships (Ferrel & Gresham, 1985).

Gardenswartz and Rowe (2003) made the following suggestions for designing and delivering diversity training: (a) ensuring that the organization is truly committed to the language or policies that are presented, (b) reading and understanding the diversity policies or statements, (c) making the training accessible and accommodating, (d) linking diversity skills to job requirements and behavioral expectations, (e) asking the legal department to check for consistency, (f) watching for discriminatory tone, (g) avoiding immediate commitments to changes in policies and practices without review, and (h) ensuring that no new terminology is introduced to the company's lexicon, presumably because these new terms have not been tested and there is no precedent supporting their usage (Gardenswartz & Rowe, 2003).

Similarly, suggestions for managers when implementing diversity include (a) remaining nondefensive, (b) challenging stereotypic comments and assumptions, (c) spending time with employees different from them, (d) soliciting diversity when hiring, (e) consciously mixing employees when forming task forces and project teams, (f) sending mixed groups to training sessions or conferences to give staff a way to naturally build new common ground and break down barriers between groups, (g) mentoring beyond the familiar, (h) addressing conflicts and complaints, (i) involving staff in building the workplace culture, (j) maximizing the effect of staff meetings, (k) showing support and communicating about diversity, (l) measuring and rewarding successes and achievements in reaching diversity goals, and (m) routinely surveying policies and practices for equity in opportunities for career advancement, training, and other perks (Gardenswartz & Rowe, 2003). Managers play a key role in setting the tone of organizational culture. Thus, taking actions such as these will demonstrate that they "walk the talk" of inclusiveness and respect. This will pay big dividends every day on the job (Gardenswartz & Rowe, 2003), including reduction of burnout and increased staff productivity.

## Employee Burnout and Job Productivity

In a study of 203 self-identified lesbians, three fifths reported that they expected job discrimination if their sexual orientation were known to others. Of these, most (90%) anticipated taunts, ostracism, or even violence; 75% anticipated problems with their immediate supervisors, 66% expected termination, and 13% expected harassment (Levine & Leonard, 1984). In an investigation assessing the effect of self-identified gay men and lesbians working in a nonembracing environment, Irwin (1999) found that many participants reported profound negative effects on their overall mental and physical health, including illness, loss of confidence, and increased anxiety and depression. In addition, some participants acknowledged that their work performance was negatively affected, given that they were often ill, took extensive sick leaves, or merely did not want to go to work (Irwin, 1999). Human resources professionals are responsible for resolving employee behaviors that affect work environment (e.g., stress) and developing employee management practices that reduce attrition (O'Conner, 2000). A part of risk management involves understanding how employees' mental health and behaviors affect productivity, attrition, and employee management costs. For human resources management, this means that its emerging responsibility is to provide a return on investment that can be realized. More important, in larger self-insured companies, human resources can recast its role as the guardian of management practices and work culture into a role that is more sensitive to risk, wellness, and costs (O'Conner, 2000).

Burnout is defined as a psychological process, brought about by unveiled work stress, which results in emotional exhaustion, depersonalization, and feelings of decreased accomplishments (Ivancevich & Matteson, 1987). It is described as a stress condition brought on by being involved in an intense situation for a long period, without adequate rest and recreation (Business Health Services, 2005). Lesbians of color experience chronic depression from homophobic discrimination, and this stress is compounded by job-related stress and burnout that might stem from alienation regarding their sexual orientation (Bridges, Selvidge, & Matthews, 2003). Warning signs of burnout include (a) exhaustion; (b) detachment; (c) boredom; (d) cynicism; (e) an inability to catch up; (f) body, mind, spirits, and emotions wearing low; (g) slow ailment recovery; (h) decreased patience; (i) increased irritability; (j) change in work style; (k) physical pain; (l) paranoia; (m) disorientation; and (n) depression (Business Health Services, 2005).

According to Business Health Services (2005), successful burnout management strategies can include encouraging employees to (a) seek intervention, (b) know their limits, (c) take care of themselves, (d) get managerial support, (e) participate in focus groups, (f) initiate change, and (g) talk with others. Burnout occurs when repeated stress is not balanced by healthy timeouts for genuine relaxation. Thus, other successful management strategies can include (a) vacation, (b) rest, (c) laughter, (d) eating balanced meals in peaceful environments, (e) listening to soothing music and relaxation tapes, (f) reaching out to others and spending time with people, (g) avoiding numbing emotional pain with drugs or alcohol, and (h) reducing self-deprecating thoughts (Business Health Services, 2005).

Organizations contribute to employee burnout in a variety of ways; Cordes and Dougherty (1993) identified four particular examples: (a) high levels of work overload, (b) dead-end jobs, (c) excessive red tape and paperwork, and (d) poor communication and feedback about job performance. Lesbians of color in the workforce may seek professional help to find their way through possible stressful challenges of being a triple minority (Bridges, Selvidge, & Matthews, 2003), and stress also costs organizations money. In fact, the cost of workplace stress has been estimated to be about $150 billion annually (Ivancevich & Matteson, 1996). This amount includes reductions in operational effectives, poor decision making, and decreased creativity, as well as mental and physical health issues from stress (e.g., hospital costs, workers compensation, lost work time, turnover, sabotage; Ivancevich & Matteson, 1996). It is important to note that burnout is not inevitable in work life, and it heavily affects women of color (Fine, 2002). Burnout, isolation, and feelings of hopelessness are significant issues for African American women (Belenky, 1996). The sense of burnout, isolation, and hopelessness faced by some African American women can be broken by the process of sharing their unique experiences as women of color leaders and discussing the meaning of those events (Fine, 2002).

Cultures often socialize women to be in a mind-set of placing their primary focus on attending to the collective needs of the family and community (Matias, 2005). Women of color leaders in nonprofit organizations have described feeling overwhelmed by the enormity of need within their communities and the struggle to meet those needs (Matias, 2005). The nonprofit sector represents work that can institute change in terms of it also supporting leadership, but this arena of work, however, is characterized by limited resources and unlimited need (Matias, 2005). Thus, work in the nonprofit sectors consists of an environment characterized by long hours, low pay, lack of security, and lack of respect—all conditions that can also easily lead to or contribute to burnout. Unfortunately, little is known about how to alleviate these conditions for those working in the nonprofit sector while allowing them to sustain passion for their work (Kovan, 2002).

People differ in the manner in which they respond to organizational stressors, with a classic distinction referred to as Type A versus Type B behavior. Individuals characterized as Type A like to do things their way and are willing to exert a lot of effort to ensure that trivial tasks are performed in the manner they prefer. They also often fail to distinguish between important and unimportant situations. In contrast, individuals characterized as Type B are generally much more tolerant of stress than Type A individuals, and they are not as easily frustrated or angered in response to noncompliance (Ivancevich & Matteson, 1996).

According to Ivancevich and Matteson (1996), job burnout is a particular type of stress often experienced by people who work in the human service industry, such as health, education, or ministry. Job burnout includes attitudinal and emotional reactions that result from job-related experiences. The first sign of burnout is usually a feeling of emotional exhaust because of one's work. One common reaction of individuals in the human service industry who are feeling burned out is to place psychological distance between their clients and themselves. Indeed, burned out individuals in this field often report feeling that they have become calloused by their jobs and that they have grown cynical about their clients. In addition, such individuals also report emotional exhaustion and a feeling of low personal accomplishment (Ivancevich & Matteson, 1996).

Many human service professionals begin careers with great expectations that they will be able to improve the human condition through their work, within a few years, they begin to realize they are not living up to these expectations (Ivancevich & Matteson, 1996). There are many systemic reasons for the gap between a novice's goals and a veteran's accomplishments. Such reasons include (a) unrealistically high expectations due to a lack of exposure to the job during training, (b) constraints on the worker through the rules and regulations of the job, (c) inadequate resources for performing one's job, (d) clients who are frequently uncooperative and occasionally rebellious, and (e) a lack of feedback about one's successes (Ivancevich & Matteson, 1996). These and other characteristics of human service organizations almost guarantee that some employees will be frustrated in their attempts to reach their goals. Unfortunately, workers may not recognize the role of the system in producing this frustration; rather, the worker may feel personally responsible and begin to think of himself or herself as a failure (Ivancevich & Matteson, 1996).

Ivancevich and Matteson (1996) noted that burnout is a barrier to career development. When combined with emotional exhaustion, feelings of low personal accomplishment may reduce motivation to a point where performance is, in fact, impaired (Ivancevich & Matteson, 1996). In addition to poor job performance, burned-out staff members may also experience deterioration of their relationships with coworkers (Ivancevich & Matteson, 1996). Those suffering from burnout also are absent from work more often and take more frequent work breaks, thereby affecting the quality of one's work life. Similarly, burnout can also lead to behaviors that cause a deterioration of the quality of one's home life (Ivancevich & Matteson, 1996).

In an investigation of burnout among 142 married, male police officers, Ivancevich and Matteson (1996) asked the police officers' wives to describe how their husbands behaved at home. Emotionally exhausted officers were described as coming home tense, anxious, upset, and angry, as well as often complaining about the problems they faced at work. These officers were also described as more withdrawn while at home, preferring to be left alone rather than share time with the family. The wives' reports also revealed that officers who had developed negative attitudes toward the people they dealt with also had fewer close friends (Ivancevich & Matteson, 1996).

Excessive stress increases job dissatisfaction and is associated with a number of dysfunctional outcomes, including increased turnover and absenteeism and reduced job performance. If productivity is reduced just 3%, for example, an organization employing 1,000 people would need to hire an additional 30 employees to compensate for that lost productivity (Ivancevich & Matteson, 1996). Similarly, if annual employee costs are $40,000, including wages and benefits, stress is costing the company $1.2 million just to replace lost productivity. This figure does not include costs associated with recruitment and training, nor does it consider that decreases in quality of performance may be more costly for an organization than decreases in quantity (Ivancevich & Matteson, 1996).

Further examples of the organizational costs associated with stress are found in research conducted by the National Safety Council, the College of Insurance, and the National Institute for Occupational Safety and Health (W. Jones, 1984). For example, approximately 75% to 85% of all industrial accidents are caused by an inability to cope with stress, and these cost U.S. companies in excess of $32 billion annually. Heart disease, which is associated with stress, is responsible for an annual loss of more than 185 million work days; similarly, stress-related headaches are the leading cause of lost work hours in American industry. Moreover, psychological or psychosomatic problems contribute to more than 60% of long-term employee disability cases, and $26 billion is spent annually on disability payments and medical bills (W. Jones, 1984).

The consequences of excessive stress are significant in both individual and organizational terms, as work stressors evoke different responses from different people. Some individuals are more able than others to cope with a stressor. They can adapt their behavior in such a way to meet the stressor head-on. On the other hand, some individuals are predisposed to stress and are not able to adapt to the stressor, which can lead to physical or emotional exhaustion, lack of motivation or decreased morale, work pressures, and/or financial difficulties.

According to O'Conner (2000), employers frequently address physical health issues with various health and disease management resources, including wellness programs and modified work or lighter assignment of duties. However, O'Conner (2000) stated that mental health remains an isolated concern that has yet to be fully included within employee health management paradigms. There is growing evidence of its effect on human resources concerns such as attrition, lost productivity, and job satisfaction. Comparing most companies' physical health and disability interventions to their mental-health-related practices provides human resources personnel with a simple, yet important, insight into the evolution of cost-driven employee management practices (Greenberg, 1999).

Human resources can actively participate in absence and disability management planning by understanding how employees with stress, depression, or other mental-health-related problems drive up employee management costs. By understanding these cost and risk variables, human resources departments can devise strategies to enhance job satisfaction and ultimately improve productivity (Greenberg, 1999). Unlike employees with physical injuries who return to work only when medically able, workers with stress-related or mental-health-related conditions bring their diminished stamina to work every day. Therefore, human resources must reshape employee management practices to respond to these employees and to address the cost of lost productivity, attrition, and disability (Greenberg, 1999).

*EAPs*

According to Smoyer (1998) small companies can reduce workers' compensation costs by $75,000 by establishing an EAP with an emphasis on safety awareness. In fact, studies conducted at Crestar Bank showed that average mental health costs were 58% less for EAP participants, as compared with those who did not use the EAP. Marsh & McLennan Companies also reported evidence of savings achieved through drug-free workplace programs that included EAPs (Employee

Assistance Programs Association, 2002). A study of 122 staff members who used the EAP at the University of Michigan showed that the university saved a minimum of $65,341 over a five-year period for those employees because of improved retention rates and reduced sick leave (Employee Assistance Programs Association, 2002). The Staying at Work Survey (Wyatt, 1999), reported that the factors cited most often in rising disability costs were (a) poor plan design, (b) lack of supervisor involvement in the return-to-work process, (c) abuse of sick leave, (d) job dissatisfaction, and (e) preventable health problems. Notably, with the exception of plan design, each of these factors has a behavioral management component. Thus, human resources can design alternative approaches to confront unhealthy behaviors or ineffective performance, including poor communication and teamwork. Human resources interventions must address the work environment because the environment affects mental health and adaptive behavior (O'Conner, 2000).

EAPs have been the most dynamic employee benefit to emerge over the past 20 years. In their infancy, EAPs provided two benefits: (a) a confidential, clinical resource to the employee and (b) an educational resource on substance abuse and mental health issues to the employer. According to O'Conner (2000) once the human resources department chooses to confront mental wellness factors in the workforce, it can do four specific things to reduce costs related to mental health and behavioral disabilities.

First, the human resources department can generate feedback from employees and supervisors about practices and work culture traits that contribute to stress or depression. This provides the human resources department with ratings of its disability management practices, its mental-health-related resources like the EAP, and its policies related to the American With Disabilities Act (ADA) and the Family and Medical Leave Act (FMLA). Second, the human resources department can conduct audits of training and consultant resources in order to gauge its success in reducing work culture variables that contribute to mental-health-related disability. Third, the human resources department can analyze medical and EAP vendor data to assess the vendors' ability to manage disability and subsequently improve mental wellness in the workforce. This will provide the human resources department with the necessary information to make management and environmental changes to reduce these costs.

Understanding the uses of this data reinforces the value of the human resource department in the disability management team dynamic alongside risk management and benefits administration. Finally, the human resources department can implement a plan for modifying the work culture and employee management protocols in response to the overall assessment. Such a plan could include (a) staff training, (b) behavioral performance standards for supervisors, and (c) proactive (e.g., not response oriented) strategies for reducing disability-related events or behaviors in the workplace (O'Conner, 2000).

Traditionally, human resources professionals have relied on the company's benefit plans and EAPs to manage the mental health concerns of employees. Human resource professionals must now meet the challenge of reducing the risk factors in the work environment and creating employee management practices that reinforce employees' adaptive and healthy behavior. Work relationships and environment consistently rank above compensation in relative importance to employee retention (Wyatt, 1999). Building healthy relationships among employees within organizations aids cross-departmental communication, cooperation, and team building.

*Stress Reduction and Burnout Management*

One thing that organizations can do, in addition to offering EAPs, is to unexpectedly engage in an activity that does not reduce productivity in the office yet breaks any associated tension (Wyatt, 1999). New hire orientation programs present opportunities to share the organization's culture and build relationships. Orientation presentations should optimally include employees from across the organization, in order to enhance buy-in and promote mentoring. Celebrating diversity, wellness programs, promoting staff appreciation, and community involvement can also be great ways for an organization to reinforce a positive message about the company's role in the community or to allow employees to keep a suitable work–family balance. Employees who feel better about themselves and support each other's efforts are more effective (Wyatt, 1999).

Employees also should take responsibility for identifying the jobs that will help them thrive. Employees should be trained in how to assess their individual characteristics and skills by prompting them to ask themselves the following: (a) "What skills am I currently using in my job that I enjoy using?" (b) "What skills am I currently not using that I enjoy using?" (c) "What skills am I currently required to use that I do not enjoy using?" and (d) "What skills am I currently not required to use that I do enjoy using?" (Prochaska, 2003). Assessing their own skills and preferences can help employees understand why they find some tasks or roles more stressful than others; it is important to help employees identify their behavioral limits in dealing with stressors (Prochaska, 2003).

Time management can also be an effective individual strategy to deal with organizational stress (Ivancevich & Matteson, 1996). It is based, in large part, on an initial identification of an individual's personal goals and other strategies that should be part of individual stress management. Examples of such personal goals include (a) following a good diet, (b) getting regular exercise, (c) monitoring physical health, and (d) building social support groups (Ivancevich & Matteson, 1996).

According to Ivancevich and Matteson (1996) increasing employees' participation in the decision-making process, and thus increasing the amount of control they have, can be an effective way to prevent some forms of burnout from occurring. For example, a study of hospital nurses found that feelings of emotional exhaustion were linked to perceptions of a lack of control (Ivancevich & Matteson, 1996). Nurses reported often being unable to exercise control, either over the behavior of physicians on whom they closely depend or over the decisions of administrators who determine hours and conditions of their work. Specifically, emotional exhaustion was greater for nurses who were less able to influence policies and decisions and for those who had bureaucratic hassles. Emotional exhaustion was also greater for nurses who perceived fewer opportunities to illustrate creativity in carrying out their work (Ivancevich & Matteson, 1996). According to Ivancevich and Matteson (1996), besides giving workers a feeling of control, participation in decision making gives them the power to remove obstacles to effective performance, thereby reducing frustration and strain. One effective use of influence is to persuade others to change their conflicting role expectations for one's own behavior. Participative decision making can also allow members of the organization to gain a better understanding of the demands and constraints faced by others. Thus, when work-related conflicts appear, negotiation is likely to commence over which expectations should be changed in order to reduce inherent conflicts (Ivancevich & Matteson, 1996).

Another important consequence of participative decision making is that individuals become less isolated from their coworkers and supervisors; thus, through discussion, employees learn about the formal and informal expectations held by others (Ivancevich & Matteson, 1996). Employees also learn about the formal and informal policies and procedures of the organization, and this information can help reduce feelings of role ambiguity, as well as make it easier for the person to perform his or her job effectively (Ivancevich & Matteson, 1996). Finally, participation in decision making helps prevent burnout by encouraging the development of a social support network among coworkers. Social support networks help people cope effectively with the stressors they experience on the job (Ivancevich & Matteson, 1996).

According to Srinivas (1991), employers need to provide clear role expectations to their employees and to reduce conflicting role demands to the greatest extent possible. Role ambiguity is a major contributor to employee burnout in nonprofit organizations (Srinivas, 1991). In order to reduce employee burnout, there are a number of approaches to take: (a) garnering top-level support, (b) building a mission and vision statement, (c) integrating wellness into the company's strategic vision by building a wellness committee and planning a wellness program plan based on needs assessments, (d) attaching gender neutrality to company benefits, and (e) surrounding programs with policies and procedures. Measurable outcomes related to burnout reduction may include improved health care and associated costs; increased stability; decreased turnover, absenteeism, and claims data; and decreased risk factors and associated costs.

A natural connection exists between healthy employees and company benefit and according to Ivancevich & Matteson (1996), companies with wellness programs often find that they have better attendance, lower medical and workers' compensation costs, and happier, more productive employees. Employees with healthy lifestyles have fewer illnesses and injuries than other workers, and they recover from illnesses and injuries quicker. Employees who participate in regular physical activity also demonstrate increased cardiovascular endurance. In addition, those who eat low-fat diets, refrain from smoking, and get adequate rest are adding years to their lives. Collectively, employees who engage in all of the aforementioned behaviors are more alert, more positive in outlook, and better able to deal effectively with the stress and rapid change of today's world.

## Career Development Theory

Employment discrimination has been discussed in research addressing oppressed groups, such as women, ethnic minorities, and people with disabilities, but there is a lack of conceptualization (Chung, 2001). There are numerous studies researching career development theories, but the extent to which there is applicability to minorities similar to that of White males is limited. According to M. T. Brown (1995), "many of the current theories of career development have not been empirically tested using African Americans" (p. 10). Little literature was located, however, with regard to lesbian women of color, specifically African Americans. Theoretical and conceptual research addresses some issues pertaining to both gay men and lesbians, but lesbian women are underrepresented in empirical research (Chung, 2003). Research has examined gay men's vocational aspirations and interests (Chung & Harmon, 1994) whereas research on the vocational preferences of lesbians could not be found.

In the past few years, more authors have researched lesbian issues specifically (Boatwright et al., 1996; Driscoll et al., 1996) or have included both gay men and lesbians in their studies (Rostosky &

Riggle, 2002). A balanced treatment of issues regarding gay men and lesbians is encouraged in future efforts.

Only a small amount of empirical data was located on lesbian career development. J. E. Elliott (1993) found that vocational literature about lesbians and gay men was almost nonexistent until the 1970s. He emphasized that career information needs to reflect the current multiculturalism, which acknowledges the effect of discrimination on the needs of minorities, gay men, and lesbians (J. E. Elliot, 1993).

Lent, Brown, and Hackett (1994) developed a theory of career development based on Bandura's social cognitive theory that incorporates the influence of environmental factors on one's career development. Lent et al. (1994) argued that, through an interaction of personal, contextual, and experiential factors, one's "self-efficacy beliefs, outcome expectations, and goal representations" are expressed (p. 83). Self-efficacy beliefs can be acquired vicariously, for example, through witnessing the success or failure of someone who appears to resemble oneself (Lent et al., 1994).

Issues such as sex discrimination, structure of opportunities, equal opportunities, and family demands change the process of women's career development from that of men (Cox, White, & Cooper,

1992), and sexual orientation further compounds the issue (E. White, 2007). As nonethnic minority members, lesbians and gay men face barriers to career development that can be affected by outcome expectations. Many of the concerns around being out at work, identity confusion, prejudice, and discrimination can be thought to be barriers to accessing and succeeding in careers. Sociocognitive career theory (Lent et al., 1994) has been applied to a number of oppressed groups to facilitate the understanding of the unique career barriers encountered by these individuals. Morrow, Gore, and Campbell (1996) suggested the use of this theory for the LGBT community. A lot of emotional energy is required for LGBT identity management, which makes the career development process become more complex and receive less attention (Belz, 1993; D'Augelli, 1996; Fassinger, 1996a). The lack of such exploration can later lead a sense of being behind heterosexual peers in career development or being inadequate (Fassinger, 1996a).

In a qualitative study of 10 adult lesbians, Boatwright et al. (1996) found that six reported educational delays during the time period when they came "out." Six felt that this process had derailed their career path, and nine reported a feeling of being behind their peers in career development. Career barriers, such as these, can be proximal or distal (Lent et al., 2000). Distal factors exist in the background of one's career decision-making process, including factors that affect self-efficacy and outcome expectations. These may include the presence or lack of role models or support for career-related behaviors and are thought to shape career-related interest and choices. Proximal factors come into play at career decision-making junctures and may include "informal career contacts or exposure to discriminatory hiring practices" (p. 38). Both types of factors are likely to affect the translation of interest to goals or goal-directed behavior (Lent et al., 2000).

LGBT oppression potentially affects many career-related factors such as self-efficacy, outcome expectancies, interest formation, goal setting, goal-directed behavior, and skill development (Chung, 2003). Additionally, lesbians must contend with external factors that make career progress difficult, including homophobic attitudes, harassment, and discrimination (Fassinger, 1996a). All of these factors can be seen as barriers to lesbian career development or progress. The career development process is critical to the success of organizations (Society for Human Resources Management, 2001) and the implicit assumption is that career development models are generalized across both gender and race (B. Greene, 1994b).

Consequently, models of career development do not sufficiently address the realities of and process of women's careers. Research suggested that a person engages in career development activities on the basis of his or her experiences. In particular, an African American woman's career development process may differ from that of others, and race and gender may account for some differences (Betters-Reed & Moore, 1995; Diamond, 1987; Marshall & Rossman, 1995). Gay men and lesbians, specifically, face distinct issues when negotiating a positive self-concept that will counteract views of their devalued gender and sexual orientation, leaving them with little energy for career development tasks (Fassinger, 1996b).

*Career Development Barriers*

"The career is the individually perceived sequence of attitudes and behaviors associated with work-related experiences and activities over the span of the person's life" (D. T. Hall, 2002, p. 12). Missing from this definition is the sociological view of career development where educational opportunities, socioeconomic status, race, and gender influence career development (Rocco & Gallagher, 2006). Advancement is an increase in status, salary, and scope of responsibility (Rocco & Gallagher, 2006). Friskopp and Silverstein (1996) found that heterosexism limits the career advancement of gay men and lesbians. Corporations and even gay executives preferred LGBT people to stay in the closet (Miller, 1995). Workplace heterosexism resulted in fewer promotions over a ten-year period for LGBT people (Ragins & Cornwell, 2001). Ragins and Wiethoff reported that "heterosexism had a negative relationship with job satisfaction, organizational commitment, career commitment, organization-based self-esteem, and satisfaction with opportunities for promotion" (Ragins & Wiethoff, 2005, p. 187).

Barriers to career development can be defined as "external conditions or internal states that make career progress difficult" (Swanson, 1995, p. 236). A review of the literature suggested career-related barriers to be an important area of inquiry for the career development of oppressed persons, but despite recent trends and increasing attention to career concerns and decision-making processes of minority groups, little attention has been given to lesbian groups in career-counseling literature (Barret & Logan, 2002). The fear, discrimination, and prejudice portrayed by society are more cruelly expressed toward lesbian and gay men than toward any other minority group (Israel & Selvidge, 2003). Unlike dealing with other social factors (e.g., gender and race), Israel and Selvidge (2003) stated, the idea of addressing one's sexual orientation in counseling can become a particularly difficult topic for many people.

A review of literature suggested that work discrimination is multifaceted. H. A. Brown and Ford (1977) reviewed employment discrimination: Access (e.g., discrimination during hiring, such as denial of job offer or lower starting salary) and treatment, such as discrimination after the person is hired. According to Chung (2001), Chojnacki and Gelberg (1994) identified four contrasting levels of work discrimination: Overt (or the presence of explicit formal and informal discrimination), covert (e.g., the presence of discrimination in the absence of a formal antidiscrimination policy), tolerance (e.g., the presence of formal antidiscrimination policy but lacking informal support), and affirmation (e.g., presence of both formal and informal support). Chung (2001) further points to the presence of discriminatory practices against individuals who are labeled as being lesbian, gay, or bisexual. For instance, Levine and Leonard (1984) found that self-identified lesbians reported experiences consistent with verbal harassment (e.g., gossip, taunts, and ridicule), nonverbal harassment (e.g., hard stares, ostracism, and damages to personal belongings), physical harassment, and violence. Notably, formal discrimination is presumed to directly affect an individual's vocational achievement or status, whereas informal discrimination may affect a person's morale, mental health, and work performance, which may indirectly influence his or her level of career advancement.

The risk factor regarding how much a person is willing to endure depends on a number of factors, including his or her level of sexual identity development, potential for discrimination, relative importance between sexual orientation and other considerations, and self-efficacy of coping with discrimination (Chung, 2001). These factors should be carefully explored and fully acknowledged when making vocational decisions. The application of sociocognitive career theory (Lent et al., 1996) may be helpful in such efforts (Morrow et al., 1996). According to Chung (2001) and this theoretical framework, vocational choice is influenced by previous learning experiences, self-efficacy, outcome expectations, interests, goals, and contextual factors, such as perceived potential discrimination.

## *Sociocognitive Career Theory*

Sociocognitive career theory (Lent et al., 1994) describes three career-related processes and how they are affected by three social–cognitive factors. According to this model, self-efficacy beliefs, outcome expectations, and goal representations reciprocally influence the development of career-related interests, the selection of career-related choices, and engagement in career-related endeavors. This theory is unique in its incorporation of the influence of background and environmental factors on career development. Such factors include gender, race or ethnicity, and contextual affordances (e.g., opportunities and barriers). Sociocognitive career theory is groundbreaking in its recognition of oppression as a formative influence in career development (Lent et al., 1994). According to Morrow et al. (1996), sociocognitive career theory may be appropriate for an LGBT population. These researchers summarized sociocognitive career theory as the idea that vocational interests are generally formed around activities and skills for which a person anticipates success. Given the presence of prejudice against LGBT individuals in some fields, they may not anticipate positive outcomes even when they are competent to perform the job. Therefore, anticipated barriers to career achievement may cause a foreclosure of career options.

Sociocognitive career theory (Lent et al., 1996) assumes a circular model of vocational development beginning with the formation of career-related interests, which are heavily influenced by self-efficacy and outcome expectations. This theory posits that to achieve a particular task, an individual must possess not only the requisite ability but also a sense of self-efficacy. Thus, individuals are likely to become interested in activities in which they anticipate efficacious and successful outcomes. In the case of lowered self-efficacy or less than positive predicted outcomes, "it may be difficult for robust interests to blossom" (Lent et al., 1994, p. 89). The development of career-related interests is followed by goal-setting and goal-directed behavior. This allows the individual to gain exposure and practice career-related activities. Such practice leads to increased skill attainment, which directly influences individuals' self-efficacy and outcome expectations related to the task. Many of these concerns around passing as straight, identity confusion, prejudice, and discrimination can be perceived as barriers to accessing and succeeding in careers. In fact, as Swanson, Daniels, and Tokar (1996) stated, barriers to career development can be defined as "external conditions or internal states that make career progress difficult" (p. 236). It is important to note that this definition does not conceive barriers as impenetrable but rather as obstacles that "are capable of being overcome, although with varying degrees of difficulty, according to the specific barrier and the particular individual" (Swanson et al., 1996, p. 236). A number of researchers have recently begun to examine the phenomenon of career barriers, and a review of the literature suggested that career-related barriers represent an important area of inquiry, especially for the career development of oppressed persons. For example, if there is low self-efficacy or expectations of negative outcomes, the entire developmental process may be affected. For LGBT youth, two important processes characterize the period of adolescence: crystallization of career interests and the discovery of sexual identity (Morrow et al., 1996). During this crucial time, barriers may be internal or external and can potentially restrict career development in a variety of ways. Internally, the individual may suffer from a loss of self-confidence and decision-making abilities (Fassinger, 1996a). Belz (1993) stated, that the decision to choose a career path is a difficult one for many students, and this difficulty is increased if one is also facing prejudice, negative stereotypes, discrimination, and homophobia in family, friends, and even oneself. In this regard, "sexual identity can become the core of self-definition and thereby affect all other factors in the career planning process" (p. 198). Externally, harassment, negative societal attitudes, and a lack of role models can have a grave effect both on developing a positive identity and on support for career choices (Fassinger, 1996a. Because of the emotional energy required for LGBT identity management, the career development process may become more complex and receive less attention (Belz, 1993; D'Augelli, 1996; Fassinger, 1996a). The lack of such attention can later lead to feelings of anxiety, indecision, and a sense of being behind or inadequate (Fassinger, 1996a). For instance, in a qualitative study of self-identified adult lesbians, Boatwright et al. (1996) found that 6 individuals reported educational delays during the time period when they came "out." In particular, these six individuals indicated that they felt this process had derailed their career path, whereas nine individuals reported a feeling of lagging behind their peers in career development.

Barriers to career development can also be distal or proximal (Lent et al., 2000). Distal factors exist in the background of one's career decision-making process, including factors that affect self-efficacy and outcome expectations. These factors may include the presence or lack of role models or support for career-related behaviors and are thought to shape career-related interests and choices. In contrast, proximal factors emerge at career decision-making junctures and may include "informal career contacts or exposure to discriminatory hiring practices" (Lent et al., 2000, p. 38). Both types of factors are likely to affect the translation of interests to goals or goal-directed behavior.

Lent et al. (2000) conceptualized the environment effect on an individual on three related, yet distinct, levels. Personal factors (e.g., gender, sexual orientation, self-efficacy) exist on the first level, the immediate social environment (e.g., family, friends) exists on the second level, and the larger society in which the individual resides constitutes the third and final level. LGBT individuals may potentially face barriers at all three levels. On the first level, minority sexual orientation may lead to internalized homophobia, resulting in decreased career self-efficacy and foreclosed career options. On the second level, the LGBT individual may encounter barriers in the form of discrimination or homophobia from significant others, which may affect support for pursuing certain career options. Finally, the LGBT individual may face barriers in the larger heterosexist society, which may affect job attainment or present discrimination at work. All three levels may result in messages to the individual that certain career paths are unacceptable or difficult to succeed in for a nonheterosexual. These expectations and performance standards may also blend with social realities to enhance or delimit academic or career options. Thus, impediments to career development may stem both from environmentally precipitated forces "and from the internalization of these forces" (Lent et al., 1994, p. 105).

Many LGBT individuals face oppressive circumstances that might have a negative effect on their vocational development process (Chung, Loeb, & Gonzo, 1996). Indeed, oppression may potentially affect many career-related factors such as self-efficacy, outcome expectancies, interest formation, goal setting, goal-directed behavior, and skill development. In addition, LGBT individuals must contend with external factors that make career progress difficult, including homophobic attitudes, harassment, and discrimination. All of these factors can be conceived of as barriers to career development or progress. Although a growing body of research on career barriers exists, minimal studies to date have focused on an LGBT population. Moreover, the majority of empirical work on career-related barriers has focused on person factors at the exclusion of contextual factors (Lent et al., 2000). This study will contribute to the knowledge of lesbian and gay vocational issues through an exploration of career-related barriers, at both internal and external levels, thereby addressing limitations in existing work.

## The Effect of Employment Discrimination on African American Lesbian Career Development

The focus of the research is not on mental health, but career advancement is tied specifically to its subcategory of vocational counseling. This research may also be a portal to assist vocational counselors in career-related mental health services for African American women. Past negative experiences often discourage lesbians from seeking mental health care services, inclusive of vocational counseling, and when they do, lesbians are at times fearful and often are not open about their sexual orientation, identity, and behavior (Saulnier, 2002). Growing evidence suggested that lesbian, gay, and bisexual adults are at increased risk for mental health disorders than heterosexuals (Cochran, Mays, Alegria, Ortega, & Takeuchi, 2007). These mental disorders may not be to the level of a serious pathology, but employment discrimination may contribute to these higher rates (DeAngelis, 2002; Cochran & Mays, 2000). Increased risk is possibly due to anti-gay stigma, but little of this work has examined minorities' experience of multiple sources of discrimination (Cochran et al., 2007). Anti-gay stigma is compounded by the United States mental health system and vocational counselors not being well equipped to meet the needs of minority populations (Takeuchi & Uehara, 1996). In addition to the elimination of employment discrimination, negative stereotyping, discrimination, and limited role models, mental health effects are another concern that the LGBT population may face given possible employment discrimination.

African American lesbians use mental health services more than any other racial group of lesbians (Morris, 1997), and they constitute 47% of the lesbian population who seek mental health counseling (Morris, 1997). According to researchers on the Chicago Health and Life Experiences of Women Study, 69% of African American lesbians report use of mental health services such as vocational therapy and career counseling (Hughes, 2001). Vocational and career development counseling is a subset of mental health counseling and there is a need for specific research that can also be used to support the vocational development of African American lesbians that is provided by mental health professionals. Homophobia is possibly one reason that the mental health needs of African American lesbians are often not addressed (Fassinger, 1991), and this may suggest another social and emotional effect of sexual orientation employment discrimination. More recent research also points out that social stressors, such as homophobia, can influence some mental disorders, mainly anxiety and substance abuse disorders (Dohrenwend, 2000). However, with regard to racial and ethnic groups, little research has considered minority psychological health in conjunction with other oppressed identities, including sexuality and gender (Bowleg et al., 2003). With this in mind, because of the history of (a) social stigmatization, violence, and discrimination against gay men and lesbians, and (b) the oppression of women in general, lesbians of

African descent are seemingly vulnerable and may be at risk for high rates of psychological distress.

Hetherington, Hillerbrand, and Etringer (1989) addressed the career issues of people in the gay community, who are reputed to be more uncertain about their career choices and less satisfied in their jobs than are heterosexual individuals. Hetherington, Hillerbrand, and Etringer (1989) found that counselors need to know three issues regarding support needed by gay men and lesbians from mental health professionals. One issue is negative stereotyping (e.g., equating homosexuality with mental illness or assuming that gay men and lesbians dominate certain occupations). A second issue is employment discrimination, because the legal status of those having a different sexual orientation from the majority is not clearly established and is still evolving. A third issue concerns the fact that there are limited role models or mentors for gay men and lesbians. Limited role models appear to have the same effect on the gay community as the absence of appropriate role models has on any minority population (Hetherington, Hillerbrand, & Etringer, 1989). More recent research also shows the need for health professionals to address career-related issues that affect African American lesbians—sexual and ethnic minorities at risk of experiencing discrimination and oppression (Boatwright, Gilbert, Forrest, & Ketzenberger, 1996).

In summarizing the relation of employment issues, gender, race, and sexuality for African American lesbians, one can describe career-identity development as needing to include dealing with the process of coming out and effectively handling experiences with overt and internalized homophobia. Many lesbians are faced with this challenge during young adulthood, and given the difficulty many have with coming "out," making career decisions at this time period becomes an added difficulty (Barret & Logan, 2002). While an African American lesbian is developing a lesbian identity, she is also developing an African American identity. One identity is not exclusive of the other each, and both are involved in the development of an overall identity. For example, self-sustaining the identity of being African American may clash with the identity of being lesbian.

Research by Bridges et al. (2003) implies that many lesbian women of color seek professional counseling to deal with their triple minority status in society. All lesbian women of color from different racial and religious backgrounds struggle to live in a society that is described as racist, sexist, heterosexist, and that promotes considerable challenges for people of multiple minority statuses (Barret & Logan, 2002). With these challenges, some may develop negative beliefs about potential careers and are less apt to take advantage of professional opportunities for advancement (Barret & Logan, 2002).

There is very little known about the effects of sexism and racism on career development, and the extent to which existing models accurately describe the experiences of African American women is still unclear (Richie et al., 1997). There is not a comprehensive model of career development of racial and ethnic minorities, and there is even less attention devoted to models of career development of racial and ethnic minority women (Betz, 1994) and there is a strong need to extend the research of the career decision self-efficacy to other populations, especially those that are not White (Betz, Klein, & Taylor, 1996). African American women could be perceived to view their career development process differently from their White counterparts because of their unique backgrounds and views. More needs to be known about the career development of African American women, because knowing this will help organizations and researchers develop appropriate theories, research, and interventions.

The importance of a person's environmental context to career development, such as Savickas's (2002) career construction theory, is consistent with the literature that has demonstrated a clear relationship between social support and career variables (Harris, Moritzen, Robitschek, Imhoff, & Lynch, 2001; Swanson, 1995). In a 2005 study, Savickas examined the idea that external contextual variables, such as social support, contribute to the way an individual progresses and constructs his or her career development. Savickas (2005) found that social support predicted career maturity and vocational indecision. Social support has also been shown to be an important variable related to healthy adjustment in several facets of development, including sexual identity and career development processes (Schultheiss, Kress, Manzi, & Glasscock, 2001). Social support among LGBT individuals has been associated with lower levels of internalized homophobia, higher levels of identity expression, and higher levels of disclosure (Szymanski, Chung, & Balsam, 2001).

"African Americans often cite that one of the barriers to career advancement is being viewed as having divergent cultural norms from their White peers and I think the same is true for gay employees," according to H. Alexander Robinson, CEO of the National Black

Justice Coalition, a civil rights organization that supports African American LGBT people (E. White, 2007, p. 66). Robinson points out that for African American LGBT employees, it may be even more difficult to advance because being in a management position would be one more thing that might make them different from their coworkers (E. White, 2007, p. 66).

# CHAPTER 3. METHODOLOGY

## Methodology Introduction

This doctoral studies research considered ethical issues related to both content and research protocol. The university Institutional Review Board (IRB) approved the research proposal and helped the researcher ensure that the problem studied benefits the participants. This dissertation's IRB approval required participant consent forms, confidentiality protection and procedures, such as data storage, that consider the needs of and risks to all participants. The only potential risk to the participants was their identification; however every effort was made to protect privacy and confidentiality by using a self-selected pseudonym during the form completion, interview, and in the dissertation document. Place of employment was not identified and the audiotapes, notes, signed consent and demographic forms, and transcripts are retained in the researcher's secure residential office location in a locked fireproof safe deposit in for a minimum of seven years with the key only available to the researcher. Seven years after publication of the dissertation, all tapes, notes, transcripts, etc. will be destroyed by erasure and/or shredding disposal. Those procedures were reviewed in detail with the participants and are discussed throughout this chapter.

Norms and organizational values are socially constructed by dominant groups and are usually composed of the views of those who are White, male, heterosexual, and mentally and physically able (Croteau, Talbot, Lance, & Evans, 2002). Minorities are often minimized, and there may be informal social behavior, such as organizational marginalization of racial minorities, women, LGBT individuals, and/or members of disabled groups (Agocs, 2004). White, male culture remains the norm in American culture today, and women, people of color, and other nonmajority groups often recognize this as the situation. This has left many minorities feeling that White men have always had a seat at the corporate table (K. Greene, 2006).

Unfortunately, many White male managers are only subconsciously aware of the sometimes unspoken rules and double standards that can affect African American lesbians. Managers should consider learning to identify their organization's culture and rules, which can then be passed down to women and minorities (K. Greene, 2006). Knowledge sharing refers to providing all employees with what they need to know about career advancement, communication, leadership, management, organizational culture, power, networking, interpersonal skills, and all other unwritten rules, norms, and cues for success.

Even with empowerment of minority and female employees, the hardest and most controversial questions among employee rights are those having to do with LGBT employees. Sexual minority employees have been denied promotions or lost jobs because many organizations do not have policies against discrimination on the basis of sexual orientation, and some organizations do not promote diversity awareness (Daly & Simon, 1992). According to Agocs (2004), the culture of an organization or department may render minority group members invisible, creating a glass ceiling, and perpetuating a poisoned environment that is intimidating, abusive, hostile, humiliating, or offensive. Individual, situational, and cultural factors influence the extent to which individuals will regard themselves as victims of discrimination. Because discrimination perceptions involve the subjective, it is often difficult to determine whether individual perception of the amount of discrimination he or she is experiencing accurately reflects the level of discrimination that truly exists in a given context (Kaiser & Major, 2006). The most direct way to assess whether individuals report or suppress their discrimination perceptions is to simply ask them to reflect on how they handled past experiences with discrimination (Kaiser & Major, 2006). For example, a recent telephone survey of roughly 1,000 Americans revealed that 28% of the African American respondents believed that they experienced workplace discrimination within the past year with being passed over for a promotion, being assigned undesirable tasks, and hearing inappropriate comments were the most frequent complaints (Dixon, Storen, & Van Horn, 2002).

There is a need for a greater understanding and awareness of diversity in sexual orientation, a segment of diversity in the workplace (Society for Human Resource Management, 2001). Companies that understand the importance of managing diversity in the organization have a better chance of attracting the best employees (Luthans, 2002). According to Chin (2005), cultural competence is vital in organizations, and activities should include training, using self-assessment tools, and implementing goals and objectives to ensure that policies and practices are responsive to diversity within the work population.

Although there is greater acceptance for gay men and lesbians, there are still highly controversial questions about their employee rights given the lack of federal support (Human Rights Campaign Foundation, 2003). Organizations need to understand the needs of their LGBT workforce in order to create policies and programs that protect them and other minorities from discrimination. Recent qualitative studies have documented the persistence of discrimination among minorities, especially African Americans, in many different social settings (Cose, 1993; Essed, 1991; Feagin, 1991).

This research will broaden the current qualitative research and provide greater insight into the possible employment discrimination faced by self-identified African American lesbians. To date, apparently little attention has been paid to how an individual's multiple social and cultural group statuses shape that individual's multicultural experiences. A few conceptual works have focused on the interactive effect of multiple oppressed statuses (Fukuyama & Ferguson, 2000; Reynolds & Pope, 1991). However, it remains notable that few investigations have examined how multiple group statuses work in combination, particularly the combination of oppressed and privileged statuses.

Research Design

Although commonly used interchangeably, the terms *Black* and *African American* have different definitions. African Americans are persons who self-identify with African ancestry who were kin to involuntary immigrants to the United States (Ogbu, 1990). The term *African American* refers only to U.S. citizens, but is often applied to Black residents who are not citizens. Some people who perceive themselves or are perceived by others as members of a dark complexion cultural group often are called *Black* but may not be African American (Ogbu, 1990). The term *African American* is used in this research, given the commonality of its usage in earlier research when describing similar research participants. The research participants will have spent the majority of their adult life living in the United States.

Racial discrimination has received a great deal of attention in existing literature given the history of slavery and segregation and documented racial discrimination affecting advancement of African Americans (Jaynes & Williams, 1989). Race and sexual orientation are importantly linked and intertwined in identity development. Every individual belongs to several different social and cultural statuses; that is, each individual has a race or ethnicity, gender, sexual orientation, and economic status. Status within each of these dimensions corresponds to a different rank and value in society, resulting in privilege, such as White, male, and heterosexual status, or oppression, such as African American, female, and LGBT status (Fukuyama & Ferguson, 2000; Robinson & Howard-Hamilton, 2000).

Some research suggested that reported levels of discrimination are linked to methodological issues, such as the manner in which discrimination is assessed (D. Williams, 1998). In debating whether qualitative or quantitative research is superior, Tashakkori and Teddlie (1998) appeared to be swayed by the pragmatist philosophy of "what works" (p. 21). The idea of wanting to understand the qualitative dynamics of one's lived experiences can best be done by utilizing a framework that focuses on personal viewpoints of human behavior. One of the significant differences between the positivist and constructivist points of view is conceptualization of human behavior (Glesne, 1999). The overall purpose of qualitative research is to explore and describe socially constructed realities (Denzen & Lincoln, 1994). Validity within this qualitative constructivist paradigm is one of meaning (Moustakas, 1990). Guba and Lincoln (1994) two criteria for validity, "trustworthiness and authenticity" (p. 114). According to these authors, trustworthiness, or credibility, as an indication of validation in the constructivist paradigm, is an internal process in which the researcher creates legitimacy. A researcher can require validation, objectivity, and reliability. They further stated that authenticity, defined as fairness, addresses the question of validity. Authenticity also leads to improved understanding of constructions of others and is relevant to this phenomenological study, given that it examined the lived experiences of the participants. The positivist position contends that behavior is quantifiable and determined by external laws, whereas the constructivist position contends that individuals' behavior can only be understood within their personal contexts (Moustakas, 1990).

Psychologists often evaluate an individual's experience to guide treatment, and this research also aims to try to understand individuals' meanings as they relate to their lived experiences (McMahon, Patton, & Watson, 2003). The emergence of constructivism has affected many areas of psychology, including vocational psychology, which is very relevant in discussions of employment discrimination. Mays & Cochran (2001)offered that psychology must be willing to teach and develop a body of science that is informed by principles of social justice and equity. Given the lack of employment focused legislative initiatives can result in career-related psychological distress for LGBT people and consequences include fear, sadness, alienation, anger, and an increase in internalized homophobia (Russell, 2000; Russell & Richards, 2003). In addition, LGBT minority stress can increase given the lack of federal protection and fear that revolves around it (Cochran & Mays, 2000; Mays & Cochran, 2001).

Constructivists within vocational psychology have a fundamental goal to understand the manner in which individuals make meaning of career issues within the context of their lived experiences (Lyddon & Alford, 1993). Career and personal contexts are blended, and meaning is dictated by the individual. The individual tells his or her stories while the investigator seeks to understand meaning within the individual's experience (McMahon et al., 2003). In this manner, qualitative research can focus on the participant's lived experiences.

Methods of conducting qualitative research include use of narratives, phenomenology, ethnography, grounded theory, and case studies (Creswell, 2003). Qualitative methods are appropriate for the current study because they allow for examination of collective cultural characteristics, including how individuals personally transform such cultural characteristics (Kleinman & Kleinman, 1991). In addition, qualitative methods are appropriate for the current study because they allow one to explore particularly intractable problems of human experience, as interacting cultures are realized, expressed, and interact on individual and collective levels. According to Creswell (2003), "qualitative research can be less objectifying and more concerned with cultural and political means, thus conveying the voices and experiences of individuals who have been suppressed" (p. 10). Individuals from minority groups can fit into that context. In fact, according to Subich (1996), qualitative research, in general, serves well the needs of diverse populations, such as those of ethnic and sexual minorities.

The research study focused on the experiences of ethnic and sexual minority participants using phenomenological research that examined human experiences through detailed descriptions of the individuals being studied. Qualitative phenomenological research can be useful when personal meaning and lived experience are the foci of inquiry, such as employment discrimination due to issues related to race, ethnicity, religion, politics, veteran status, age, disability, and sexual orientation. Within phenomenology, the goal is not to eliminate subjectivity but rather to clarify its role when knowledge is attained. However, qualitative research still possesses some disadvantages, including (a) the need for extensive data collection, (b) the potential for researcher bias, (c) labor intensity, (d) data overload, (e) adequacy of sampling with only a few participants, (f) credibility and quality of conclusions, and (g) the reliability, validity, and generalizability of findings (Miles & Huberman, 1994). Overall, in qualitative research, trustworthiness is vital and means being faithful to the data or having what is often referred to as *validity* in quantitative research (Glesne, 1999).

In an effort to help discover key phenomena that would support tracking career development and describe a population that has rarely been studied, the experiences of the participants are interpreted through a qualitative research contained within the phenomenological philosophy. The goal of a phenomenological approach to scientific research is to give an accurate description of a specific aspect of subjective human experience (Polkinghorne, 1988). Phenomenologists believe that humans interpret our experiences in multiple ways through our interactions with the world. In turn, the meaning we attribute to our experiences constitutes our reality. A phenomenological study, therefore, is one which seeks to explore the conceptual world of the participants in order to understand how they construct meaning in relation to specific event (Bogdan & Bilken, 1992).

In terms of validity, the cause-and-effect thinking of qualitative social science data analysis can be effectively utilized when assessing employment discrimination (Creswell, 2003). The research study aimed to generate explanations regarding potential career hindrances among self-identified African American lesbians. Because of this the researcher can use epoche bracketing as a means to reduce threats to validity or researcher bias. This bracketing method highlights a particular period when significant events occurred in the experiences of a researcher, but any impact from the memory of these events needs to be placed aside during data collection (Morse, 1994). To further eliminate threats to validity, researchers have also advocated for rapport building between the interviewer and interviewee (Blumer, 1956; Bogdan & Bilken, 1992; Stebbins, 1972), given that validity is often increased by pursuing subjectivity, as opposed to objectivity.

Ethics revolves around researchers being actively involved in disclosing the assumptions, values and interests into the design, implementation and use of the research. The task of ethics is not to prescribe policies or corrective action, but to continue to open the discussion for scrutiny and ethical consideration and deliberation. The task of ethics is to point back to the thoughts that made particular inquiries show up as meaningful and necessary. It seeks to interrogate these assumptions and attitudes.

In terms of ethical liability, researchers ensure that the data obtained are stored with all the precautions appropriate to the sensitivity of the data. Data released should not contain names, initials or other identifying information. Dignity and autonomy of human subjects is the ethical basis of respect for the privacy of research subjects. Privacy is a fundamental value, perceived by many as essential for the protection and promotion of human dignity. Hence, the access, control and dissemination of personal information are essential to ethical research. Information that is disclosed in the context of a professional or research relationship must be held confidential. Thus, when a research subject confides personal information to a researcher, the researcher has a duty not to share the information with others without the subject's free and informed consent. Breaches of confidentiality are against IRB protocol and may cause harm: to the trust relationship between the researcher and the research subject; to other individuals or groups; and/or to the reputation of the research community. Confidentiality in this researcher's study applies to information obtained directly from subjects and has a legal obligation to maintain personal records confidential. In this regard, a subject-centered perspective on the nature of the research, its aims and its potential to invade sensitive interests may help better design and conduct research.

The research indicated to research subjects the extent of the confidentiality that can be promised. Good ethical reasoning requires thought, insight and sensitivity to context, which in turn help to refine the roles and application of norms that govern relationships. There are several reasons why it is important to adhere to ethical norms in research (National Institutes of Health, 2008). First, some of these norms promote the aims of research, such as knowledge, truth, and avoidance of error. For example, prohibitions against fabricating, falsifying, or misrepresenting research data promote the truth and avoid error. Second, since research often involves a great deal of cooperation and coordination among many different people in different disciplines and institutions, many of these ethical standards promote the values that are essential to collaborative work, such as trust, accountability, mutual respect, and fairness. For example, many ethical norms in research, such as guidelines for authorship, copyright and patenting policies, data sharing policies, and confidentiality rules in peer review, are designed to protect intellectual property interests while encouraging collaboration. Most researchers want to receive credit for their contributions and do not want to have their ideas stolen or disclosed prematurely. Third, many of the ethical norms help to ensure that researchers can be held accountable to the public. For instance, federal policies on research misconduct, on conflicts of interest, on the human subjects' protections, and use are necessary in order to make sure that researchers who are funded by public money can be held accountable to the public. Fourth, ethical norms in research also help to build public support for research. People are more likely to fund research project if they can trust the quality and integrity of research. Finally, many of the norms of research promote a variety of other important moral and social values, such as social responsibility and human rights.

## Sampling Approach

Subich (1996) noted that qualitative research fits well with the needs of diverse population, such as ethnic and sexual minorities. The best method for social science study is one that answers the research question(s) most efficiently and with foremost inference quality; the method should also include dimensions of trustworthiness and internal validity. The research study utilized a qualitative research method, phenomenology, and participant interviews to explore the issues related to the career advancement of self-identified African American lesbians.

The phenomenological approach to be used in this study will incorporate multiple-participant research. This will potentially allow for strong inferences to be made once factors start to recur with more than 1 participant. Within constructivist research, the participant will become the expert on her lived experience, and the investigator will become a curious inquirer (McMahon et al., 2003). The research methodology will consist of semi-structured questions, as constructivism requires active work on the parts of both researcher and participant. Accordingly, the participant fills the role of teacher, whereas the researcher fills the role of learner (Peavy, 1997).

Creswell (1994) emphasized that phenomenological research involves "studying a small number of subjects through extensive and prolonged engagement in order to develop patterns and relations of meaning" (p. 12). Snowball sampling, a nonprobability sample, was used in this study to recruit participants, because this method is recommended when the group under study is invisible, group membership is not obvious, and/or when access to the group is limited (Sommer & Sommer, 1991). Phenomenology can be associated with single cases or a selected study sample. With single-case studies, phenomenology can illustrate issues that describe failures in systems and discrepancies; it may also convey attention to different situations, suggesting that positive inference is more difficult to make with a small participant sample (Warren, 1977). In multiple-participant research, the strength of inference, which can be made, increases rapidly once factors or themes start to recur with more than one participant (Warren, 1977).

Phenomenological research can be quite robust in indicating the presence of factors and their related effects in individual cases, but is also tentative in suggesting the extent of such factors in relation to the population from which the participants or cases were drawn (Creswell, 1994). Thus, phenomenological research may be used to illustrate that thematic factors are present and demonstrate their effects but should not be used to draw cause-and-effect references with respect to the study's population (Creswell, 1994).

"Purposeful sampling focuses on selecting information-rich cases whose study will illuminate the questions under study" (Patton, 2002, p. 230). Polkinghorne (2005) recommended a sample size of 5 to 25 participants in qualitative research, although Patton (2002) stated that there are no specific rules for sample size. "Sample size depends on what you want to know, the purpose of the inquiry, what's at stake, what will be useful, what will have credibility, and what can be done with available time and resources" (Paton, 2002, p. 244). Following the guidance of both authors, the sample size of the study consisted of eight lesbian women who identified as African Americans in managerial positions at work. In addition, interviews continued until data saturation was reached. Data saturation in the current study was reached by participant eight and data saturation is obtained when the interviews stop producing new information or insights that add to the themes captured in previous interviews. Data saturation is a subjective determination made by the researcher (Creswell, 2005). Qualitative research and phenomenological research designs typically employ a purposeful sampling strategy, as opposed to the random sampling used in quantitative designs (Creswell, Plano Clark, & Garrett, 2007; Haverkamp & Young, 2007; Patton, 2002). Purposeful sampling was used to identify participants for the study. Purposeful sampling, or snowball sampling, as it is sometimes referred to-involved direct outreach toward individuals who self-identified as African American, a manager, and lesbian. The researcher relied on her own membership in this community to use word of mouth, etc. to recruit participants. The most effective strategy was word of mouth and mass email, as many of the participants had relationships or knowledge of others in the context of the community of self-identified African American lesbian managers.

The selected method of additional convenience sampling is described as nonrandom sampling in which individuals are sampled because they are the only ones available (Glicken, 2003). The second stage of sampling was snowball sampling due to suggestions that it would be difficult to locate out lesbians who meet eligibility criteria.

As described, snowball sampling is a nonprobability method used to recruit a sample (Walters & Simoni, 1993). In the snowball sampling method for this study, the researcher asked participants to identify other potential participants.

Targeted participants for the study were self-identified African American lesbian managers, although it is acknowledged by the researcher that this may not be an easily attained group. Accordingly, a nonprobability sampling method was used, which involves study of groups of the general population that are generally unknown and inaccessible (Glicken, 2003). Convenience sampling methods were utilized initially in the study, with potential participants to be recruited at the National Black Lesbian Conference held in Las Vegas, Nevada. This annual summer conference is composed of self-identified African American lesbians from all over the United States. Conference participants are generally at the managerial level and above, from both public and private organizations. The national conference typically attracts over 500 African American women who identify as lesbian and the program guide reaches as many as 10,000 people and it had the researcher's contact information and research details for those that might be interested in being a participant. In an effort to recruit participants, e-mails were sent to various LGBT-related organizations to be forwarded by the organization itself to its electronic mailing lists so that the need for study participants can pass by word of mouth. LGBT organizations and networking groups were contacted via email and asked to forward the consent letter and research details to its membership.

Participants were also recruited by online resourcing such as LGBT contact websites. Gay and lesbian organizations such as the Audre Lorde Project, NIA Collective, LGBT Meetup Groups, Human Rights Campaign, Astrea , Blacklight , The International Federation of Black Prides , Operation Rebirth , Fierce , Zami , Griot , People of Color Political Action Club , People of Color in Crisis , HirShe , Women of Color Resources , Sisters in the Life , Half-n-Half Productions , Shadee Productions, Women of Distinction , United Lesbians of African Heritage , FemmeNoir , Sable , Girlzparty , African Ancestral Lesbians United for Social Change, Sisters in Search of Truth and Harmony ,Sophisticated Aggressive Gents, Brooklyn Pride ,  Heritage of Pride, Go , National Black Lesbian and Gay Lesbian Leadership Forum , Out Professionals (, National Gay and Lesbian Task Force , Black Gay and Lesbian Leadership Forum ,

National Black Justice Foundation , Lesbian Alliance and National Center for Lesbian Rights , Zuna Institute , Let's Talk National LGBT Community Centers, Inhertwined , Jasmyne Cannick , DC Black Pride Promoters , African Asian Latina Lesbians United , Black Lesbian Support Group , Lovergirl , National Center for Lesbian Rights , and Women in the Life , and so forth were resources via e-mail contact and they forwarded the consent letter to their membership via their electronic mailing list forwarding and listserves. The organizations were sent study objectives, Internal Review Board information, and researcher contact information.

    The consent letter also indicated for recipients to forward the letter and consent form to others that might have interest and be qualified. The research study looked to enroll a minimum of 8 and a maximum of 12 participants, up to the point of saturation. Researchers utilize diverse strategies when faced with issues of sample size in qualitative research, and there are no set rules for sample size in qualitative inquiry. Rather, sample size depends upon what the researcher wants to know, what will have credibility, and what can be done with available time and resources (Patton, 1990). According to Creswell (1998), sample sizes in phenomenological research are usually "small, with up to 10 participants" (pp. 65, 113). There is no formula to determine the size of a nonrandom sample, and researchers have found that their phenomenological study topics were saturated after interviewing only fix to six individuals (Gayle, 1997; Savage, 1973). As noted, saturation is the point at which the interviews fail to reveal additional themes. Given the limited amount of research in this area, sample size was slightly larger than the standard of six participants. However, this would be the case only if saturation was not encountered after interviewing the recommended six participants. Other factors that impacted sample size include time, resources, participant geographic location, and availability of participants.

## Participants

Each participant in this study self-identified as an out African American lesbian that is currently or was previously employed in a managerial position. To be selected for participation in this study, each participant defined herself as (a) African American, (b) an out lesbian, (c) currently or previously employed as a manager or retired for no more than two years, and (d) between the ages of 32 and 72 years, in order to allow for progressive work experience and managerial-level growth and progression. Those interested in participating in the study had to select a pseudonym for confidentiality, return a demographics form, allowing the researcher to know whether they fit the study criteria. The demographics form asked for information on age, marital status, previous and current positions, tenure in the organizations, the number of people supervised, and so forth (Appendix A). Selection of participants was based on their being self-identified African American lesbian managers in the workforce in which their experiences are investigated. Participants were sought openly to discuss their experiences, beliefs, and articulate their feelings, and the use of managers may allow for greater insight into career development trends that allow for professional advancement.

The investigation involved two parts: (a) An explanation of this study and gaining the participant's informed consent, and (b) a discussion of the participant's experiences related to being out at work. The length of the interview was anticipated to be approximately between 2 and 4 hours; however, the timeframe was flexible, to provide adequate time for the interview questions to be answered thoroughly. The interview questions were open-ended, informal, and conversational in nature, and the interviews were scheduled for weekdays after 5:00 pm, for the weekend, or for mutually convenient times. There were 25 interview questions, but this number varied based on the flow of the interview and thoroughness of the participant responses. Interviews took take place in wheelchair accessible space at the X or at a mutually convenient location, such as the X events, if more feasible for the participant.

This phenomenological study described and interprets the experiences of participants in order to seek understanding of their perspectives. Accordingly, the study was based on the belief that there are multiple ways of interpreting the same experience, and the meaning of that experience is what constitutes the participant's reality. This research question was focused on ascertaining the thematic codes regarding the trends in meaning of the event, episode, or interaction.

Factors that have informed the targeted sample size include the purpose and focus of the study, primary data collection strategies, and participant availability. It is essential to the design of the study that those who might volunteer to participate meet certain inclusion criteria. Consequently, the study was designed to include only those who, at minimum, have been employed in the workforce at a managerial level or higher and, if retired, must have done so within the past two years. The latter criterion is to ensure that recollections of their career experiences remain relatively fresh in their minds. It is also critical that all potential participants indicate their willingness to engage in active self-reflection and self-disclosure about their work experiences as an out lesbian and be open to sharing information related to the research question: "How does employment discrimination, or the fear of such discrimination, affect African American lesbian managers' perceptions of their career advancement?"

## Instrumentation and Overview

A variety of methods can be used in phenomenological-based research, including interviews, conversations, participant observation, action research, focus meetings, and analysis of personal text journals. To strike a balance between keeping a focus on the research issues and avoiding undue influence by the researcher, good rapport and empathy are vital to gaining depth of information, particularly where investigating issues for which the participant has a strong personal stake.

This dissertation study explored the nature of the participant's subjective interpretation of the various types of social interactions that have shaped her career advancement and professional development. Phenomenology designates and permits the understanding of the lived experiences. These lived experiences are the core foundation of inquiry into the varied interpretations, the emic or personal interpretation or understanding of what appears to others as not the monocular single portrait or presentation of a single universal truth but rather the creation of multiple truths encountered within a binocular landscape (Walzer, 1987). Phenomenology is concerned with the understanding of a reality embodied in human experience and expressed in categories of understanding that are social in origin and shared with others (Holstein & Gubrium, 1996). In the case of a phenomenological study, the data consists of the participants' descriptions of their subjective experience of a particular event. Although descriptions can be gathered in a variety of ways, interviews are the most common. Interviews are preferable when a large amount of information is needed, when there is a need to be flexible in gathering data from each respondent, and, finally, when sensitive topics are to be probed.

Patton (1990) outlined three basic approaches to interviewing, namely the informal conversational interview, the standardized open-ended interview, and the general interview guide approach. For the purpose of this study, the general interview guide was selected. This approach to interviewing called for the preparation of a list of questions or areas of inquiry that need to be explored with each participant. Using an interview guide was a way to provide the researcher with more control over data gathering than one would have with an informal conversational interview. The interview guide approach allowed the researcher to structure each interview so that the same topics were covered and the same type of information is gathered from each respondent (Patton, 1990). The interview guide served as a checklist to be used during the interview while giving the interviewer the freedom to be spontaneous and to adapt the wording of each question to the personality of each respondent. In addition, it offered the possibility to explore a specific area further if needed (Patton, 1990). The researcher developed an interview checklist (Appendix A) in order to keep track of the questions asked and of the areas covered during the interview. To ensure that the same type of information was obtained from all participants, the researcher placed check marks in front of each area of inquiries once it had been satisfactorily covered. The interview guide was a resource tool and it did not mandate that each question was asked if the participant hadalready covered the content in a previous response.

Reinharz (1992) contended that interviewing is particularly important for the study of women, "because in this way learning from women is an antidote to centuries of ignoring women's ideas altogether or having men speak for women" (p. 19). Anderson, Armitage, Jack, and Wittner (1990) suggested that "interviewing is a method used to incorporate the previously overlooked lives, activities, and feelings of women into our understanding of the past and present" (p. 95). Interviews tell how women feel and can interpret the personal meaning and value of particular activities. It was suggested by Anderson et al. (1990) that "oral interviews not only allow women to articulate their own experiences, but also allow reflection upon the meaning of those experiences" (p. 102).

This research used open-ended questions to minimize simple "yes" or "no" responses and consistent questioning of each participant will provide more efficient time usage. Interview questions regarding the main area of inquiry were constructed around the research question and consisted of the following major categories: Career development, career path, workforce interactions, barriers to career progression, and facilitators to career progression. Patton (1990) contended that the "interview guide presumes there is common information that should be obtained from each person interviewed" (p. 280).

Throughout the interviews in this study, the researcher sought to establish an atmosphere of trust so that the participants will feel comfortable talking about their personal experiences. Because the setting plays a major part in creating an atmosphere conducive to a relaxed conversational exchange, all the interviews were conducted in a relaxed, informal private conference room atmosphere, that was booked by the researcher or selected by the participant, to allow for non-interruption.

Participants received an introductory letter that described the study, and they were asked to sign the letter to document informed consent. Thereafter, in-person, audio taped interviews took place in less than a 12-week period, with consideration given to those in the X Tri-State area proximity or attending X Conference. The interviews were projected to last between 2 and 4 hours, and the average interview was actually 1 hour and 15 minutes, with no strict minimum or maximum timeframe. Participants also had the opportunity to send any additional interview response feedback via e-mail as a supplement to the in-person interview, with the rationale that some individuals express themselves better in writing than in verbal conversations. After in-person interviews were conducted, the researcher confidentially conversed with the subjects regarding the written the written transcript that they had the option of verifying, adding to, and/ or correcting and returning.

The interview questions centered on career development, professional advancement, the work environment, and coming out at work. Pretests were completed to preview the interview guides for language and ease of understanding. The field test, not a pilot study, used five people, such as professors to gauge the ease of grammatical question construction and interview question comprehension, professional women managers who are familiar with the research topic, and people similar to those who are most likely to inquire about being a research participant. External factors that are purported to threaten the validity of the study include (a) interactions between the researcher and participants, (b) participants' reaction to the topic being discussed, (c) the setting of the interview, (d) preexisting participant perceptions regarding the outcome of the study, and (e) participants' willingness to share their experiences openly and honestly.

## Data Collection

Phenomenology concerns itself with exploring an experience from all sides until the true essence of the experience is recognized. The exploration creates vivid and complete descriptions of experiences (Moustakas, 1994). Other qualitative methods were evaluated for their appropriateness to the current study. Although a case study method was considered as a possible methodology, case study research focuses on a bounded system and a specific identified issue (Creswell, et. al. 2007) and given the study sought to understand the lived experiences of the women, an alternative method, such as surveys, would not provide the breadth and depth of information sought. Phenomenology permits researchers to cultivate an "objective 'essence' through aggregating subjective experiences of a number of individuals. Phenomenology is useful to use when the researcher has identified a phenomenon to understand, and has individuals who can provide a description of what they have experienced" (Moerer-Urdahl & Creswell, 2004, p. 23).

Qualitative methods are appropriate to capture detailed and in-depth information from a small sample of individuals (Patton, 2002). A qualitative approach was appropriate given little is known about this specific concept or "central phenomenon" (Creswell, 2005) and therefore, a phenomenological approach was suitable for this study. Phenomenology focuses on "exploring how human beings make sense of experience and transform experience into consciousness-how they perceive it, describe it, feel about it, judge it, remember it, and make sense of it, and talk about it with others" (Patton, 2002, p. 104).

The primary source of knowledge according to phenomenology is perception (Moustakas, 1994). Perceptions translate into a comprehensive description of the lived experiences of individuals in relation to a central phenomenon, which allows the researcher to unearth underlying themes of meanings (Gibson & Hanes, 2003). After gaining the perceptions of the women through the semi-structured interviews, phenomenological analysis occurred by incorporating four steps. The four steps included (a) the epoche and focus on trying to reduce preconceptions of the researcher, (b) phenomenological reduction or bracketing to get an account of the actual participants' experiences, (c) imaginative variance to obtain textual descriptions from each participant, and (d) synthesis of meaning and essences to unify the individual experience group as a whole (Moustakas, 1994).

Resulting from first-person information of life experiences, phenomenological analysis incorporates the four steps described above (Moustakas, 1994). Epoche, the Greek term regarding to stay away from or abstain, according to Moustakas (1994), requires the researcher to refrain from judgment and view the phenomenon without bias or preconceived notions, as if to see it for the first time. The epoche is not a single fixed step and the process is ongoing and occurs even as the second step of phenomenological reduction begins. Phenomenological reduction requires the researcher to discover the data in their purest form by bracketing out presuppositions and assumptions (Patton, 2002). "Phenomenological reduction is not only a way of seeing but a way of listening with a conscious and deliberate intention of opening urselves to phenomena as phenomena, in their own right, with their own textures and meanings" (Moustakas, 1994, p. 92). In addition to bracketing the data, phenomenological reduction involves its horizontal placement, which requires the researcher to treat all of the data as equally important. Themes extracted from different frames of reference and divergent perspectives during the reduction phase were also analyzed resulting in a structural description of the phenomenon (Moustakas, 1994; Patton, 2002). The themes were enhanced and expanded, which provided a textual depiction of the theme. "The textual portrayal is an abstraction of the experience that provides content and illustration, but not yet essence" (Patton, 2002, p. 486). In addition to the structural description, the researcher discovers the underlying and precipitating factors, which answer the question "how did the experience of the phenomenon come to be what it is?" (Moustakas, 1994, p. 98) after imaginative variation, which is aimed at generating the structural meanings behind the statements of thee participants. The intuitive integration of the fundamental textual and structural descriptions into a unified statement of the essences of the experience of the phenomenon as a whole (Moustakas, 1994, p. 100) was vital. These steps, in addition to the use of the Van Kaam analysis method modified by Moustakas (1994), provided systematic data collection techniques to accomplish a phenomenological analysis.

Interviews are the typical phenomenological investigation method (Moustakas, 1994).

Phenomenological research methods can include research based on interviews, participant observation, conversations, action research, focus groups, and review of personal statement transcriptions (Moustakas, 1994). In this study, however, to illustrate thematic patterns, the researcher utilized semi-structured interviews to gain insight into participants' experiences. The semi-structured interviews used open-ended questions and a purposeful sampling strategy among eight African American lesbian managers in X states and the analysis was inductive in that it sought to discover the premises and categories that emerged from the data (Patton, 2002). Qualitative methods are appropriate to capture detailed and in-depth information from a small sample of individuals (Patton, 2002). A qualitative approach was appropriate given little is known about this specific concept or "central phenomenon" (Creswell, 2005) and therefore, a phenomenological approach was suitable for this study. Given phenomenology focuses on "exploring how human beings make sense of experience and transform experience into consciousness-how they perceive it, describe it, feel about it, judge it, remember it, and make sense of it, and talk about it with others" (Patton, 2002, p. 104), the interviewing required the researcher to be try to be very empathic in nature. According to Lester (1999), the establishment of a good level of rapport and empathy is critical to gaining depth of information when looking at issues in which the subject has a strong personal stake.

Creswell (1994) indicated, "Qualitative researchers have no single stance or consensus on addressing traditional topics such as reliability and validity in qualitative studies" (p. 157). This research process was supported by aforementioned utilization of bracketing, a process of rigorous self-reflection in which the researcher makes every effort to suspend bias, knowledge, and notions about the phenomenon under investigation (Creswell, 1994). Through this process of holding knowledge lightly, the researcher sought to be empathic (Mertens, 1998). In this manner, the researcher attempted to suspend personal beliefs but build rapport (Mertens, 1998). Colaizzi (1978) suggested that this inventory of personal researcher bias take place to assist a researcher in recognizing his or her own experiences, assumptions, and biases.

The study's purpose, procedure, benefits, and implications were orally outlined for participants as well as written in an informed consent form. Participation benefits include contributing to an understanding of the topic, adding to the knowledge, updating the research literature, and learning something about oneself by virtue of the interview process. There were no monetary rewards for study participation.

Participants were asked to sign the consent form, complete the attached demographics survey, and return both (Appendix B) to Denalerie Johnson-Faniel via toll-free fax at 1-888-X or mail to P.O. Box X. Only the researcher could access the confidential fax machine and private mailbox. Entries had to be received via fax by 5:00 pm eastern standard time, Friday, October 16, 2009. Late or incomplete submissions were not accepted. Those selected to be research participants were contacted on or before January 1, 2010, to further discuss the study and to set up the interview. Each participant received a copy of her signed consent form; the originals are now kept on file in a confidential fireproof safe to which only the researcher has access. Study participation was voluntary, and it was each participant's option to terminate participation at any time without penalty or prejudice. Participants could freely choose to avoid any specific question in the study and continue with the rest. Participants were encouraged to ask any questions at any time about the nature of the study and the methods used. Each had the opportunity to suggest transcript changes to the researcher, if necessary. Participants are able to read a copy of the final dissertation before the summer of 2011.

When each participant was contacted, the researcher addressed any questions regarding the purpose of the study, taping and transcription of interviews, analysis of interviews, confidentiality, and other concerns that participants expressed. A date, time, and location confirmation was set for the in-person interviews to occur. The first submissions that met the criteria were noted for individual follow-up via phone to discuss the research project, consent, and verbally verify interest in being a research participant. Interviews were completed before mid-January 2010.

Before interviews began, participants were reminded of the purpose and focus of the research and were given copies of their previously signed and returned consent form and demographic information form. The interviews allowed the researcher to probe for more explanation, more clarification, and better descriptions of their responses. The researcher also kept the signed copy for her records and gave each participant a copy.

Each participant was asked to select a pseudonym so that her identity and participation is kept in confidence. Matheson and Zanna (1990) explained that individuals feel less of a personal risk in disclosing personal information when true identities are not revealed and they are able to select their own pseudonyms. Pseudonymous communication makes participants more comfortable and more willing to reveal personal information with the anonymity (Matheson & Zanna, 1990) and this study's participant pool agreed.

Participants were advised that the interview was estimated to be 2 to 4 hours, but additional time was given if deemed beneficial by the researcher. Interviews began with a request for the participant to talk about time(s) when they experienced the phenomenon of interest. The aim was to help participants expand upon their experiences. Thus, "what was that like?" and "how did that feel for you?" were deemed important follow-up probes to the semi-structured interview questions. Probes followed directly from the participant's response and were intended to be conversational in nature. Each of the participants were asked the same questions from the interview guide, and the researcher responded with follow-up questions to clarify points that were made, encouraged the participant to expand on what she said, and summarized and paraphrased to check the understanding of the participant's experience. The advantages of the open-ended questions to the researcher were that they enabled the study of complex experiences. The advantages for respondents were (a) the ability to qualify or explain answers (b) the opportunity to express ambivalent or contradictory feelings, and (c) the freedom to answer as they wish, using their own spontaneous language (Miles & Huberman, 1994).

The main disadvantage of the open-ended questions is that it might be more difficult to evaluate the reliability and validity of verbal data. It is hard to ascertain the extent of such potential problems as interviewer bias and variability, and respondent deception, exaggeration, fabrication, and forgetting. Careful examination by the researcher of the participant's manner and word choice can provide important hints about the credibility of the verbal data. Another issue, according to Miles and Huberman (1994), is that open-ended questions tend to produce a great variability in the amount of data across respondents. Verbally fluent respondents may provide very full answers, whereas less fluent respondents may find open-ended questions demanding to answer. Open-ended questions also typically generate large amounts of data, which are usually very time consuming to analyze (Miles & Huberman, 1994).

Following the individual interviews, each tape was reviewed and transcribed verbatim with Naturally Speaking transcription software (Nuance Computer Software, Burlington, MA, Version 9), and identifying data was eliminated during the transcription process. After transcription and coding, each participant was communicated with confidentially for the purpose of solidifying trustworthiness of the data. In qualitative research, *trustworthiness* refers to being faithful to the data; this is referred to as *validity* in quantitative research (Glesne, 1999). Participants were presented with the opportunity to inform the researcher of any changes or additions that might be needed regarding their interview data.

## Data Analysis Plan

As outlined by Corbin and Strauss (1990), procedures and techniques grounded in theory were used for data analysis. According to Giorgi (1985), the theme of phenomenology is to return to the mundane world where phenomena exist. In terms of data analysis, this involves four steps: (a) review of the entire description or protocol, (b) re-review of the description for the purpose of finding themes, (c) review of themes in search for psychological insights, and (d) synthesis of those themes and insights into a cohesive statement about the participants' experiences (Giorgi, 1985). Colaizzi (1978) included these steps but also incorporated two additional specifications: (a) The themes must include ideas from the words of the participants, and (b) the themes must develop into a structure by which experience can be understood.

Data obtained via open-ended interviews was analyzed using phenomenological analysis, as discussed by Colaizzi (1978). First, significant statements were extracted and used to build meaningful statements of the participant's experiences. Clusters were then expanded upon to describe the overall experience of the participant and to define the fundamental structure of the participant's experiences.

In an attempt to reduce statistical bias and under-coverage variability within the lesbian sample, complete information about the research study and participant solicitations was advertised through Web-based electronic bulletin boards, electronic mailing lists, and group e-mails of several LGBT organizations and groups. Sometimes not considered a reliable statistically unbiased sample, snowball sampling techniques are most often used in studies to create a sample (Buhrke, Ben-Ezra, Hurley, & Ruprecht, 1992; Phillips et al., 2003). This makes it one of the most appropriate sampling methods for assessing populations with hidden characteristics and memberships—thus appropriate for the LGBT population. This method includes the use of self-identified lesbians who were asked to pass along information about the study and the researcher's contact information to other self-identified lesbians that they know.

Throughout the process the researcher kept a journal to write thoughts on the research process that might be difficult to remember at a later time; the journal included notes on the interviews and the researcher's reaction to certain items. The journal was also used to help vent frustrations and record personal biases. The confidentially kept journal also providedan organized method to keep notes on committee member feedback.

Glesne and Peshkin (1992) suggested that data analysis involves organizing what one has seen, heard, and read so that sense can be made about what was learned. As a result of analyzing the data, the researcher created explanations, posed hypotheses, developed a theory, and linked stories to one another. Themes were used as a method of understanding the career development process of African American lesbians. Interview responses were transcribed verbatim from the interviews and loaded into the software program ATLAS.ti (ATLAS Computer Software, Berlin, Germany: Student Version) for analysis. The software looks for correspondence, similarities, accordance, analogies, or homologies within the varied sets of data and assists in discovering patterns. ATLAS.ti (ATLAS Computer Software, Berlin, Germany: Student Version) is ideal for making linkages between different elements of the data, and it is helpful for making distinct the connections between data elements (Barry, 1998).

The themes that emerged were regarding what statements or phases that seem essential or revealing about the career development experiences are being described. The qualitative data analysis software also helped identify and organize the material by themes. The researcher then further reviewed the themes and meanings and subsequently note meanings found by the software that were salient to the experiences that the participants were conveying.

Data analyses were derived from observations, interviews, and document analyses. The analysis included critically examining, summarizing, and synthesizing the data, followed by three stages of analysis. Coding involved organizing the data into reasonable, meaningful units in which words or very short phrases signified a category. Emic, or personal accounts of experience or behavior, categories emerged from information provided by the participants in their own language, whereas etic categories emerged from the researcher's interpretation of the emic data. For data analysis the researcher used major codes and subcodes, followed by summarization of the coded data with a sentence or two that reflects its essence. The researcher then used computerized sorting of data and pattern seeking and synthesizing. The researcher also sought to synthesize the relationships among the categories and patterns that suggested generalization and then interpretedd the findings inductively, synthesize the information, and drew inferences. Inferences were drawn from pattern seeking and from the researcher's ideas developed during the literature review. These tentative patterns were identified and additional data was collected to determine if they are consistent with those patterns.

In summary, this research study utilized a phenomenological interviewing approach, using open-ended questions to obtain a comprehensive description of the lived experiences (Moustakas, 1994). Data collection procedures ensured the confidentiality of the participants and the Van Kaam phenomenological analysis method, as modified by Moustakas (1994), and the ATLAS.ti software, a program that stores, organizes, and represents qualitative and demographic data, allowed for the analysis of the qualitative interview information and data.

The following is an overview of the phenomenological approach that was used to capture the subjective experience of self-identified African American lesbians and the aim was to determine "what an experience means for the persons who have had the experience and are able to provide a comprehensive description of it" (Birzer & Smith-Mahdi, 2006). The study attempted to understand participant perceptions and their understanding of particular life situations (Birzer & Smith-Mahdi, 2006). The findings of the study were derived from semi-structured interviews and the research question, from a phenomenological perspective, sought to expose the essences and meanings of human experiences and be stated in clear and concrete terms (Moustakas, 1994), in an effort for the researcher to then obtain vital information regarding the central phenomenon identified by using a phenomenological design and analysis strategy. Given the very personal topic, ethical considerations were a serious concern. As in any qualitative, phenomenological interviewing, the researcher inquired into the real world of the participants (Patton, 2002). To ensure an ethical study and participants' rights to privacy, the study followed the informed consent recommendations of Patton (2002). Pseudonym names were used and confidentiality involved keeping participants' names from public disclosure and directly linking the responses to the specific participant (Neuman, 2007). Providing confidentiality is imperative when seeking honest and open responses from participants in interviews (Patton, 2002). The introductory letter and informed consent form were the first steps in ensuring confidentiality and interviews began with providing a discussion of both items as well as the purpose of the study and a description of how the data obtained will remain confidential. If the participants agreed to continue with the study, the participant left the signed the research study informed consent form with the researcher.

All forms and data including written notes, audio recording and transcripts obtained from interviews, were kept in a locked file to maintain confidentiality. The information will be retained for a period of seven years from collection and destroyed after that period. The researcher handled the data and the data collected from each participant was coded to maintain its confidentiality and only minimal risks to the participants in the study existed. The geographic locations of the interviewed participants were in X states and the data collection process began after this research study received formal committee, university and Institutional Review Board (IRB) approval.

Based on the literature, "Qualitative data is gathered primarily in the form of spoken or written language rather than in the form of numbers" (Polkinghorne, 2005, p. 137). The goal of the qualitative, phenomenological study was to capture the lived experiences in relation to the central phenomenon (Newman, Thompson, & Roberts, 2006), in this case career barriers and this was reiterated throughout the interviews. As mentioned, interviews were the appropriate approach for the study for several reasons and the phenomenological research design most often employs interviews as its source of data (Moustakas, 1994; Patton, 2002; Van Manen, 1990).

The data collection process provided answers to the research question and illuminated the issue of career barriers for African American managerial level lesbians as defined by the problem statement. The phenomenological research design provided the structure and detailed the essential assumptions for exploring the central phenomenon of the perceived career barriers (Van Manen, 1990). The study employed a phenomenological interview procedure, as identified by Moustakas (1994). The phenomenological interviews allowed for an informal, interactive process. Although the primary researcher developed a series of questions aimed at evoking a comprehensive account of the person's experience of the phenomenon, the interviews began with a social conversation, and then the interviewer asked the participant to reflect on the central phenomenon. The task of the researcher was to create a comfortable climate in which the participant would respond thoroughly and truthfully (Moustakas, 1994). Again, to accomplish this goal, the interviews took place face to face on at a location selected by the participant. In-person interviews provided an advantage to researchers in that the nonverbal communication and nonverbal cues help to guide the interview process and the selection of interview questions to reach the lived experiences of the participants (Suzuki, Ahluwalia, Arora, & Mattis, 2007). The study's semi-structured interview format with open-ended questions was "designed to cover a common set of themes but allowed for changes in sequencing of questions and the forms of questions, enabling the interviewer to follow up on the participants' answers" (Suzuki et al., 2007, p. 311). In addition, it allowed for a natural conversation flow (Suzuki et al., 2007). In creating the interview questions for the current study, Van Manen (1990) recommended asking questions about phenomenon by asking for concrete examples of the experience or situation, thus the participant lives or relives the experience as she talks about it. The intent of the interview questions was to elicit the lived experiences of the women in relation to their perceived career barriers, perception of overcoming the barriers, mentoring, and career aspirations. The list of questions was the primary instrument used to gather the data from participants (see Appendix B).

The first method of collecting data was the actual interviewing, and for those women who agreed to participate, a confidential interview was scheduled at the location of her choice. All interviews and follow-up occurred between June 2009 and December 2009. Each participant was interviewed in a conversational style, using open-ended questions from an interview guide (See Appendix A). The data were transcribed and then coded for themes identified by similarities and differences in responses, perspectives, life course markers, and experiences. The responses were coded to represent common themes and areas of difference. The respondents selected a pseudonym name to be represented by and any identifying information was removed from their responses to protect their identity. Identification consisted of the date and time the interview was conducted and this study sought to answer the research question.

Finally, using the Van Kaam method, as modified by Moustakas (1994), and ATLAS.ti software, the data collected from the eight participants was recorded and transcribed interviews were coded and then analyzed after the data was organized and assembled to allow for coding using the ATLAS.ti software. The software synthesized the data and allowed for a comprehensive phenomenological analysis. Phenomenological analysis "seeks to grasp and elucidate the meaning, structure, and essence of lived experience of a phenomenon for a person or group of people" (Patton, 2002, p. 482).

Because phenomenological analysis is not just a description of the phenomenon, but an "interpretive process" (Creswell et al., 2007, p. 253), the data analysis phase used the seven-step process designed by Van Kaam and modified by Moustakas (1994).

1. Listing and preliminary grouping via horizontal placement: List every expression relevant to the experience.

2. Reduction and elimination: To determine the invariant constituents: Test each expression for two requirements:

    a. Does it contain a moment of the experience that is a necessary and sufficient constituent for understanding it?

    b. Is it possible to abstract and label it? If so, it is a horizon of the experience. Expressions not meeting the above requirements are eliminated. Overlapping, repetitive, and vague expressions are also eliminated or presented in more exact descriptive terms. The horizons that remain are the invariant constituents of the experience.

3. Clustering and thematizing the invariant constituents: Cluster the invariant constituents of the experience that are related into a thematic label. The clustered and labeled constituents are the core themes of the experience.

4. Final identification of the invariant constituents and themes by application: Validation: Check the invariant constituents and their accompanying theme against the complete record of the research participant.

(a) Are the themes expressed explicitly in the complete transcription? (b) Are they compatible if not explicitly expressed?

(c) If they are not explicit or compatible, they are not relevant to the participant's experience and should be deleted.

5. Using the relevant and validated invariant constituents and themes, construct for each participant's individual textural description of their experience. Include verbatim examples from the transcribed interview.

6. Construct for each participant's experience based on the individual textural description and imaginative variation.

7. Construct for each research participant a textural-structural description of the meanings and essences of the experience, incorporating the invariant constituents and themes.

From the individual textural structured descriptions, the researcher developed a composite description of the meanings and essences of the experience, representing the group as whole. (Moustakas, 1994, p. 121). This process was appropriate as it allowed the researcher, through clearly defined steps, to be able to extract the essences and lived experiences of the participants. Although the ATLAS.ti software assisted in "data storage, coding, retrieval, comparing, and linking" (Patton, 2002, p. 442), the researcher laid out the actual analysis by using the steps outlined above as a framework for a proper, effective, and valid research analysis.

Using the phenomenological interviewing technique (Moustakas, 1994), each participant was asked the 25 interview questions (see Appendix B) in a semi-structured fashion. Patton (2002) highlighted the importance of in-depth interviews when using phenomenology given that to truly understand what an individual experiences, the researcher must experience the phenomenon as directly as possible. The following participant data relied on broad, open-ended questions (Creswell, 2005), thus the interview process included open-ended questions relevant to the research questions.

The interviews lasted an average of 90 minutes, with the shortest being 47 minutes and the longest 120 minutes. The eight selected participants shared their lived experiences in relation to career barriers, career decision-making, "isms", professional goal setting, mentoring, and future career aspirations. Following the completion of the semi-structured interview questions, each participant shared feedback regarding the interview questions and process. The sample size of the phenomenological study consisted of eight women, which was in alignment with the sample size recommendations of Patton (2002) and Polkinghorne (2005) and saturation was reached in this study.

The prescreening of possible participants via telephone, where information was shared about the study, provided an opportunity to seek out those women who understood the central phenomenon and had information-rich experiences to share. The interested women and the interviewer selected a date for the interview during the telephone call or email. The researcher provided informed consent forms via email and again at the beginning of the actual in-person interview introduction (sees Appendix A). The form allowed the participants to sign and consent to the interview and the use of a recording device. The general dissertation data collection and publication process was also explained to each participant. The snowball sampled participants initially received a telephone call and/or email inviting them to participate in the study and they were then emailed an introductory letter (see Appendix A) and informed consent form (see Appendix A). The letter and informed consent included the following information:

the purpose of the study and why it is important; whom the information was for and how it would be used; the dissertation process and university details, how the responses would be handled; and the risks and benefits for the participant (Patton, 2002).

All of the women selected a pseudonym, completed the demographics questions, and signed the informed consent (see Appendix A) before interviewing and were asked if there were any questions or concerns. In order to assess the sample better and to allow for more detailed analysis of the qualitative data, sets of demographic information were collected from each participant at the beginning of their interview. The data include educational background, years as age range, education, title of current position, etc. (see Appendix A).

In an effort to reduce the possibility of bias, the researcher also tried to adhere to epoche during the interviews, by attempting to refrain from judgment and view the phenomenon without personal bias or preconceived notions. The researcher hoped to have set aside personal previous experiences, perceptions, preferences, and feelings to receive the phenomenon in its purest form (Creswell et al., 2007; Moustakas, 1994), but researchers are not able to determine if the bias notions were fully avoided. Notes were taken during the actual interviews and the participants were asked for clarification on statements, etc. as throughout the interview process, as needed. In closing the semi-structured interviews, a final question was asked to each woman regarding if there was any additional information she would like to share and this final question provided additional data and an opportunity for the women to offer further related information. Upon completion of the interviews, the data were then transcribed into a Microsoft document from the audio digitally recorded interviews and the transcribed interviews were later reviewed and compared to the audio recorded interview to ensure accuracy.

Participant checking increased the validity of the study (Creswell, 2005) and allowed the participants to voluntarily make certain the information provided was realistic and complete, in addition to clarifying unclear statements to be incorporated into the data analysis. Due to confidentiality and the shared fear amongst the participants regarding losing their jobs the interview transcripts were not included in the written part of this study document, but the participants were made aware of the fact that their pseudonyms were used throughout the process and the transcripts would be kept on file and available for university access once the participants had been notified. The modified Van Kaam method (Moustakas, 1994) is a well-tested and reliable method of extracting key words, phrases, constituents, and themes from raw textural data, such as those provided in the eight interviews from this study. The modified Van Kaam method with Moustakas (1994) support was used in conjunction with the ATLAS.ti software and a qualitative method using a phenomenological research design addressed the specific problem.

As mentioned, all of the participants signed the informed consent form before the interview process started. The interview questions elicited responses that provided insight into the research question. This phenomenological study sought to identify the perceived career barriers among African American women in managerial roles that are out lesbians in their work environment and the research question provided the needed focus for the study (Neuman, 2007) and Creswell (2005) stated that qualitative research questions should be limited and be open-ended, neutral, and exploratory. It was anticipated that the exploration of the participants' experiences would lend insight into the research question and shed light on homophobia and its effect on the career development and professional advancement of African American lesbian managers.

# CHAPTER 4. DATA COLLECTION AND ANALYSIS

Overview

The previous chapter explored the qualitative phenomenological research methodology for this doctoral dissertation research study. This study focused on providing insight into the perceived barriers that might prevent upward professional mobility for African American lesbian managers by exploring their lived career experiences. The researcher asked participants to describe the impact of employment discrimination or the fear of such discrimination. In summary, the researcher used semistructured interviews with open-ended questions and a purposeful sampling strategy among eight self-identified African American lesbian women in managerial positions in X states. X state and the surrounding area is an ideal place to study African American lesbian populations, given that it has the largest concentration of African American, same-sex cohabiting couples in the United States (National Gay and Lesbian Task Force, 2004). Moreover, unlike most cities across the country, almost daily X state hosts at least one public social event via Meetup groups, community centers, and so forth. that specifically caters to lesbians of color, helping make it a location where gay minority populations can thrive.

The researcher discovered that traditional methods for data gathering were not appropriate for generating a large sample of African American lesbian managers and that more outreach and calls for participants were needed than originally thought. This study was found consistent with the research indicating that African American lesbians largely ignore study recruitment advertisements and related postings at LGBT community centers, so studies that use these methods do not successfully enlist large numbers of non-White participants (Blumstein & Schwartz, 1983). That finding is still valid today and is supported by data showing that (a) because of homophobia within the African American community, African Americans engaging in homosexual behavior perceive that their friends and neighbors are unsupportive (Ramsey, Hill, & Kellam, 2010; Siegel & Epstein, 1996; Stokes, Vanable, & McKirnan, 1996), and thus (b) they are often reluctant to disclose their sexual orientation and participate in research studies, especially those requiring them to be out of the closet (Adams & Kimmel, 1997; Cochran & Mays, 1994, 1988a; ; Mays et al., 1998). For this study, the researcher spent an average of at least 3 days per week at a variety of public social events that had a largely minority lesbian attendance, including after-work networking hours, religious meetings, shared meals, LGBT pride events, house events, meet-up group activities, community center activities, parties, sporting events, conference workshops, and so on. As described in the previous chapter's participant-selection overview, the study employed purposeful sampling to select the research study participants and saturation was reached.

Chapter 4 details the results of this study and provides an analysis of the collected interview data. The data include the extracted themes and lived experiences of the women recruited via snowball sampling, the descriptions of their career development experiences, and their perceptions, beliefs, and understandings of barriers that prevent their upward mobility. This chapter documents the methodical implementation of the data collection procedures and data analysis process using the Van Kaam method as modified by Moustakas (1994).

*Confirmability* refers to the degree to which others can corroborate the findings (Guba & Lincoln, 1981. Confirmability of the findings is established when the three criteria of credibility, fittingness, and auditability have been met; confirmation of the findings for this research study was established by the fact that all of the themes were accepted by the participants as part of their lived experience.

Data, which included perceptions, beliefs, and understandings of the participants, were collected during an interview. The semistructured interviews used open-ended questions and a purposeful sampling strategy among the eight African American lesbian managers, and the analysis was inductive, in that it sought to discover the premises and categories that emerged from the data (Patton, 2002). Following the phenomenological design as described in Chapter 3 and outlined by Moustakas (1994), the interviews were conducted in order to gain a deeper insight into perceived career barriers of African American managers. Following the collection and transcription of the interview data, the researcher organized that data to allow for data analysis using ATLAS.ti software. This permitted the synthesis of the participants' experiences, thus providing the essence and meaning of the phenomena around career trajectories (Moustakas, 1994). This phenomenological research used interviews "as a means for exploring and gathering experiential narrative material that may serve as a resource for developing a richer and deeper understanding of a human phenomenon" (Van Manen, 1990, p. 66). Outcomes in phenomenological research are not reached unless rich and deep descriptions are gained (Van Manen, 1990), and this study's participants were allowed to discuss the information collected in the interview and reflect upon their statements. In addition, Parrish (2008), Moustakas (1994), and Van Manen (1990) encouraged this process as a way to validate the data, ensure the participants' perspectives are represented fairly, and reduce potential bias.

The purpose of this phenomenological study was to explore the lived experiences of African American lesbian managers in relation to any perceived career barriers, and Chapter 3 provided an explanation of the qualitative research methodology and design as well as its appropriateness for the current study. "Phenomenological research seeks the meaning, structure, and essence of the lived experiences of a specific phenomenon" (Patton, 2002, p. 104), and the researcher aspired to gain a deeper understanding of the nature or meaning of everyday experiences through phenomenological methods (Van Manen, 1990).

These processes aided in the intuitive integration of the meaning of the data into a description of the essences and lived experiences of the African American lesbian managers that participated in this research study. The meanings captured will provide researchers with an added understanding of the literature on the barriers experienced by African American lesbian managers. By listening to the voices of African American lesbian managers, leaders and other scholars will better understand the impact that the systemic barriers have for this group of women. The barriers identified could help inform institutions and organizations regarding their policies, procedures, and practices that hinder midlevel managerial women leaders from advancing.

The findings from this study illuminated and clarified barriers faced by managerial women, and the information gained from the women added to the body of knowledge on the perceived effect of the glass and concrete ceiling, or the invisible barriers that block women and minorities from achieving promotions and senior leadership positions (J. Moore, 2003).

The seven steps of the modified Van Kaam method include listing and preliminary grouping, reducing and eliminating, clustering and thematizing the invariant constituents, making final identification of the invariant constituents and themes, generating individual textural descriptions, constructing individual structural descriptions, and creating textural–structural descriptions. Composite descriptions representing the group as a whole conclude the analysis. The initial four steps of the modified Van Kaam method (Moustakas, 1994) were utilized to create the invariant constituents and thematic categories. These represented the lived experiences of managerial level women that self-identified as African American lesbians.

In the data analysis process of this dissertation research study, the researcher generated 25 key invariant output code constituents and then consolidated these into 10 thematic categories. The first step of the modified Van Kaam method (Moustakas, 1994) was the listing and preliminary grouping, or horizonalization, of all expressions made by the participants that were relevant to their experiences as midlevel women administrators. This was accomplished through the aid of the ATLAS.ti qualitative software program, which was used to code the text of the interviews. The execution of the initial step of the modified Van Kaam method was a subjective process, whereby the researcher evaluated the relevance of the statements made by the participants with regard to their experience as midlevel women administrators. ATLAS.ti was used as an aid to note the location and frequency of occurrences of these statements in the text of the transcribed interviews of the participants. The second step of the data analysis, based on the modified Van Kaam method (Moustakas, 1994), was the reduction and elimination of the invariant constituents. Each invariant constituent generated in the first step of the Van Kaam method was tested against two criteria: (a) Does it contain a moment of the experience that is a necessary and sufficient constituent for understanding it? and (b) can one abstract and label it? The invariant constituents that met these requirements were considered horizons of the experiences of the participants. Once these valid invariant constituents were determined, they were evaluated in relation to one another to ensure that there were no overlapping, repetitive, and vague expressions. The third step of the modified Van Kaam method (Moustakas, 1994) required the clustering and thematizing of the invariant constituents under thematic labels or categories. Experiences of the women that were considered related, with regard to career advancement and barriers to career advancement (e.g., those concerning or related to mentors), were grouped into the thematic categories.

The 10 major thematic categories that emerged represent the core of the experiences of the African American lesbian manager participants with regard to their perceptions of personal and organizational barriers. ATLAS.ti was used to group the invariant constituents into appropriate categories and to generate frequency percentages for those invariant constituents as they were represented by the eight participants of the study. The fourth step of the modified Van Kaam method (Moustakas, 1994) involved the validation of the invariant constituents and the themes under which they were categorized. The invariant constituents were found to be valid (a) when they were explicitly expressed in the transcription (the use of ATLAS.ti ensured this step by tracking the location of the text containing the invariant constituents in the transcribed documents), and (b) when they were compatible, if not explicitly stated. Compatible constituents were responses that clearly indicated a reference to an explicit invariant constituent. From this final collection of the invariant constituents and their categorization into their thematic categories, the researcher executed the fifth step of the modified Van Kaam method. This step required the generation of individual textural description of the participants' experiences of personal and organizational barriers as African American lesbian managers. ATLAS.ti aided in the construction of these descriptions by locating textural examples of specific mentions of particular invariant constituents for each participant.

The researcher generated a more concise individual structural description for each participant to complete the sixth step of the modified Van Kaam method (Moustakas, 1994). These descriptions summarized the information of the individual textural descriptions and incorporated imaginative variation, by the researcher, to express the relevant experiences of each participant. The seventh and final step of the modified Van Kaam method called for the construction of the composite textural–structural descriptions to encapsulate the lived experiences of the midlevel women administrators effectively. The composite descriptions presented the experiences of the group of participants as a whole, which was necessary to answer the research questions of the study in a deliberate and organized fashion. This phenomenological study examined human experiences through the descriptions provided by the women involved in the research. These experiences are called *lived experiences*, and the goal of this phenomenological research was to describe the meaning that these experiences held for each participant. The framework for this research was (a) to identify the phenomenon, the lived experience, (b) to ask participants to explain the meaning of the lived experiences, and (c) to acknowledge that the participants are the only reliable source of this information. The participants interpreted the action or experience for the researcher, and then the researcher interpreted the explanation provided by the participant.

As in grounded theory, this phenomenological research was an iterative process, and data were collected until theoretical saturation occurred, duplicate themes were identified, and no new themes were discovered. Again, theoretical saturation occurs when the researcher finds only repeated patterns in the sampling process, and saturation demonstrates that the research process is complete. In this descriptive study of how individuals experience a phenomenon, data collection continued until saturation was reached, at Participant 8, and exploring further data did not add to the insight already gained. At this point, the analytical framework was saturated and further analysis was not necessary. The data analysis followed three general steps: open coding (i.e., reading transcripts line by line and identifying and coding the concepts found in the data), axial coding (i.e., organizing the concepts and making them more abstract), and selective coding (i.e., focusing on the main ideas, developing the story, and finalizing the themes). This process was considered complete when theoretical saturation occurred and the data were well validated.

The researcher provided the research question that explored the meaning of lived experiences for individuals and asked individuals to describe these experiences. The researcher (a) collected data, via long interviews, from individuals who have experienced the phenomenon under investigation, and (b) conducted data analysis by the horizonalization or extracting of significant statements from transcribed interviews. The significant statements were then transformed into clusters of meanings according to how each statement falls under specific psychological and phenomenological concepts. Finally, these transformations were tied together to make a general description of the experience, both the textural description of what was experienced and the structural description of how it was experienced. The research was written in such a way that readers should be able to understand better (a) the essential, invariant structure of the essence of the experience and (b) what it is like for someone to experience that phenomenon, as described by the participants (Polkinghorne, 1989).

The major limitation of this research was the impossibility of generalizing beyond the sample. Inferences cannot be made outside of the scope of the responses received from the respondents. Among the other limitations of this study were the time frames in which the data was collected. In addition, many African American lesbian managers wanted to participate but were not out at work and/or saturation had been reached. The limitations also included the sample size; the researcher's personal, familial, and work obligations; the funding and geographic restrictions on travel; and the researcher's own biases as a member of the group under study, given that no researcher is fully clear of all bias.

## Demographics

All of the research study participants were African American, lesbian, female-born managers, and all were American-raised citizens. The age of this research study's participants ranged from 32 to 63 years old. Fifty percent of the participants were in their early 40s, with the average age of all participants being 41 years old. Twenty-five percent were parents, and 75% were partnered in a romantic relationship. Fifty percent were managers within their organization,

25% were at the director level, and 25% were at the vice president level. The average number of direct reports per participant was five. Twenty-five percent of the participants worked for Fortune 500 companies, 25% worked for educational institutions, and 50% worked for social service agencies. The size of organizations ranged from 50 employees to 500,000 employees. The years of service on their current jobs ranged from 2 to 25 years. Education levels of the participants ranged from having attended some college to having obtained a doctoral degree.

## Coding and Emerging Themes Process

Understanding the perceived career development opportunities and career decisions of African American lesbians in management career fields provides African American lesbians beneficial directions for the focus of improvements and changes. Over time, this may help increase the percentage of African American lesbian females in management-level careers. The empirical literature review for this study provided background to the issues and factors surrounding (a) African American women's perceptions regarding management career choice and career development and (b) the shortage of out African American lesbians in management careers. African American females may be faced with several influences and career-related issues when making career choices.

The major career choice and development theories include self-concept theory, self-efficacy theory, social cognitive career theory, self-determination theory, knowledge gap theory, social learning theory, and Holland's vocational choice theory (Ivy, 2006). Although the researcher identified scholarly studies and theories in the literature review that focused on career choice and career development, an emphasis on African American women was omitted in the majority of these studies and theories. In the literature review, the researcher identified little research specific to African American female career decisions and career-decision influences. Malcolm, Hall, and Brown (1976) concluded that career development among minority women in the scientific career fields experience a double bind due to their ethnicity and gender. This double bind of being African American and female has limited opportunities for African American females in employment decisions (Alfred, 2001; Epstein, 1973). Minority female career choices may be constrained by socialization, access to guidance and assessment, tracking into certain fields, societal and self-stereotypes, isolation from networks, and early schooling experiences (Kerka, 2003). Lipsett (1971) identified six social factors that influence career development decision: community, pressure groups, home influences, role perception, and social class membership. These were also themes prevalent throughout the current research. Research has evaluated the factors that influence career choices. These factors include the influence of family, peers, school, church, mentors, and the community; one's world view; one's identity; and one's values (Alfred 2001; D. Brown, 2002; Burger, Creamer, & Meszaros, 2005; Slevin &Wingrove, 1999; Walsh, Bingham, Brown, & Ward, 2001). The literature review on influences of African American career decisions (a) includes the career decision factors as identified by Alfred (2001), D. Brown (2002), Burger et al. (2005), Slevin and Wingrove (1999), and Walsh et al. (2001), and (b) focused on race, gender, class, and support.

In this phenomenological research study, eight participants from various industries, including legal, information technology, education, social work, health, banking, community development, and religion, within the X state area, shared their career advancement experiences during individual in-depth interviews. The researcher found 25 predominant themes for the influence of career choices: (a) family values and the importance of self-identity, (b) mentor access and the reliance on self-confidence and inner strength, (c) socioeconomic factors, (d) lack of encouragement in business preparation and limited-or-no computer exposure and/or lack of training, (e) perception of professionals in management positions and/or role conflict, (f) fear of failure, lack of confidence, or assertiveness, (g) fear of success, self-expectancies, or abilities, (h) disclosure of sexual orientation, (i) relations with family and friends, (j) job supply and demand, (k) interests, (l) attitudes, (m) developed desire to pursue career field, (n) spiritual factors, (o) in-depth awareness of occupations in career field and required skills and training or achievement needs, (p) exposure to professionals in career field, or encouraged preparation, (q) mother's role model, father's role model, family guidance, or early childhood experiences, (r) career trajectory, work history, or career goals;,(s) appearance, (t) internal personal barriers, (u) gender discrimination barriers, (v) sexual orientation discrimination barriers, (w) racial discrimination barriers, (x) relations with coworkers, and (y) relations with supervisors or mentoring.

    After creating the above 25 codes, the researcher reviewed the transcripts and noted the codes that had occurred several times; these were used to determine the elimination or combining of codes. The researcher determined that codes retained would have at least five or more references and then clustered the codes based on frequency of occurrence. By this process, the researcher narrowed the relevant codes to 10 based on groundedness and density, or the number of times the code-related concept appeared and the number of times the codes appeared in relation with other codes. The researcher observed connections between the women's feelings, and key common areas of discussion were found in the 10 themes. In fact, many of the women included in the response their historical and cultural understandings of career advancement, and many were struggling with the same basic concern: how to advance in their careers without fear of employment discrimination.

Ten key codes representing the career-related characteristics of the participants emerged:

1. Disclosure of sexual orientation: any reference to coming out or "not coming out" in the workplace or the degree to which the interviewee's sexual orientation has been disclosed to the interviewee's coworkers.

2. Appearance: (a) any reference to the interviewee's appearance, particularly in regard to the influence that dress, hairstyle,

use of makeup, and so on, has on how one is treated in the workplace and what, if any, pressure one feels to alter one's appearance because of this; (b) discussions focusing on feminine versus masculine norms–stereotypes in behavior, appearance, and so on, and/or; (c) discussion of how behavior conforms to, or is a modified version of, feminine or masculine stereotypes–categories.

3. Career trajectory/work history/career goals: (a) descriptions of the jobs that the interviewee has held and the paths her career has taken, especially career successes or regrets, and (b) discussion of future career goals.

4. Internal personal barriers: any reference to internal barriers that may impede career advancement (e.g., internalized homophobia, self-esteem issues).

5. Gender discrimination barriers: discussions of discrimination against women or other barriers faced in the workplace that the interviewee has experienced or has been aware of;

6. Sexual orientation discrimination barriers: discussions of discrimination or other barriers faced by LGBT persons in the workplace, either those that the interviewee has experienced or those she has been aware of.

7. Racial discrimination barriers: discussions of discrimination or other barriers faced by racial minorities in the workplace that the interviewee has experienced or has been aware of;

8. Relations with supervisors and mentoring: references to the relationship between the interviewee and her supervisor, especially any discussions of mentoring and the beneficial effect that mentoring has on career advancement.

9. Relations with coworkers: discussions of the interviewee's relationships with coworkers or other peers and discussion of how the interviewee is either positively or negatively perceived by coworkers, especially any types of misconceptions coworkers have.

10. Relations with family and friends: discussions of the interviewee's relationships with family and/or friends.

The following section presents how participants responded to the semistructured interview questions. An important note is that one of the distinct advantages of phenomenological research is the fluidity of the data collection process. Participants sometimes touched on relevant themes in response to an interview question not directly associated with the research question to which it was linked. The process was not a detriment to the analysis; quite the opposite, it was an enhancement that allowed the full breadth of participants' perceptions, beliefs, and lived experiences to be expressed in the data analysis. Participant responses relevant to whether African American lesbian managers believe in the existence of a glass ceiling that impacts them as a triple minority (African American, female, and lesbian) were fully encompassed by the research.

The researcher further isolated the emerging themes by constructing specific categories from similar ideas across all the interview data. Miles and Huberman (1994) described this process as data linking, which involves connecting relevant segments of data from categories and clusters of information. The researcher used inductive reasoning, intuition, and reflection to further explore the data in order to refine the themes. The themes that emerged in this study provided descriptions of lived experience and revealed the essence of the participants' perceptions of their experiences.

The thematic categories found were (a) general perceptions of African American lesbian managers and (b) the influences that both personal barriers and organizational barriers to advancement have on their career decisions. The additional thematic categories are presented at the end of this section with the goal of providing context and enhancement of participant responses relating directly to the research question. Again, the research question is, "How does employment discrimination, or the fear of such discrimination, affect African American lesbian managers' perceptions of their career advancement?" The participants provided insight related to their vocational experiences.

## Voices of the Participants

To participate in the study all of the participants had to have achieved managerial leadership positions in spite of barriers to their advancement, and they discussed how these barriers shaped their career development and leadership experiences. Research suggested that traditional gender expectations and practices shape people's experiences even after they reach the top (Catalyst, 2007), and that was supported by the views of 100% of the participants in this study. A fundamental challenge to the women's leadership arises from the mismatch between the qualities traditionally associated with leaders and those traditionally associated with women (Catalyst, 2007; Eagly & Carli, 2007a). The assertive, authoritative, and dominant behaviors that people link with leadership tend not to be viewed as typical or attractive in women (Catalyst, 2007; Eagly & Carli, 2007b); 100% of the participants in this study expressed the same sentiments and also offered that they, as lesbian women, were seen as overbearing or overly aggressive at times but that they could not say whether that was based on their race or sexual orientation.

Participant 1 noted,

Gender discrimination is real and I had to actually change my name on my resume to my initials. So now all you see are my initials and my last name and that makes it a bit harder for hiring managers to tell if I am male or female and that lessened the perceived discrimination I felt I was facing and I started being offered more employment interviews.

So, according to Participant 7,

Discrimination has been a part of my being a female, and a lot of it, I think, may be the fact that many people, both men and women, look down on you because you're a woman and you're a minority. People think that you're not capable of handling the position, until you're actually thrown in and you prove it to them, then that's when I have earned their respect.

Participant 3 said,

Being a woman sometimes makes me feel like I'm invisible and that I have to get up and wave my hands to even be acknowledged and to let them know the ideas presented were mine and that I am indeed competent enough to do my job.

By the same token, participants (2, 5, and 7) that perform traditionally male roles felt that they are seen as nice and that they are liked but not as respected; that is supported in the research (Rudman & Glick, 2001). In short, it appears that women, unlike men, exchange competence (i.e., success) for likeability in traditionally male roles, according to Participants 2, 5 and 7.

Participants 1, 2, 3, 4, 5, 7, and 8 agreed that at each level of their career advancement, their qualifications for leadership were called into question. Some of their organizations consistently, if unwittingly, communicate that women are not fit for leadership roles; and, just as others may view her leadership through a cultural lens distorted by gender bias, so too, many women have difficulty developing a viable self-view as a leader. Participants 1, 3, 7, and 8 also discussed issues around internalized discrimination and self-defeating behavior. According to Participant 7,

There's no federal protection, but you have institutional protection and state protection in some states and organizations, but I still have felt that I have had to hide my sexuality before I came out of the closet in order to climb the career ladder and I have at times felt that I was less than when I compared myself to other professionals with similar qualifications and that is my own self-hatred that had been instilled based on how I thought others felt about me.

According to Participant 4,

There are all kinds of discrimination and there are strategies you have to put into place to deal with it. You have to be willing to recognize it. You also have to document it. That includes looking at patterns and you can see that some people have contempt for homosexuals and some will try to ruin your career and halt your advancement, especially if there is a chance you will be in a position of authority on the job. You have to be willing to call it out if you're in a position to call it out, but many African American lesbians, even managers, are not in the position due to fear of losing their job or not being able to advance as their straight peers might and I think adding the component of gender discrimination to the pot makes it worse.

Differential structures of opportunity and power block women's access and advancement to leadership positions (Kanter, 1997; Reskin, 1988; Ridgeway, 1993; Strober, 1984). For example, men's predominance in positions of organizational power, together with differences in the composition of men's and women's social and professional networks, give men greater access to information and support (Burt, 1992; Ibarra, 1992; Podolny & Baron, 1997). Participants 1, 4, 5, and 8 discussed their experiences around this phenomenon, as they felt women in traditionally male-dominated settings often have difficulty breaking into the good old boys club" that offers advice and professional development opportunities (Catalyst, 2003a; Heffernan, 2004; Ragins, 1998) that they were not privy to. Isolation and exclusion were central parts of the discussions with 100% of the participants, and research points to this being an issue particularly likely for women of color (American Bar Association Commission on Women in the Profession, 2006; Bell & Nkomo, 2001; Catalyst, 2003a, 2004a).

In terms of the participants' professional development, Participant 2 said,

> I worked my way up the career ladder by completing school. Every time I completed a degree I moved on to do something else to better my education and increase my market value. Even though I was faced with homophobia on the job, if I could choose, I would still be a gay, Black, female and I wouldn't hide it because that struggle made me stronger. I have to be more strategic in my career path planning than straight people, especially straight White men.

Participant 6 said,

> When it comes to being a lesbian I don't feel like anything is holding me back related to just sexuality, it is compounded again with being African American, which holds you back, regardless. I just feel like there's always more advancement for you if you're not African American and White women, lesbian or not have it easier in terms of getting ahead.

Participant 5 stated,

> A lot of Black lesbians really are not visible in corporate America. They seem to feel more comfortable in the social

services non-profit sector. I could even take it out of the lesbian women and just broaden it to Black women in general. How much corporate Black women are there? So—and that's a really good question, why is that? The first Black woman to head a Fortune 500 company was just named in 2009 and it has taken us that long and moving up the ladder is not easy especially when you do not have formal support, that type of support I have never really had.

Surveys of upper level American managers find that almost half of women of color and close to one third of White women cite a lack of influential mentors as a major barrier to advancement (Catalyst, 1999, 2000). All participants agreed that the lack of a mentor has impacted their career advancement and that when they have sought one, this behavior was met with opposition. Perhaps more important, however, removing obstacles helps to ensure that women are able to develop to their fullest potential. In order to thrive in an increasingly competitive and multicultural environment, organizations cannot squander their human resources.

All eight participants reported having few role models whose styles were feasible or congruent with their self-concepts. Participant 8 said

> I think my advancement, or anyone's advancement, being a lesbian or not, depends on how much support you're getting from your colleagues and from your bosses or your administration, and whether they're open to you, number one, being homosexual, and just being who you are and still advancing. Your advancement should be based on your own skill level and not based on race or gender or sexual orientation, but those that are out on the job seem to struggle a bit more to get to the top and I have seen African American lesbians passed over for jobs that they were qualified for and then asked to train the other person.

Participant 5 stated,

> Many lesbians that I network with have decided that they are frustrated with the prejudice and even the hidden homophobia that they felt kept them from moving as fast as they could have and obtaining the salary levels and titles they deserved. Many

decided to start their own business that did not let someone else define or stunt their career growth.

All of the participants felt that mentors would give them more courage and the inspiration that they need and that they would know they could make it because they would have someone helping set a career path for them and holding them accountable. Seventy-five percent of the participants said they felt invisible on the job and had to insert themselves into conversations to feel like part of the team. These participants indicated that after proving their capabilities it became easier to make a positive name for themselves, but it also took, for some, years longer to reach the same level as their peers. Participant 1 stated "We all need a guide; especially in male-dominated fields where straight men seem to feel intimidated by lesbian women."

Participant 1, 2, 3, 4, 6, 7, and 8 agreed that African American lesbian managers have had to fight their way to the top and fight misperceptions. Participant 6 said "I think people, as a whole, are getting more comfortable with the fact of lesbians in the workplace, but it still feels like tokenism or affirmative action." According to Participant 3 "Black women struggle with multiple barriers as it is and being a lesbian makes it harder given sexual harassment on the job and the lack of equitable benefits such as family leave, etc." Some evidence suggested that women of color are particularly likely to face challenges, given their greater responsibilities as single parents or caretakers of elderly and extended family members (Catalyst, 2003a; Hewlett, Luce, & West, 2005). This also impacted 100% of the participants, because excessive workloads leave limited time for the informal socializing and mentoring that promote professional development, given that after the workday ends, men are picking up tips over golf and drinks, whereas women, lesbian or not, are picking up laundry, dinner, and the house (Wellington & Catalyst, 2001).

In addition, other concerns around race were raised by all participants. Participant 4 stated,

> A more masculine and assertive Black woman is scary to corporate America. It's very scary, but where I save myself is by knowing how to be good with people. I know how to put people at ease and I know how to make them comfortable so I don't come across as an angry Black woman.

Participants 1, 2, 3, and 4, self-identified as more masculine than feminine in terms of their appearance and mannerisms and noted that they felt women who conform to traditional feminine stereotypes are often liked but not respected: They are judged too soft, emotional, and unassertive to make tough calls and project the necessary presence in positions of authority, and that is supported by the literature (Catalyst, 207; Eagly & Carli, 2007b). Participants 5, 6, 7, and 8 self-identified as more feminine and, by contrast, felt women who adopt more masculine traits are often respected but not liked: They are seen as domineering, strident, and cold, and that is supported by the literature as well (Babcock & Laschever, 2003; Eagly & Karau, 2002; Rhode & Kellerman, 2007). Participants 1, 3, 4, 5, 6, 7, and 8 felt that trying to move up the ladder and be promoted is a major issue for African American lesbian managers. It takes twice as long, and "we put in more hours that others and work for less pay. In terms of appearance, lesbians could not be considered for certain positions in management that would have them as visible representatives of the company.

Overall, self-promoting behavior that appears self-confident or entrepreneurial in men often look pushy and unfeminine in women, and African American women are especially vulnerable to such stereotypes and risk being seen as overly aggressive and confrontational (Catalyst, 2004b). A review of more than 100 studies found that women are rated lower when they adopt authoritative, masculine styles, particularly when the evaluators are men (Butterfield & Grinnell, 1999; Catalyst, 2007; Cleveland, Stockdale, & Murphy, 2000; Rhode & Kellerman, 2007). The participants in this study felt that they all face a trade-off between competence and likeability in circumstances where effective leadership requires both. Even in experimental situations where male and female performance is objectively equal, women are held to higher standards, and their competence is rated lower (Foschi, 2000), and women of color routinely encounter lower expectations of competence by others (Eagly & Carli, 2007b). All of the participants agreed with this and also felt that being a lesbian and being faced with homophobia created an even bigger impediment to climbing the career ladder.

Participant 5 said,

The biggest struggle is, I think, is sexism. But more about not even sexism, but more about heterosexism. Or gay male privileges as gay men, especially gay White men, are more accepted than more masculine lesbian Blacks and sometimes it feels a little bit uncomfortable and I don't always feel a part of the team.

Participant 7 was told,

> You're not going to get that position because you're an out lesbian and the stories that I hear from young, dyke lesbians is that they really have a hard time with their jobs. They pose a threat to the guys in their job, they get harassed by guys on the job, you know, "I can show you," "You think you're a man," all of that kind of stuff. There are misconceptions around some coworkers thinking that you want to be a man, but I think it's just fear of the unknown, just like a lot of people don't like Black people, because they don't know anything about them until they finally get to meet a Black person and talk to them and they're like, "Oh, they're just like me. You know can I touch your hair? I think it's the same concept with gay men and gay women. People are just uncomfortable. They don't know enough. And, this is where more gays are coming out for help so I think it's also very important that—when a person feels they're in a position where they could be discriminated against—that they're proactive. That instead of just sitting back and being discriminated against, what can be done to

> combat discrimination? I'm a masculine-looking woman in a White man's world. I'm easy prey for discrimination.

Participant 2 said,

> I was written up for being gay and ended up having to resign from my position because of the harassment and there was no protection for me because it was their word against mine and they made up false accusations. I did not have the strength to fight it nor the money, etc.

At the same time, the presence of a few highly regarded women at the top creates the illusion that the glass ceiling has been shattered for everyone else. And when superstars fail or opt out, their departures attract particular notice and reinforce stereotypes about women's lesser capabilities and commitment (Kephart & Schumacher, 2005; Stanley, 2002). This issue was seen as a burden by Participant 2, 3, 4, 5, 6, 7, and 8. These perceptions about performance can, in turn, prevent women from getting assignments that would demonstrate their abilities, thus creating a cycle of self-fulfilling prophesies. In professional contexts, women, particularly women of color, are left out, and Participants 1, 2, 3, 4, 6, and 8 felt that they less frequently receive responsibilities that lead to top executive positions, as did women of color from other studies (International Labor Organization, 2004; Rhode & Kellerman, 2007.

According to Participant 2,

You have to put in long, long hours and you have to put in face time. You have to schmooze. You have to make yourself seen, make yourself heard. You have to be with the right people. You have to grab a mentor. So if you're doing all of that, you're not having a home life. You're not having a relationship. Or if you do have a relationship, they're not seeing you. So hopefully it's already established, and so they're supportive in what you want to do. Or if it's not, then you have to be extremely patient while they wait for you to have some kind of time to see or spend with them. It is a hard fight that is unfair and burdensome and fear of discrimination is real. I feel like even with protection I have to be more discreet with my personal life just in case, especially given that is an employer at will state.

According to Participants 1, 2, 5, and 7, the increasing pace and competitiveness of organizational life, coupled with technological advances, have created a culture of total accessibility and blurred the boundaries of home and work, which leads to feelings of guilt around work and life balance. Although such technologies have made it easier for a woman to work from home, they have also made it harder not to, and excessive hours that are seen as a necessity for the company have made Participants 1 and 7 consider stepping off the leadership track, just as have other women in various research studies (Stone & Lovejoy, 2004). Although women in top managerial and professional positions often are in workplaces that offer reduced or flex-time arrangements, few of these participants take advantage of them. Literature points to any limitation in hours or availability would jeopardize their career prospects and that they would end up working more than their status and compensation justified (Crittendon, 2001; Rhode & Williams, 2007), and this is the perception of 100% of this dissertation study's participants.

Participants 2, 4, and 8 discussed internalizing stereotypes, which creates a psychological glass ceiling. In general, throughout their career, they saw themselves as less deserving than men of rewards for the same performance and less qualified for key leadership; this impact of internalized stereotypes on the creation of a psychological glass ceiling is supported by literature (Babcock &

Laschever, 2003; Barron, 2003; Rhode & Kellerman, 2007). This lesser sense of entitlement may discourage them from engaging in assertive, self-promoting behaviors and from taking risks that are likely necessary for developing key leadership skills (Hogue & Lord, 2007). They did not want to be seen as attempting to take over their boss's job or as being too difficult, and this undervaluation of their own worth often deterred them from negotiating effectively for what they wanted or needed to move their careers ahead. Their reluctance is understandable in settings where men's dislike of assertive women can undermine career advancement.

Only one third of women of color surveyed by Catalyst (1999) felt that diversity efforts created a supportive environment for their group (Giscombe & Mattis, 2002), and limited research documents improvements in the representation of women in upper level positions as a result of such training, especially lesbians of color (Kalev, Dobbin, & Kelly, 2006; Krawiec, 2003). Mentoring initiatives also merit attention, especially in light of the role they might play in the development of leadership identity. Although virtually all experts agree about the value of mentors (Catalyst, 2007), only one participant in this study, Participant 1, expressed satisfaction with the current availability of mentoring at her workplace, especially for African American lesbians. This is compounded when the issue of sexual orientation is included.

Participant 3 said,

> I think that organization heads, in general, are more receptive to White men and used to White men being in charge or in power. So I would say they definitely don't have many stop signs or yield signs in their path as, say, Black females have. It's not saying that Black females who are lesbian or heterosexual here haven't gained success, but I would say there may be a few more doors that are open being a White male.

All but one of the participants in the study agreed. Participant 7 stated, "The biggest struggle is racism and fear of being emasculated, in terms of the White males that traditionally hold most positions of power." Participant 6 said,

> I think that the way that the federal government deals with same-gender loving homes is egregious. It's a constant—it's going to be a fight, I think, and it's systemic of the way that the Constitution is written, because it was written by Puritans, fundamentalists who think, you know, read the Bible for what

it is and can't see beyond something more than man and woman. And I think that that also impedes a woman's ability to possess a true leadership and senior management position. There's still injustice and inequity in the workplace and even with government regulated protection it won't be enough given hatred that will still exist and be played out in various ways on the job.

Overall, the participants felt that if an employee is good at what she does she will be able to advance just as they have but that it will be a fight that can lead to deteriorating health, family issues, multiple jobs to find the right fit, and so on. Participants also indicated that one may have a sense of never belonging, always having to work twice as hard, and having to be more protective of one's personal life. The participants felt that their sexual orientation influenced decisions central to career growth, including: (a) family (80% of participants), (b) self-satisfaction (100% of participants), and (c) financial concerns (100% of participants). The central career decision influences are family, self-satisfaction, and financial concerns, and barriers to advancement included lack of mentoring experience, pay equity issues, organizational barriers, lack of policy on promoting women, sexism, obstinate superiors, racism, and homophobia.

The research study findings indicate that managerial level African American lesbian women should (a) seek high-visibility assignments to improve their access to corporate positions (50% of the participants); (b) set career goals and create the action plans necessary to achieve them (100% of the participants); and (c) work with sensitive executive coaches to prepare for and take full advantage of critical feedback (50% of the participants). Participants also indicated that corporations need (a) cultural change to attract minorities and African American lesbian females (80% of the participants), (b) specific training for women and African American women, and (c) senior management's complete commitment (100% of the participants).

Impediments to the career advancement of African American women, based on the literature review, include the following: relationships or networking, mentors or sponsors, work–life balance, developmental opportunities, political skills, aspirations, risk taking, feedback, commercial instinct, confidence, influence, developmental gaps, self-awareness, tokenism, alignment of values, coachability, style–fit, change agent, health or fitness, optionality, resilience, power, racism, contracting and/or just saying no, sexism, cross-cultural competence, stereotypes, competiveness, and the glass ceiling (Lott & Hutson, 2009). Many of these same impediments were also noted by this study's participants, for which a fear of employment discrimination was a key factor in the impediments to career advancement for African American lesbian managers.

## Confirmation of Validity and Reliability

In qualitative research, *validity* "refers to the bridge between a construct and the data" (Neuman, 2007, p. 120). *Validity* also means truthful and authentic. In qualitative research, a researcher seeks authenticity, which equates to providing a sincere, reasonable, and balanced description of the viewpoint of a person who lives the phenomenon every day. *Reliability* in qualitative research means dependability or consistency (Neuman, 2007). In qualitative research, reliability and validity are conceptualized as trustworthiness, rigor, and quality. Although *internal validity* and *external validity* are terms typically used in quantitative, experimental research (Neuman, 2007), internal validity in qualitative studies requires the researcher to establish that the results are "credible or believable from the perspective of the participant in the research" (Trochim, 2006, para. 3). External validity in qualitative research is the ability to transfer the results of the study to other contexts or settings (Neuman, 2007; Trochim, 2006). This research study increased validity in several ways.

The study sought to discover lived experiences of managerial women in relation to their perceived career barriers, and interviewing was the best method for the phenomenological design (Moustakas, 1994; Patton, 2002), as it increased the likelihood of capturing the lived experiences. To ensure the truthfulness of the data captured and to increase validity, Creswell (2005) recommended "member checking" (p. 252), where the researcher asks the participants to check the accuracy of the recorded and transcribed interview. With this method, the researcher ensures that the participants feel the descriptions are realistic and complete and gives him or her time to respond and clarify any unclear statements. Patton (2002) indicated that the researcher is the instrument in qualitative studies, thus he or she is an important part of increasing validity in a study. Another way to increase the validity of the researcher is the epoche, where the researcher abstains from judgment and any preconceived notions of the phenomenon (Moustakas, 1994; Patton, 2002). The researcher increases the validity of the study by strictly adhering to epoche, phenomenological reduction, imaginative variation, synthesis of meaning, and the Van Kaam (1990) method of phenomenological analysis, as modified by Moustakas (1994). To ensure that the current study's data were reliable, the researcher followed a consistent process and used the same interview questions with all participants, thus obtaining comparable descriptions of the lived experiences. The researcher, using the same set of interview questions, transcribed the confidential participant interview responses, allowing the strength and reliability of phenomenology to obtain the rich descriptions of the career barrier phenomenon under study.

## Summary

In this study the participants all felt as if they were triple outsiders, but all had a sense of personal accountability that propelled them to move forward and to be role models for other African American lesbians, especially those seeking managerial positions.

But even with seemingly dismal views of homophobia and its possible impact on career development, corporate behavior and response toward LGBT professionals seems to be changing (Lott & Hutson, 2009). According to the report Corporate Equality Index, published annually by the Human Rights Campaign, the nation's LGBT civil rights organization, 305 of 590 of the nation's top 1,000 companies received a 100% ranking for having an inclusive work environment for LGBT employees. These included General Motors Corporation; AT&T, Inc.; IBM Corporation; Bank of America Corporation, and Citigroup, Inc. Ford Motor Company; Goldman Sachs Group, Inc.; and Cardinal Health. This list was first published in 2002, when only 13 companies received a 100% ranking (Lott & Hutson, 2009). African American lesbian professionals are trying to gain more ground in corporate America, but unchecked discrimination still exists, according to all of the participants. One hundred percent of the participants felt strongly that LGBT Americans experience discrimination. When asked which groups suffer the most discrimination, all indicated African Americans and LGBT people. All felt that employment discrimination was a major issue for African American lesbians and that climbing the career ladder to managerial positions is not as easy for this group as it is for other demographics.

All of the participants also supported the central consensus theme that LGBT people should have equal rights and that they strongly support efforts to end employment discrimination and bias, which they said has halted career growth, in some cases, once a certain level has been achieved, slowed career progress, impacted personal relationships, increased mental and physical health problems, and affected their income potential. All of the participants referenced personal or tangential experience of companies violating civil rights laws by subjecting African American and lesbians to a pattern and practice of discrimination, harassment, and retaliation and similiarities have been noted in the literature (B. Greene, 2002). This adds to the already difficult fact that African American lesbians and bisexual women have multiple stigmatized identities and are affected by the conflation of institutional racism and sexism, as referenced in the literature, despite perceived progress (B. Greene, 2002).

The overarching theme from the lived experiences of the participants is that LGBT African American lesbian managers face a daily host of barriers and subtle discrimination practices, such as (a) feeling awkward and being isolated and excluded from general or specific networking opportunities and/or other company events, (b) being restricted in their contact with clients or customers, and (c) having no LGBT role models or leaders. Participants also indicated that their companies lack education and awareness on these challenges. Eighty percent of the participants felt that they might be further along in their career if they were not out on the job. As highlighted in the previous chapters, in the United States, and around the world, women are underrepresented in top leadership positions (Thomas & Bierema, 2004), and all eight participants agreed with the literature based on their personal experiences. The literature also indicates that women are underrepresented in leadership roles in the corporate setting, higher education (Catalyst, 2007), secondary education, and elementary education (Witmer, 2006), and the study participants working in those fields agreed.

In practice, the underrepresentation of women in the highest level positions continues (Witmer, 2006), and barriers such as the glass ceiling, stereotypes, personal responsibilities, networking, mentoring, and so on create a problem concerning the upward mobility of female leaders (Sagaria & Rychener, 2002). The specific focus of the study was the existence of perceived barriers that hinder the upward mobility of African American lesbian managers, and the theme of inequality was consistent in all of the interviews. The participants voiced their concerns about (a) not feeling as valued as their heterosexual peers, (b) feeling overlooked for key assignments and promotions, (c) feeling as if they were the "token" lesbian on the team, and (d) feeling that they were often asked to work on assignments that made them less visible. The participants also expressed concern that they feel years behind their equally qualified peers in terms of advancement, career growth, supervisory promotions, and so on.

Chapter 4 presented the resulting data and demographic background, described the data collection process, and explored the codes and themes that emerged from the interviews. Chapter 5 presents discussions pertaining to the emergent phenomenon and the interpretation and impact on career advancement. The researcher presents conclusions and implications of the findings; the significance of the research; recommendations for individuals, organizations, and government; and suggestions for future research from the synthesized data results presented in this chapter.

# CHAPTER 5. RESULTS, RECOMMENDATIONS, AND CONCLUSIONS

## The Discovered Phenomena

The purpose of this qualitative data research study was to explore the lived career development experiences of African American lesbian managers. Chapter 4 presented the data collection and analysis from the study exploring the career experiences of African American lesbian managers. Each participant shared many personal reflections about their professional experiences, and descriptions of these experiences and a composite description were presented. Although each participant had a unique experience, several common themes emerged from the data. Each theme was reflected to some extent in most of the lived experiences of the eight African American women that participated in this study.

Chapter 4's phenomenological data analysis shed light on the occurrences African American lesbian managers encounter when building a career path and focused on the research question, "How does employment discrimination, or the fear of such discrimination, affect African American lesbian managers' perceptions of their career advancement?" The lived experiences of the participants provided a rich source of data and information for the general public and, specifically, human resources staff, supervisors, coworkers, counseling practitioners, as well as decision makers, policy makers, and so on.

The study also added an additional perspective to the concept of the glass ceiling, which all of the participants felt they had experienced at least once on their career path. That experience combined with their experiences of discrimination based on their sexual orientation and race provided rich data for this study.

Researchers have addressed the notion of the glass ceiling's impact on women (J. R. Elliott & Smith, 2004), but these researchers have not fully explored the viewpoint of African American lesbians managers on employment, career advancement, discrimination, and the glass ceiling. The findings of the current study contribute to gender, racial, and sexual orientation discussions of professional development and of lesbian women of color in managerial roles. The study of women as managers is also important to the field of general leadership. Vinnicombe and Singh (2003) purported that organizations continue to develop male leaders while neglecting to develop female leaders to their full capacity even though women and their leadership abilities are a vital part of the nation's human capital (Catalyst, 2007). According to McKenna (2009), the continued underrepresentation of women in leadership roles throughout society is not just morally wrong, it is economically damaging. McKenna indicated that given increased globalization and internal challenges, the need to maximize the nation's human capital has never been greater. Taking full advantage of the potential and capabilities of women will greatly benefit institutions and society. The premise of the glass ceiling component of this study has three main points. First, the discrimination of women is proven by statistics, which reflect the stereotypes and injustice against women in positions of power. Second, discrimination is irrational; organizations that discriminate against women underutilize women's talents and do not optimize their workforce (Connell, 2006). Third, the shattering of the glass ceiling is possible by implementing organizational measures that remove the barriers to women's advancement, such as eliminating prejudice and enforcing equal opportunity rules in advancement (Connell, 2006).

Although the federal government instituted extensive legislation to combat discrimination against women, it continued to investigate women's issues by appointing a 21-member bipartisan body, which became the Federal Glass Ceiling Commission. Established in 1992, the Federal Glass Ceiling Commission's goal was to identify the barriers and understand the best practices and procedures that had led to career advancement for women and minorities. The commission stated that the barriers to career advancement for women and minorities were invisible and, through their research, confirmed the existence of the glass ceiling. Though it has been over 20 years since the inception of *glass ceiling* as a term, researchers continue to investigate and question its existence and the experiences of women around the world. Bowling, Kelleher, Jones, and Wright (2006) did not agree that the glass ceiling approach to exploring gender inequity is adequate. According to the glass ceiling approach, gender is understood as two fixed categories of persons, men and women, defined by biology; but, gender is a dynamic system, not a fixed dichotomy.

According to researchers, there is the feeling that the glass ceiling is cracking. Bowling, Kelleher, Jones, and Wright (2006) found that women were facing fewer barriers when securing top positions in state agencies. Women's ascension to these positions was partly a result of their education and career background. Personal choice, not the glass ceiling, is another possible explanation for the statistical difference between men and women in top leadership positions. Stolba, a former senior fellow at the Independent Women's Forum, testified at a 2003 House of Representatives hearing that women make personal choices and decisions that pull them away from executive level positions (Solba, 2003). Current research still addresses the glass ceiling, and Marschke, Laursen, Nielsen, and Dunn-Rankin (2007) found at a large research institution that only a "purposeful and radical intervention" would create gender integration among tenure-track faculty (Marschke et al., 2007, p. 20). Although more women are receiving higher education, Oliveira and Sadler (2008) cited concerns regarding the lack of women in managerial areas and discussed that although the gender gap is closing the glass ceiling is still apparent in the business world. McKenna (2009) emphasized the persistence of the glass ceiling by pointing out the dearth of women in positions of power in spite of the great number of powerful women in the country. As highlighted by the glass ceiling, gender negatively influences the advancement of women.

The glass ceiling can be understood by three possible theoretical explanations: biology, socialization, and structural–cultural influences (Weyer, 2006, 2007). Biological differences in men and women stem from genetic, hormonal, and brain structure–function. These biological differences influence the behaviors of men and women (Yoder & Sinnett, 1995). Individuals learn, directly or indirectly, and are socialized toward specific gender-appropriate behaviors (Yoder & Sinnett, 1995). Men and women acquire gender identity, and differences between the genders, through developmental processes. These processes include upbringing, educational experiences, and work (Bartol, Martin, & Kromkowski, 2003). Bartol et al. (2003), in their study of middle and executive managers in business organizations, found support for the socialization explanation of the glass ceiling. In the structural–cultural explanation of gender differences and the glass ceiling, "men and women are allocated different roles in society due to their gender. In particular, family and occupational setting contribute to the allocation of roles defined solely on the basis of gender" (Weyer, 2006, p. 443). These traits create stereotypical beliefs about each sex, and the roles have pervasive effects on the lives of women and how others interact with women (Stenius, Veysey, Hamilton, & Andersen, 2005). These three theoretical explanations provide merit to the existence of the glass ceiling. Exploration of the lived experiences of managerial-level lesbians that identify as African American, in relation to their perceived career barriers, provided further information regarding the status of the glass ceiling as well as the impact they feel from the lack of federal protection against employment discrimination for the LGBT community.

In 1956, only a few years after the *Journal of Counseling Psychology* was founded, it published an article on the vocational interests of gay men (Haselkorn, 1956). However, after this early beginning, 25 years elapsed before the second empirical article to study gay, lesbian, or bisexual persons appeared in the journal (Atkinson, Brady, & Casas, 1981). The literature review indicated that less than 20 articles with a focus on LGBT individuals appeared in the *Journal of Counseling Psychology* during the 40 years that followed the 1956 publication. The journal has published even fewer empirical studies with women and people of color as the target population of the research, and half of those articles appeared after 2002. Even if articles about counselor perceptions of clients and studies of heterosexism in the general population are included, only about 27 articles fit that broader criterion, with half of those articles appearing between 2001 and 2008.

Although the total number of research articles on LGBT people of color is small, an exciting new period appears to be emerging, in which the discouraging lack of research and the slow pace of advance that marked previous decades have come to an end. Studies examining the experiences of bisexual people, distinct from combined samples that include bisexual, gay, and lesbian individuals, have also begun to appear, and that level of inclusivity is vital to the understanding of career and vocational development (Balsam & Mohr, 2007).

There are also encouraging signs that vocational counseling psychology researchers are interested in moving past lesbians, gays, and occasionally bisexuals to study a wider range of sexual minority people. Certainly, the trends toward increased research interest in sexual minority people and a broadening of focus are evident in the contributions of vocational counseling psychologists to a variety of publication outlets (Bieschke, Hardy, Fassinger, & Croteau, 2008; Bieschke, Paul, & Blasko, 2007), but research on the African American LGBT community is still extremely limited.

Most research on European Americans as well as on African Americans has used primarily heterosexual samples. Thus, research has largely failed to attend to and investigate the complexity of African American LGBT people's experiences, especially those of African American lesbians (Szymanski & Gupta, 2009); even less research has been conducted on the career experiences of African American lesbian managers. Research on African American lesbians is critical, given the changing labor market trends that will include an increased number of women and minorities in the workforce and the increased number of out lesbians in the workplace (Bureau of Labor Statistics, 2008).

## Summary Discussion of Results

This qualitative phenomenological research explored the lived experiences of African American, lesbian, female-born managers' perceived career development opportunities and career decisions specific to management careers. The research study explored the lived experiences of eight African American women in the X tristate areas who made the career choice, or were systematically or socially directed, to seek management-level careers. The United States may face severe shortages in lesbian management in both nonprofit, government, and for-profit entities unless society becomes more understanding of the general U.S. workforce that African American women are a part of. Of all women of color, African American women continue to represent the highest rate of employment, at 7.6% of the total work force. However, during the past decade, they have made the smallest gains with regard to total employment and higher level positions. The largest percentage of all employed women, 39%, worked in management, professional, and related occupations (U.S. Equal Employment Opportunity Commission, 2010). African American women were not typically found in the management category, and 34% of them worked in sales and office occupations. Phenomenological interviews were conducted for this research study, and the study used the modified Van Kaam method of analysis of phenomenological data described by Moustakas, with taped and transcribed structured interviews. The ATLAS.ti qualitative software program was used to assist with data analysis. Patterns and themes were identified that revealed a new understanding of the critical factors and barriers to reducing underrepresentation of African American lesbian women in management. The study findings identified the critical need to focus on the value of this group, as well as to eliminate homophobic values within the workforce, to further increase the desire of African American lesbians to pursue management-level careers. Companies should demonstrate consistent and proactive approaches to attracting, retaining, and promoting qualified lesbian minority women, and specific recommended actions are presented (in the Recommendations and Future Research section) to reduce underrepresentation of African American lesbian managers in general.

This qualitative research supports the findings from the literature review: that race, gender, and sexual orientation are important factors in the analysis of African American women in the workplace. The respondents' answers support a perception of an intersection of race, gender, and sexual orientation. Although race was the dominant factor attributed to affecting success in the workplace, sexual orientation and fear of employment discrimination even further impacted the career paths of the participants and their perception of success. The participants were also asked to define success. This component of success is a contributing factor as to why the participants feel they are successful. Getting the job done, enjoying one's job, being happy, and recognition and promotions are factors that the participants consider important. Working in an environment with minimal stress was also an important factor, and that factor was often impeded when faced with homophobia. Racism, sexism, and homophobia each represented significant factors through which African American women view their experiences. Considering each of these variables in isolation fails to accurately reflect the complexities and life experiences of most people (Constantine, 2001).

Failing to recognize the intersection of race, gender, and sexual orientation fails to acknowledge the unique interrelationships among the three variables (Burgis, 2009). Lorde (1998) addressed and criticized the view that all women are seen as representing one truth as opposed to a view that multiple and diverse truths are represented in diverse groups of women. The responses of the women in this study indicate that African American women in the United States still face discrimination on account of their race, sex, and sexual orientation and that this discrimination has (a) prevented them from reaching goals on their designated timelines, (b) caused feelings of insecurity, (c) caused them to be overlooked for promotions and advancement, and (d) required them to work much harder than their peers.

Recent research is unsettling in terms of the advancement of African American lesbians. Searles's (2009) research showed that African American women are less likely to be promoted than are men and European American women. Economists, human resource specialists, and scholars have gathered data that point to African American women being least likely to be promoted when compared to those with equitable skills (Searles, 2009).

That research was supported by the experiences of the participants in this research study but magnified given their perceptions of discriminatory practices based on their sexual orientation. Bias in the workplace exists, and no reasonable explanation for the disparity could be given despite corporate policies meant to promote and encourage diversity (Searles, 2009). In fact, a large, multiple-firms study led by Rutgers University professors located in proximity to this study's research participants demonstrated that African American women actually suffered doubly from the disparity. They showed that not only are African American women last to be promoted, they also suffer financially because European American men earned more, on average. On average, European

American men in the study earned $68,000. Minority men earned $64,000, and minority women earned $54,300 (Searles, 2009).

Searles (2009) also found that men had more control over their work, which possibly led to greater job satisfaction that results in better-than-average performance ratings from other European American men and from minority women. Only African American women were disadvantaged in this setting, whereas all others were neither advantaged nor disadvantaged. Participants in this study felt that their work was either overlooked or overly scrutinized, which added additional pressure to succeed and even to feel equal to their peers.

Another recent study, conducted by Harris Interactive (Williams, 2009), was a poll of 150 executives from a broad range of industries, services, and locales. The findings showed that 75% of corporate executives believed that having minorities in senior executive positions is particularly important to providing new ideas and innovation and to better reflect the diversity of customers, but with that, LGBT people can still be fired on the job for simply being who they are. Again, inost recent literature, Human Rights Campaign (2010), indicates that in 2010, in 29 states, companies may legally fire someone because of their sexual orientation, and in 38 states companies may legally fire someone because of their gender identity or expression. Because of federal marriage laws, same-sex couples are denied access to 1,138 rights and responsibilities (National Gay and Lesbian Task Force, 2010).

The highest ranking openly gay appointee in the Obama administration is still encouraging LGBT Americans to make passing ENDA their top civil rights priority (National Gay and Lesbian Task Force, 2010). John Berry, director of the U.S. Office of Personnel Management, called for greater focus on ENDA in 2009 following his keynote address at Out for Work's national convention. Berry commended President Obama for being clearly on the record in support of ENDA but also noted that administration support alone is insufficient to advance the law (National Gay and Lesbian Task Force, 2010).

This comes at a time when LGBT employees report unique experiences of exclusion and echo similar workplace hurdles to women. Even in Canada, a country with legislated human rights protections for LGBT individuals, LGBT employees face workplace barriers that limit career advancement and, therefore, restrict potential contributions to organizational success, according to Catalyst's report on building LGBT-inclusive workplaces (National Gay and Lesbian Task Force, 2010).

This dissertation research study found that a lack of awareness, which may cause other employees to rely on stereotypes, can lead to a hostile work environment for LGBT employees, including discriminatory behaviors such as inappropriate humor or derogatory language, exclusion from important relationships and advancement opportunities, and a lack of role models. This conclusion was supported by all study participants, as they discussed feeling overlooked for training opportunities, not advancing as fast as equally qualified heterosexual colleagues, and feeling fearful of losing employment at some point in their career because they are out on the job.

Other findings of this study include that the participants do not always feel fully comfortable bringing their same-sex partner to company events or displaying pictures on their desk, feel like the "token" minority, are not invited to lunch or work functions, do not having equal workplace benefits, have strained relations with their direct reports, do not feel fully supported by supervisors, and are left out of key work conversations—all problems that impact their performance and/or career advancement.

The participants pointed out that their fears of discriminatory practices have decreased with time but that they feel more of a need to have strong educational credentials that might not be required for the job. The need for the credentials was based on their wanting to have additional skills to fall back on and speak to their true qualifications just in case they are faced with obstacles that impede their career growth. The participants have also had to create their own informal network of supporters to obtain true mentorship, and that need developed from the participants' feeling underdeveloped and nonsupported at various stages throughout their careers. Three of the participants expressed a desire to start their own business to avoid what they perceive as discriminatory practices on their current jobs.

This dissertation research study addressed the problems that precipitated the study and has added much to the body of knowledge on the subject of career-related issues impacting African American lesbian managers. Through the participants' recollections of their experiences and their sharing their stories, insight was specifically provided to the research question "How does employment discrimination, or the fear of such discrimination, affect African American lesbian managers' perceptions of their career advancement?"

The participants' attitudes, behaviors, and experiences reflected their desire to be treated in a manner that lets them know they are valued as human beings. All participants have been seeking work environments that allow them to enjoy a freedom that comes from having the chance to interact and communicate openly at all levels throughout the organization and felt that freedom enables one to develop deeper, more trusting, productive, and effective relationships. This freedom finding is supported by the literature, and the participants also fear possibly slowing down their career track, given the lack of protection on the job and feelings of inequity around race, gender, and sexual orientation.

Overall, the participants' experienced perceived discrimination that they felt could not be solely tied to their sexual orientation, given that race and gender had impacted them all at various stages of their lives and sexual orientation confounded the perceived discrimination. Their fear of this discrimination was made stronger given the lack of federal protection and the blatant discrimination that can be seen in hate crimes, and so on, against the LGBT community. All of the participants felt that their being out on the job has slowed their career path but that navigating that stumbling block has made them stronger individuals and increased their perceived value as an employee and a manager.

## Recommendations and Future Research

Further company activities that will strengthen disciplinary knowledge of the topic include (a) organizations making concerted efforts to create LGBT-inclusive workplaces, such as diversity training, employee networks, and mentoring programs, and (b) organizations helping to raise awareness and dispel myths, which would result in better workplace relationships, improved perceptions about workplace fairness, and increased career satisfaction and organizational commitment for LGBT employees.

This study focused on the experiences of African American lesbian managers that reported that LGBT employees working in organizations with effective and inclusive diversity practices experience better workplace relationships and greater organizational commitment and career satisfaction. Organizational commitment and career satisfaction are linked to greater productivity, especially for employees that have worked at organizations without the effective and inclusive diversity practices, and this was also supported by the literature (Catalyst, 2007). To become more inclusive and increase their brand as an employer of choice, organizations should increase their awareness of the LGBT community, implement diversity training to help dispel LGBT myths and stereotypes, help LGBT employees find mentors and employee groups, and make consistent and inclusive communications a core goal. A general recommendation for additional studies that came from, but was not incorporated in the current study or supported by the data, encompasses the following: African American lesbian managers should come to really know themselves and should explore their career paths and life goals in detail and journal their life experiences for future generations. This includes noting road blocks in professional advancement, understanding what might be a self-deterrent, ensuring that they are surrounded by positivity, and increasing self-promotion. Additional research is needed of (a) to study African American lesbians that have other LGBT mentors of color, and (b) to examine what, if any, impact those relationships have on career growth.

This study's findings were consistent with other research that showed African American women face serious challenges in their climb up the corporate ladder. The literature, Catalyst (2007), indicated that the top three issues cited as preventing or slowing the rise of African American women are (a) weaker or less strategic networks available to African American women (31% of the surveyed executives), (b) inaccurate perceptions of African American women's capabilities (24%), and (c) work–life balance demands (23%). "Frankly, the findings confirm what we found in our in-depth research completed earlier in 2008," said Carl Brooks, President and CEO of The Executive Leadership Council, the leading organization for the most senior level African American executives in corporate America. Brooks said,

> Not only should senior executives cultivate more trusted and strategic relationships with high-potential African American women managers, it is important for African American women managers to have and execute detailed plans for advancement

and demonstrate a passion for the values and culture of their companies. (Williams, 2009)

Many say African American women managers need to find opportunities to be more visible and to be seen as successful risk takers (Williams, 2009) and Katherine Giscombe, Vice President of Catalyst Women of Color Research (Catalyst, 2007), believes that the responsibility is also on companies to change the dynamics in their organizations that create and support barriers to women's advancement in the workplace. She said that more companies need to expand formal networks to decrease workplace exclusion and institute mentoring programs. African American women should build a corporate image of themselves that demonstrates their leadership skills. Companies can help them do this by facilitating contacts between women of color and key influential leaders within a company, giving African American women greater access to high visibility assignments, and by conducting rigorous assessments of the success of networks (Williams, 2009).

This was consistent with this study's participants noting that they often were given assignments that would take them out of the spotlight instead of showcasing their skills. An overarching issue for the participants was that they do not feel safe in their work environments and that they have feelings of mistrust, inferiority, inequity, depression, and insecurity, as well as increased health issues and stress, based on their efforts to find a comfort level at work.

Lott and Hutson (2009) pointed out that research outlines the following recommendations African American women executives must act on to increase their chances of reaching career objectives: stay in line positions as long as possible or negotiate for profit and loss or operating roles, leverage experience by strengthening internal relationships with senior management, find mentors to give constructive feedback, self-promote and discuss personal goals, apply for international experience in the emerging markets, expand responsibilities to become a bigger player in the organization, and seek risks to get accomplishments on the radar screen of CEOs and peers, and thus combat misperceptions.

But even with the literature recommendations, this study's participants felt it is not that easy, it takes longer to advance than equally qualified peers, and that achievements are not always recognized, even when self-promoted. Those factors led to participants feeling out of place, unwanted, judged, and devalued, and only when they aged a bit did they come to accept that they might have to find numerous companies of employment before finally reaching the plateau they were seeking. Some participants also pointed out that other African American women were often the ones making them feel devalued.

One participant described the difference between her current work environment and past ones this way:

> I'm a highly productive individual today. Yesterday that wasn't necessarily the case. Prior to that, it was less because I kept my entire private life private. Have I been promoted? Yes, I have gone through a series of promotions in my career. Am I able to express myself openly? Yes, absolutely, but I wasn't necessarily open about who I am at work. Years ago I would never have discussed, even casually, as co-workers often do, plans enjoyed over the weekend or details about partners, for two reasons. One was fear of violence. The other was concern over the potentially adverse impact such disclosures might have on my career.

Promoting and working to build an open, free workplace can have strategic bottom-line impact on areas such as career advancement and turnover as well as productivity. A study conducted by Harris Interactive (Williams, 2009) included a poll of 150 executives from a broad range of industries, services, and locales, taken between November 4 and December 2, 2008. The findings show that 75% of corporate executives believe that having minorities in senior executive positions is particularly important to providing new ideas and innovation and to better reflect the diversity of customers.

The poll, conducted immediately following the election of Barack Obama, occurred at a time when there was increased discussion of how the election of the first African American President of the United States would impact opportunities for minorities seeking to move into the corporate suite and on to corporate boards. The findings also showed that African American women in particular face serious challenges in their climb up the corporate ladder, and 31% of the surveyed executives attribute those challenges to weaker or less strategic networks available to African American women. Brooks said,

> Not only should senior executives cultivate more trusted and strategic relationships with high-potential African American women executives, it is important for African American

women executives to have and execute detailed plans for advancement and demonstrate a passion for the values and culture of their companies. (Williams, 2009)

Findings of published research (Williams, 2009) as well as the findings of this dissertation research study indicate that African American women should seek high-visibility assignments to improve their access to corporate positions (73%); African American women should set career goals and create the action plans necessary to achieve them (67%); and African American women should work with executive coaches to prepare for and take full advantage of critical feedback (57%). The current research indicates that corporations need (a) cultural change to attract African American females, and females in general, (b) specific training for women and African American women, especially lesbians, and (c) senior management's complete commitment.

For African American women, the reluctance to 'play' and the frustration with the corporate 'game' was part of the focus of this study, and among the dynamics covered were the importance of relationship building, mentorship and sponsorship, and finding work–life balance. "Because both their race and gender are beyond the norm in corporate America, African American women, like other women of color face the burden of being 'double outsiders,'" cited Williams's (2009) report.

Previous studies addressing the shortage of management workers of color in the United States did not focus specifically on African American lesbian women. This indicated the need for additional focused studies to add to this body of knowledge and understanding. This study's findings add a deeper understanding of the perceptions of African American women in making career decisions in the challenging U.S. economy. The study findings of the main drivers of African American women's career decisions and the recommended use of the derived African American female career decision-making model add to the scholarly body of knowledge on African American women's career choice decisions.

Although women make up 47% of the U.S. workforce, women make up just 3% of Fortune 500 CEOs. In addition, women who worked full time earned an average of just 80% of what men earned in the same positions in 2008, according to the U.S. Equal Employment Opportunity Commission (2010). By the end of 2010, the number of women in the workforce is expected to increase by 10 million, a growth rate one third higher than that of men, with women of color representing the fastest growing segment (excluding the recession impact; Fullerton & Toosi, 2001). The segment classified as women of color generally includes women who are African American, Hispanic, Native American, and Asian American (Parker, 2001). The growth projections of this segment may be attributed in large part to increased immigration and higher birth rates than those of White women (Fullerton & Toosi, 2001). Thus, additional studies of African American women's career decisions, with expanded study of lesbian women of color, are recommended.

Considering the number of women of color projected to constitute the future workforce, the ability of members of this group to assume leadership roles in organizations is a critical issue for U.S. businesses (Betters-Reed & Moore, 1995). The career development of women of color, however, continues to lag behind that of other groups by a considerable margin. African American women in particular seem to be uniquely challenged to advance in organizations (Avery & Thomas, 2004). The most influential members of the organization are most likely to be White men; however, confronted with elements of racism and sexism, African American women are frequently excluded from relationships with these individuals (Combs, 2003; Hill & Gant, 2000).

Mentors and the reliance on self-confidence and inner strength impacted career choices of the participants. The influence of mentors in assisting with career directions and career growth directions of the participants was very significant. Although the career decision directions of participants were influenced by the support of mentors, the participants also had to depend on their self-confidence and inner strength to overcome barriers, to seek career advancements, and to make career changes. The eight study participants displayed a strong presence of self-concept and self-efficacy. The participants' high level of self-efficacy helped to drive their future. Socioeconomic factors also have an impact on career decisions. The socioeconomic factors relate to the society's economic condition (supply and demand of jobs); sex discrimination; and social, racial, and ethnic group membership (Alston, 2006). But despite these factors, the participants all found themselves able to preserve past socioeconomic status and obtain management positions.

Lack of encouragement and limited-or-no computer exposure as a youth can also influence people to seek careers in management fields. Underrepresentation of minorities in management often begins with lack of resource access, but the participants identified several other specific barriers to the career growth of African American lesbian women in management fields, including the following: not wanting to be labeled as trying to act as if they are White, male dominance, the feeling of not being accepted, lack of exposure, stereotypes impeding hiring and advancement opportunities, and the belief that the management is not protective of the LGBT community. These items were captured in the 10 themes noted in Chapter 4.

LGBT people of color are often invisible, and LGBT organizations of color are so underfunded and hidden from the media that negative stereotypes of this group continue to be reinforced. Lack of support also heightens the problem. The literature suggests that mentoring African American women may provide maximum developmental benefit to individuals early in their management careers (Alleman & Clarke, 2000; Hegstad & Wentling, 2004; Hood, 2004). During the 1990s, organizations acknowledging both the business and the moral imperative addressed the glaring disparities in career development opportunities for women and minorities by launching formal diversity initiatives (Darwin, 2000; Young & Wright, 2001). Although these initiatives have had some success in improving the general organizational awareness of diversity issues and the need for greater inclusion, the 1999 Catalyst study found that most African American women did not believe that these initiatives had any significant impact on their career growth (Lach, 1999), and the feeling was similar within this study.

Research has shown that African American women are also frequently subjected to biases attributable to both racism and sexism; therefore, they arguably face more substantial career obstacles than do White women and African American men (Bell & Nkomo, 2003; Blake-Beard, 1999; Combs, 2003). For compensation, African American women continue to lag behind White men, White women, and African American men (Cook, Heppner, & O'Brien, 2002). The literature suggests that, for African American women, attaining an influential mentor may provide maximum developmental benefit early in their management careers (Alleman & Clarke, 2000; Hegstad & Wentling, 2004; Hood, 2004). The inability to attain a mentor has been identified as a key impediment in the professional development of African American women. Attaining an influential mentor, particularly early in their management careers, appears to be essential for propelling African American women to overcome the barriers that block their professional development and to assert themselves for equitable salaries.

As evident in this study, having a mentor while in their management role positively affected the women's ability to adapt to their management roles and their subsequent career development. The women spoke of unique challenges they faced in their organizations that were attributable to their sexual orientation, race, and sex. Several participants were able to form strong mentoring relationships across racial and/or gender lines. Several participants were also able to form strong mentoring relationships with individuals that were their direct supervisors. The mentoring relationships in which all the participants engaged were informal. They received significant emotional support from their mentors that enabled them to cope with the challenges, and they felt both that these mentoring relations allowed them to advance in their careers and that those without mentors might not advance or advance as quickly. Participants indicated that trust and honesty with their mentors was a key element in building strong mentoring relationships. The participants received vital coaching and support from their mentors to improve their job performance. The mentors assisted the participants in building the networking relationships necessary to effectively navigate organizational politics. The participants believed that the mentoring they received in their first management role was a catalyst for their subsequent career progression. All of the participants were inspired by their experiences with mentoring to give back by mentoring others.

The participants in the study began their management careers in the 1970s through the 2000s. Regardless of the decade when they first became managers, the participants were one of the few and sometimes the only African American woman in a management role within their organization. Several participants noted that they worked in organizations and/or industries that were dominated by White men and at times name-calling and harassment has ocurred. The participants faced challenges that ranged from general feelings of isolation to peers who deliberately provided misinformation to disrupt the work of the participant. According to the literature, one of the most distinct challenges faced by many managers is a loss of self-confidence and self-esteem. African American women in a management role may find the loss of self-confidence and self-esteem is compounded by feelings of isolation.

One of the dominant themes that surfaced over the course of the study was the lack of equitable treatment experienced by African American lesbian managers. All eight desire an intellectual challenge, continuation of growth opportunities, and recognition. With respect to long-term aspirations, all eight seek greater workload challenge, increased quality of life, and financial security. The needs to be respected and seen as credible are equally important. So, the myth that African Americans are somehow prone to lethargy and lack ambition (Carr-Ruffino, 2003) is not borne out in this study, and participants also felt that was a myth; however, strong desires to be seen otherwise did little to promote the expectation of fair treatment. The lack of equitable treatment manifested through (a) a lack of critical consideration for advancement opportunities, (b) a lack of strategic task assignments, and (c) a lack of extended trust and confidence.

However, this study's participants voiced their observations that their mainstream

counterparts exhibit a blending of the two realities: the work environment is not exclusively the work environment; it is also the social environment. Whereas these
African American engineering professionals go to the workplace with the expectation of engaging in work-related matters, their mainstream colleagues go not only to engage in work-related matters but also to socialize. Although these African American professionals demonstrate proficiency toward their tasks, they did not necessarily fashion stronger ties with their mainstream colleagues, thus they were less strongly aligned employees. Given the task complexities and interpersonal dynamics at play in the engineering environment of the industry, clear distinctions between work-related and non-work-related exchanges are no longer readily discernable. Consequently, a reduced presence and standoffish personality as the enduring image of an African American lesbian professional may be mistakenly viewed as one less committed and difficult to engage in meaningful exchange, serving to further perpetuate the exclusion of African Americans in the work environment. This was a challenge to the participants, but discrimination based on race, gender, and sexual orientation combined with the lack of true mentorships impacted their career growth, with

discrimination based on sexual orientation creating a true level of fear, given the lack of federal protection.

Some of this study's key findings include the following: (a) relationships with senior executives need more work; (b) African American women executives suffer from the lack of comfortable, trusted, and strategic relationships at the senior level with those who are most different from themselves, most notably European American men; (c) employees need feedback about their job performance, yet internal networks for African American women executives do not provide enough strategic conversations about how they are doing and how best to advance; and (d) experiences that lead to high level corporate positions are not visible enough, and African American female executives oftentimes do not have the opportunity to showcase the breadth of their skills and experience to the people in higher levels of the organization. It was also noted that work–life balance is an individual responsibility and being proactive about managing the integration of work and life increases the ability of African American women executives to compete at the highest levels. Those interviewed for the study believe that many African American women get a late start in strategically positioning themselves for advancement in areas such as securing profit and loss positions and operating roles as well as in developing the important relationships that provide guidance, strategy, and feedback. Many say African American women executives need to find opportunities to be more visible and to be seen as successful risk takers (Williams, 2009). According to the participants, the workplace is becoming less intimidating to nonheterosexuals, and that is supported by the literature and is an overarching theme, given that the participants acknowledge continued career growth and access to benefits, and so on, that did not exist a few years ago.

Catalyst (2007) pointed out that the onus is also on corporations to change the dynamics in their organizations that create and support barriers to women's advancement in the workplace and that more companies need to expand formal networks, to decrease workplace exclusion, and institute mentoring programs. African American women should build a corporate image of themselves that demonstrates their leadership skills; companies can help them do this by facilitating contacts between women of color and key influential leaders within a company, giving African American women greater access to high visibility assignments, and by conducting rigorous assessments of the success of networks (Williams, 2009).

An additional recommendation includes supervisors acknowledging their own personal bias and behaviors. This process might be difficult at first, but it will be a beneficial process that will allow leaders to identify with the experiences of their employees on a more personal and sensitive level. That might lead to supervisors creating a nonthreatening, safe, and comfortable environment for their staff, opening lines of communication, and learning more about employees. The knowledge gained from coming to know staff members and direct reports enables leaders to be mentors, coaches, and support systems by motivating employees, especially those that identify as LGBT. Supervisors' efforts in staff support can show staff that their appreciation goes beyond graciousness because of task accomplishment but also includes caring about personal well-being and career advancement. As supervisors and staff trust each other, build respect, and share vision and inclusive behavior, they are increasingly committed to both each other and the goals of the company.

Even though federal legislation and affirmative action policies aim to eliminate employment discrimination (Glazer-Raymo, 2003), equal representation in the workforce is not yet a reality. Many women face a glass ceiling in their career pursuits (Blum, Fields, & Goodman, 2003; Thomas & Bierema, 2004). Women also encounter numerous barriers that prohibit them from advancing to higher level positions in their careers (Catalyst, 2007).

Barriers identified by this research and supported by the literature are (a) stereotypes about women's suitability for leadership careers (Sczesny, 2003), (b) exclusion of formal and informal networks, (c) lack of accountability of senior executives to assist in the advancement of women, (d) lack of mentoring and role models, and (e) gender stereotypes (Catalyst, 2007). Noticeably absent from the literature is a current and specific analysis of the career barriers that African American lesbian managers may face, especially given that federal legislation and affirmative action policies enacted over approximately the past 50 years have attempted to thwart discrimination, but fail to include protection based on sexual orientation (Burleson, Hallett, & Park, 2007).

Given the lack of federal protection, organizations should focus on building relationships based on emotional intelligence of both supervisors and employees and identifying emotion-friendly or welcoming behavior that reduces the fear of job loss, retaliation, and isolation. This research suggested that there is a gap between supervisors' and companies' attitudes and behaviors and the emotional needs of their LGBT employees, and even if federal regulation is soon passed, it will not dismiss the undercurrents of sexual-orientation-based discriminatory practices. The gap between employers and staff is present when one adopts leadership approaches such as discrimination that dismiss the humanness of employees.

According to the results of a new African American lesbian needs-assessment study (Ramsey et al., 2010), for many in the LGBT community, disclosure of one's sexual identity on the job is often accompanied by harassment, mental and/or physical abuse, as well as alienation and isolation from the dominant culture. Consequently, disclosing one's sexual identity in the workplace can often lead to exclusion from networking opportunities and/or company events, being restricted in contracts with clients and customers, or even termination (Hutson, 2009). Respondents were most likely to rate jobs and financial security, civil rights, and mental health highly as areas of concern that also affect career advancement (Ramsey et al., 2010).

Based on the literature, in the fields of sociology and psychology (Wilson & Miller, 2002), the majority of literature on African American homosexual identity focuses primarily on gay men. The literature shows that African American lesbian identity is also shaped by social, economic, and cultural forces (Henderson, 2009), and those factors impact career advancement of this population, as shown in this dissertation research study. Many of the participants agreed that African American lesbians are severely disadvantaged in contemporary American society. In areas of family, health, visibility, identity, class, and aging, African American lesbians suffer disproportionately in comparison to straight Whites and Blacks as well as compared to the broader LGBT community (Ramsey et al., 2010). Based on Ramsey et al.'s (2010) data, as research on LGBT communities continues to burgeon, the experiences of African American lesbians must remain at the heart of advocacy, funding, and research, and that sentiment is reflected in this research as well. Future studies can also include looking at the long-term approaches that seek to promote the well-being of employees as a means for accomplishing organizational goals. Future research can also look at how leadership approaches that have negative influence of relations at work are systemic through many organizational cultures. This can provide insight into leadership and its effect on employee motivation, employee perception, employee productivity, and so on, especially when there is little regard for inclusiveness and employee well-being. Addiitonal research into the perceptions of race, gender, and sexual orientation regarding how they each impact career development is needed, especially given how phenomenological research revolves arounds ones' awareness. This study on women will add to the growing body of literature on lesbians, African-American women and career development. Additionally, this study will offer greater insight into how factors such as race, gender, and sexuality impact the lives of female managers. This research has implications for helping organizations in program planning and long-term strategies should be used to address the needs of African American lesbians, especially around the growing needs of workforce development, financial security, healthcare, and access to education. I hope that this work builds strategic partnerships that can be cultivated to provide support and focus on civil rights for lesbians and their families.

This research study creates a vision for leaders seeking to be mentors and adopt a leadership approach that will help retain and develop the talent to LGBT managers. Future research could also focus on what happens when there is lack of support for supportive mentoring on the job. Delving into the career development of college age African American lesbians as they move through their careers will also expand the breadth of knowledge around the subject.

## Conclusion

Chapter 5 presented an interpretation of the collected data and the themes that emerged. The value and success of companies and LGBT managers is contingent upon how leaders interact with employees and the adaptation of leadership approaches that promote the well-being of staff along with growing the inclusivity of companies.

The purpose of this phenomenological study was to understand the lived experience of African American lesbian managers, and this research can assist vocational counselors and organizational manager interactions with this vulnerable population. Data gathered from interviews with the eight participants revealed features of their everyday experiences in the dimensions of temporality, spatiality, corporeality, and relationality. Many of the conclusions were reminiscent of extremely limited previously published findings; many of the individual datum, however, were newly insightful, having the ability to impact changes in practice, vocational theory, policy, business management, counseling, human services, and education.

The data analysis suggested that African American females aspiring to the role of management in the United States should prepare themselves professionally and academically. They should engage in career mapping to gain a fuller perspective of personal needs and needs of the institution. The study addressed (a) the major influences that led the study participants to careers in management, (b) the challenges that study participants experienced in gaining and retaining successful management careers, (c) the ways in which study participants were able to overcome career path challenges, and (d) the advice that study participants would offer to African American lesbians who aspire to careers in management.

This research topic is meant to convey not only the individual need to be included, regardless of differences in appearance, but also the collective need of organizations in the industry that rely on the optimal utilization of a talented workforce to maintain a level of productivity that enables competitive and economic viability which promotes a forward progression toward success. African American female leadership studies would benefit greatly with further research in the area of mentoring and mentorship programs. This chapter presented a summary of Chapters 1–4. The chapter also illustrated the significance of this study to leadership. Finally, Chapter 5 provided a strong recommendation for further research of the specific benefits of mentoring and mentorship programs and updates of the data based on the new 2010 census data is encouraged.

In summary, there is no secret that African American women, in general, have been overlooked when it comes to career advancement and impediments to their success based on the literature (Alston, 2006) include relationships or networking, mentors or sponsors, work–life balance, developmental opportunities, political skills, aspirations, risk taking, feedback, commercial instinct, confidence, influence, developmental gaps, self-awareness, tokenism, alignment of values, coachability, style and/or fit, change agent, health and/or fitness, optionality, resilience, power, racism, contracting or just saying no, sexism, cross-cultural competence, stereotypes, competiveness, and the glass ceiling (Lott & Hutson, 2009). In addition, some avenues of discriminatory behaviors are nonverbal, and this study's participants felt that they were conveyed through gestures, eye contact, touch, facial expression, and/or lack of spatial proximity. They also indicated that lesbian persons, just like anyone else, like to feel validated, including lesbians that have felt shunned

Companies should demonstrate consistent and proactive approaches to attracting, retaining, and promoting qualified lesbian minority women, and specific recommended actions are presented to reduce underrepresentation of African American lesbian managers. Based on this research study, practical and supportive practices should include creating an inclusive and supportive workplace involving leading by example with a clear commitment from the top down that diversity is important; public praise and acknowledgement, adopting policies and procedures to support diversity, antidiscrimination and antiharassment; promoting (both internally and externally) the organization's commitment to diversity; holding all staff and volunteers accountable; and providing training and awareness in the workplace. The focus must be on building an inclusive environment that is welcoming to people regardless of sexual orientation or gender identity.

The following is a list of practical and supportive practices: Make reference to sexual orientation and gender identity in workplace diversity policies; do not assume heterosexuality; when one interacts with a job seeker or new employee, ask inclusive questions that do not assume that the person has a spouse of the opposite gender; offer mentors; review human resources orientation sessions to make sure they reflect more than just heterosexual examples, and use the inclusive term *partner* rather than *husband* or *wife*; and extend employment and pension benefits, emergency leave, group life insurance, maternity–parental leave, pension plan, and so on, to same-sex partners. In addition to this, more than half of the participants said that they had experienced racism from the European American LGBT communities and offered that cultural sensitivity and race-related trainingbe incorporated as well.

One limitation of this phenomenological study was that it may not have relevance to all African American LGBT persons. Going forward it is vital to explore the complexity of gay identity development in African American gay men and lesbian women. This study's participants identified three specific issues as adding the most complexity and as differentiating their identity development from most gay or lesbian identity-development models, and this is consistent with the limited literature: racial prejudice, limited acceptance by the African American community, and a lack of integration into the larger European American LGBT community.

Women's representation still has not grown significantly in corporate boardrooms, executive office suites or the ranks of companies' top earners in the last year and this is the fifth report where the annual change in female leadership remained flat according to Catalyst (2010). Delving deeper into the effects on career development of ethnic and sexual minorities is more than needed and complex given that identity status such as race, gender, and sexual orientation are not simply additives but interactive parts of a person that play a defining role in his or her overall career advancement and professional development. The consistent theme from all of the participants in this study was fear and isolation and daunting barriers to achieving their career goals because of homophobia, which is even more magnified by gender and, more so, race. If managers can attend thoughtfully to the person and their conception of career advancement needs, the quality of life in all professional development dimensions may improve for the entire LGBT community.

# REFERENCES

Abu-Bader, S., & Crewe, S. (2006). Predictors of depression among African American women who were former welfare recipients: A path diagram. *Best Practice in Mental Health: An International Journal, 2*(2), 1–22.

Accenture. (2008). *The anatomy of the glass ceiling.* Retrieved from http://www.accenture.com/NR/rdonlyres/9A504280-5296-43E5-B197-AE1FC48866F3/0/glass_ceiling.pdf

Adams, C., & Kimmel, D. (1997). Exploring the lives of older African American gay men. Ethnic and cultural diversity among lesbians and gay men. In B. Greene (Ed.), *Psychological perspectives on lesbian and gay issues* (pp. 132–151). Thousand Oaks, CA: Sage.

Adams, M. (1998). Building a rainbow one stripe at a time. *HR Magazine, 43*(7), 72–79.

African American. (n.d.). In *Merriam-Webster's online dictionary*. Retrieved from http://www.m-w.com/dictionary/

Agocs, C. (2004). Surfacing racism in the workplace: Qualitative and quantitative evidence of systemic discrimination. *Canadian Diversity, 3*, 25–28.

Agrast, M. (2003). Unfinished journey. *Journal of the Section of Individual Rights & Responsibilities, 30,* 3–6.

Alfred, M. V. (2001). Expanding theories of career development: Adding the voices of African American women in the White academy. *Adult Education Quarterly, 51*(2), 108–127.

Alfred, M. (2007, August). Welfare reform and Black women's economic development. *Adult Education Quarterly, 57*(4), 293–311. doi:10.1177/0741713607302685

Alleman, E., & Clarke, D. L. (2000). Accountability: Measuring mentoring and its bottom line impact. *Review of Business, 21*(1/2), 62–67.

Alliance for Full Acceptance. (2003). *For therapists and counselors* [Brochure]. Charleston, SC: Author.

Alston, C. M. (2006). *The impact of mentoring on African American women in their first management position: A phenomenological study* (Doctoral dissertation). Available from ProQuest Dissertations and Theses database. (Publication No. AAT 3215994)

American Bar Association Commission on Women in the Profession. (2006). *Visible invisibility: Women of color in law firms*. Chicago, IL: ABA Foundation.

American Civil Liberties Union. (2002). *Questions and answers about the Employment Non-Discrimination Act (ENDA), S. 1284/H.R. 2692*. Retrieved from http://www.aclu.org/lgbt/discrim/11853leg20020226.html

American Civil Liberties Union. (2003). *Lesbian and gay rights*. Retrieved from http://www.aclu.org/LesbianGayRights/LesbianGayRightsMain.cfm

American Psychological Association. (1997). *Sexual orientation and homosexuality*. Retrieved from http://helping.apa.org/articles/article.php?id=31

Anderson, K., Armitage, S., Jack, D., & Wittner, J. (1990). Beginning where we are: Feminist methodology in oral history. In J. Nielsen (Ed.), *Feminist research methods* (pp. 103–127). Boulder, CO: Westview.

Atkinson, D. R., Brady, S., & Casas, J. M. (1981). Sexual preference similarity, attitude similarity, and perceived counseling credibility and attractiveness. *Journal of Counseling Psychology, 28*(6), 504-509.

Avery, D. R., & Thomas, K. M. (2004). Blending content and contact: The roles of diversity curriculum and campus homogeneity in fostering diversity management competence. *Academy of Management Learning & Education, 3*(4), 390–396.

Babcock, L., & Laschever, S. (2003). *Women don't ask: Negotiation and the gender divide.* NJ: Princeton University Press.

Bailey, R. (2000). *Out and voting part two: The gay, lesbian, and bisexual vote in congressional elections, 1990–1998.* New York, NY: Policy Institute of the National Gay and Lesbian Task Force.

Balsam, K. F., & Mohr, J. J. (2007). Adaptation to sexual orientation stigma: A comparison of bisexual and lesbian/gay adults. *Journal of Counseling Psychology, 54,* 306-319.

Barret, B., & Logan, C. (2002). *Counseling gay men and lesbian: A practical primer.* Pacific Grove, CA: Brooks/Cole.

Barrier, M. (2001). Mixed signals. *HR Magazine, 46*(12), 64–69.

Barron, L. (2003). Ask and you shall receive? Gender differences in negotiators' beliefs about requests for a higher salary. *Human Relations, 56,* 635–662.

Barry, C. A. (1998). Choosing qualitative data analysis software: Atlas/ti and Nudist compared. *Sociological Research Online, 3*(3).

Bartol, K. M., Martin, D. C., & Kromkowski, J. A. (2003). Leadership and the glass ceiling: Gender and ethnic group influences on leader behaviors at middle and executive managerial levels. *Journal of Leadership and Organizational Studies, 9,* 8–20.

Battle, J., Cohen, C. J., Warren, D., Fergerson, G., & Audam, S. (2002). *Say it loud: I'm Black and I'm proud: Black Pride Survey 2000*. New York: Policy Institute of the National Gay and Lesbian Task Force.

Bauer, M., & Kleiner, B. (2001). New developments concerning sexual orientation issues in the workplace. *Equal Opportunities International, 20*(5–7), 27–31.

Bieschke, K. J., Paul, P.L., & Blasko, K. A. (2007). Review of empirical research focused on the experience of lesbian, gay, and bisexual clients in counseling and psychotherapy. In K.Bieschke, R. Perez, & K. DeBord (Eds.), *Handbook of counseling and psychotherapy with lesbian, gay, bisexual, and transgender clients* (2nd ed., pp. 293-316). American Psychological Association: Washington DC.

Bieschke, K. J., Fassinger, R. F., Hardy, J., & Croteau, J. M. (2008). Intersecting identities of gender-transgressive sexual minorities: Toward a new paradigm of affirmative psychology. *Biennial review of counseling psychology* (pp. 177-208). New York, New York: Taylor & Francis.

Belenky, M. F. (1996). Public homeplaces: Nurturing the development of people, families, and communities. In N. Goldberger, J. Tarule, B. Clinchy, & M. Belenky (Eds.), *Knowledge, difference and power* (pp. 393–430). New York, NY: Basic Books.

Bell, E. L. J. E., & Nkomo, S. (2001). *Our separate ways*. Cambridge, MA: Harvard Business School Press.

Bell, E. L. J. E., & Nkomo, S. M. (2003). Our separate ways: Black and White women and the struggle for professional identity. *The Diversity Factor, 11*(1), 11–15.

Belz, J. R. (1993). Sexual orientation as a factor in career development. *Career Development Quarterly, 41*, 197–200.

Betters-Reed, B. L., & Moore, L. L. (1995). Shifting the management development paradigm for women. *Journal of Management Development, 14*(2), 24–38.

Betz, N. E. (1989). Implications of the null environment hypothesis for women's career development and for counseling psychology. *The Counseling Psychologist, 17*, 136–144.

Betz, N. E. (1994). Basic issues and concepts in career counseling for women. In W. B. Walsh & S. H. Osipow (Eds.), *Career counseling for women* (pp. 1–41). Hillsdale, NJ: Erlbaum.

Betz, N. E., Klein, K. L., & Taylor, K. M. (1996). Evaluation of a short form of the Career Decision-Making Self-Efficacy Scale. *Journal of Career Assessment, 4*, 47–57.

Bierema, L. L. (1994). *How executive business women develop and function in male dominated organizational culture* (Unpublished doctoral dissertation). University of Georgia, Athens, GA.

Bierema, L. L. (2002). A feminist approach to HRD research. *Human Resource Development Quarterly, 1*(2), 244–268.

Birzer, M.L., & Smith-Mahdi, J. (2006). Does race matter? The phenomenology of discrimination experienced among African Americans. *Journal of African American Studies, 10*(2), 22–37.

Blake-Beard, S. D. (1999). The costs of living as an outsider within: An analysis of the mentoring relationships and career success of Black and White women in the corporate sector. *Journal of Career Development, 26*(1), 21–36.

Blum, T. C., Fields, D. L., & Goodman, J. S. (1994). Organization level determinants of women in management. *Academy of Management Journal, 37*(2), 241–

Blumer, H. (1956). Sociological analysis and the variable. *American Sociological Review, 21,* 683–690.

Blumstein, P., & Schwartz, R. (1983). *American couples: Money, work, sex*. New York, NY: Pocket Books.

Boatwright, K. J., Gilbert, M. S., Forrest, L., & Ketzenberger, K. (1996). Affect of identity development upon career trajectory: Listening to the voices of lesbian women. *Journal of Vocational Behavior, 48*, 210–228.

Bogdan, R., & Bilken, S. K. (1992). *Qualitative research for education: An introduction to theory and methods* (2nd ed.). Boston, MA: Allyn & Bacon.

Bowleg, L., Craig, M., & Burkholder, G. (2004, August). Rising and surviving: A conceptual model of active coping among Black lesbians. *Cultural Diversity and Ethnic Minority Psychology, 10*(3), 229–240. doi:10.1037/1099-9809.10.3.229

Bowleg, L., Huang, J., Brooks, K., Black, A., & Burkholder, G. (2003). Triple jeopardy and beyond: Multiple minority stress and resilience among Black lesbians. *Journal of Lesbian Studies, 7*(4), 87–108.

Bowling, C. J., Kelleher, C. A., Jones, J., & Wright, D. S. (2006). Cracked ceilings, firmer floors, and weakening walls: Trends and patterns in gender representation among executives leading American state agencies. *Public Administration Review, 66*(6), 823–836.

Bridges. S., Selvidge, M., & Matthews, C. (2003). Lesbian women of color: Therapeutic issues and challenges. *Journal of Multicultural Counseling, 31*, 113–130.

Brown, D. (2002). The role of work and cultural values in occupational choice, satisfaction, and success: A theoretical statement. *Journal of Counseling & Development, 80*(1), 48–56.

Brown, H. A., & Ford, D. L. (1977). An exploratory analysis of discrimination in the employment of Black MBA graduates. *Journal of Applied Psychology, 62,* 50–56.

Brown, M. T. (1995). The career development of African Americans: Theoretical and empirical issues. In F. T. L. Leong (Ed.), *Career development and vocational behavior of racial and ethnic minorities* (pp. 7–36). Mahwah, NJ: Erlbaum.

Browne, I. (1999). *Latinas and African-American women at work: Race, gender, and economic inequality.* New York, NY: Russell Sage Foundation.

Buchanan, N., & Fitzgerald, L. (2008). Effects of racial and sexual harassment on work and the psychological well-being of African American women. *Journal of Occupational Health Psychology, 13*(2), 137–151. doi:10.1037/1076-8998.13.2.137

Buhrke, R. A., Ben-Ezra, L. A., Hurley, M. E., & Ruprecht, L. J. (1992). Content analysis and methodological critique of articles concerning lesbian and gay male issues in counseling journals. *Journal of Counseling Psychology, 39,* 91–99.

Bureau of Labor Statistics. (2001). *Manager definition.* Retrieved from http://stats.bls.gov/soc/soc_a1c1.htm

Bureau of Labor Statistics. (2008). *Working in the 21st century.* Retrieved from http://www.bls.gov/opub/working/page3a.htm

Burger, C. J., Creamer, E., & Meszaros, P. (2005). *Women in information technology: Pivotal transitions from school to careers.* Blacksburg, VA: Virginia Tech University.

Burgis, C. (2009). *Black women in the workplace: A perception of how race, gender, and age affect success, fulfillment, job satisfaction, and stress* (Doctoral dissertation). Available from ProQuest Dissertations and Theses. (Publication No. AAT 3339461)

Burleson, D. A., Hallett, R. E., & Park, D. K. (2007, November). *What do students know? Evaluation of urban high school students' knowledge of college processes.* Presented at the annual meeting of the Association for the Study of Higher Education, Louisville, KY.

Burt, R. (1992). *Structural holes.* Cambridge, MA: Harvard University Press.

Business Health Services. (2005). *Physical signs of stress.* Retrieved from http://www.bhsonline.com

Business Training Media. (2004). *Affirmative action vs. diversity.* Retrieved from http://www.business-marketing.com/store/affirmvsdiv.html

Butterfield, D. A., & Grinnell, J. P. (1999). Reviewing gender, leadership, and managerial behavior: Do the decades of research tell us anything? In G. Powell (Ed.), *Handbook of gender and work* (pp. 223–238). Thousand Oaks, CA: Sage.

Cadrain, D. (2003). Equalities last frontier. *HR Magazine, 48*(3). Retrieved from http://www.shrm.org

Cammermeyer, M. (1994). *Serving in silence.* New York, NY: Viking Penguin .

Carbado, D., & Gulati, M. (2003). What exactly is racial diversity? *California Law Review, 91,* 1149–1165.

Career advancement. (n.d.). In *Merriam-Webster's online dictionary.* Retrieved from http://www.m-w.com/dictionary/careeradvancement

Carr-Ruffino, N. (2002). *Managing diversity: People skills for a multicultural workplace.* Boston, MA: Pearson .

Catalyst. (1999). *Women of color in corporate management: Opportunities and barriers.* New York, NY: Author.

Catalyst. (2000). *Cracking the glass ceiling: Strategies for success.* Retrieved from http://www.catalyst.org

Catalyst. (2002). *Women and men MBA graduates satisfied with value of MBA degree and with careers overall.* Retrieved from http://www.umich.edu/~cew/mba2.html

Catalyst. (2003a). *Advancing Asian women in the workplace: What managers need to know.* New York, NY: Author.

Catalyst. (2003b). *Women of color in corporate management: Three years later.* Retrieved from www.catalyst.org

Catalyst. (2004a). *Advancing African-American women in the workplace: What managers need to know.* New York, NY: Author.

Catalyst. (2004b). *Catalyst report outlines unique challenges faced by African-American women in business.* Retrieved from http://www.catalyst.org

Catalyst. (2004c). *Women and men in U.S. corporate leadership: Same workforce, different realities.* New York, NY: Author.

Catalyst. (2007). *The double bind dilemma for women in leadership: Damned if you do; doomed if you don't.* New York, NY: Author.

Catalyst. (2010). 2010 *Catalyst census: Fortune 500 women board directors.* Retrieved from http://diversity-executive.com/article.php?article=1051

Chapman, A. (2008). Race and gender. *Black Enterprise Magazine, 38,* 82–86.

Chin, J. (2005). *The psychology of prejudice and discrimination: Bias based on gender and sexual orientation.* Westport, CT: Praeger.

Chojnacki, J. T., & Gelberg, S. (1994). Toward a conceptualization of career counseling with gay/lesbian/bisexual persons. *Journal of Career Development, 21,* 3–10.

Chung, Y. B. (2001). Work discrimination and coping strategies: Conceptual frameworks for counseling lesbian, gay, and bisexual clients. *The Career Development Quarterly, 50,* 33–44.

Chung, Y. B. (2003). Career counseling with lesbian, gay, bisexual, and transgender persons: The next decade. *The Career Development Quarterly, 52,* 78–86.

Chung, Y. B., & Harmon, L. W. (1994). The career interests and aspirations of gay men: How sex-role orientation is related. *Journal of Vocational Behavior, 45,* 223–239.

Chung, Y. B., Loeb, J. W., & Gonzo, S. T. (1996). Factors predicting the educational and career aspirations of Black college freshmen. *Journal of Career Development, 23*(2), 127–135.

Ciazza, A., Shaw, A., & Werschkul, M. (2004). *Women's economic status in the United States: Wide disparities by race, ethnicity, and region.* Washington, DC: Institute for Women's Policy Research.

Clair, J., Beatty, J., & MacLean, T. (2005). Out of sight but not out of mind: Managing invisible social identities in the workplace. *Academy of Management Review, 30*(1), 78–95.

Cleveland, J., Stockdale, M., & Murphy, K. (2000). *Women and men in organizations: Sex and gender issues at work.* Mahwah, NJ: Erlbaum.

Cochran, S. D., & Mays, V. M. (1988a). Disclosure of sexual preference to physicians by Black lesbian and bisexual women. *Western Journal of Medicine, 149,* 616–619.

Cochran, S. D., & Mays, V. (1988b). Epidemiological and sociocultural factors in the transmission of HIV infection in Black gay and bisexual men. In M. Shernoff & W. Scott (Eds.), *The sourcebook of lesbian/gay health care* (pp. 202–211). Washington, DC: National Gay and Lesbian Health Foundation.

Cochran, S. D., & Mays, V. M. (1994). Depressive distress among homosexually active African-American men and women. *American Journal of Psychiatry, 151*(4), 524–529.

Cochran, S. D., & Mays, V. M. (2000). Relation between psychiatric syndromes and behaviorally defined sexual orientation in a sample of the US population. *Journal of Epidemiology, 151*, 516–523.

Cochran, S. D., Mays, V. M., Alegria, M., Ortega, A. N., & Takeuchi, D. (2007). Mental health and substance use disorders among Latino and Asian American lesbian, gay, and bisexual adults. *Journal of Consulting and Clinical Psychology, 75*(5), 785–794.

Colaizzi, P. F. (1978). Psychological research as the phenomenologist sees it. In R. S. Valle & M. King (Eds.), *Existential-phenomenological alternatives for psychology* (pp. 48–71). New York, NY: Oxford.

Coleman, D. (1990, July 10). Homophobia: Scientists find clues to its roots. *The New York Times,* pp. C1, C11.

Collins, P. H. (1990). Black feminist thought in the matrix of domination. In *Black feminist thought: Knowledge, consciousness, and the politics of empowerment* (pp. 221–238). Boston, MA: Unwin Hyman.

Comas-Diaz, L., & Greene, B. (Eds.). (1994). *Women of color: Integrating ethnic and gender identities in psychotherapy.* New York, NY: Gilford Press.

Combs, G. M. (2003). The duality of race and gender for managerial African American women: Implications of informal social networks on career advancement. *Human Resource Development Review, 2*(4), 385–405.

Comstock, G. D. (1991). *Violence against lesbians and gay men.* New York, NY: Columbia University Press.

Conklin, W. (2000). Out and equal employee resource groups: A foundation for support and change. *Sexual Orientation in the Workplace, 9*(1), 14–23.

Connell, J. (2006). Recruiting agencies in the global health care chain.*Merchants of labour* (pp. 239–253, ). C. Kuptsch, ed. Geneva, Switzerland: International Labour Organization.

Constantine, M. G. (2001). Addressing racial, ethnic, gender, and social class issues in counselor training and practice. In D. B. Pope-Davis & H. L. K. Coleman (Eds.), *The intersection of race, class, and gender in multicultural counseling* (pp. 341–350). Thousand Oaks, CA: Sage.

Cook, E. P., Heppner, M. J., & O'Brien, K. M. (2002). Career development of women of color and White women: Assumptions, conceptualization, and interventions from an ecological perspective. *The Career Development Quarterly, 50*(4), 291–305.

Corbin, J., & Strauss, A. (1990). Grounded theory research: Procedures, canons, and evaluative criteria. *Qualitative Sociology, 13,* 3–21.

Cordes, C., & Dougherty, T. (1993). A review and integration of research on job burnout. *Academy of Management Review, 18,* 621–656.

Cose, E. (1993). *The rage of a privileged class.* New York, NY: Harper Collins.

Cox, T., Jr. (1994). *Cultural diversity in organizations: Theory, research, and practice.* San Francisco, CA: Berrett-Koehler.

Crampton, S., & Mishra, J. (1999). Women in management. *Public Personnel Management, 28,* 87–106.

Creed, W. E. D. (2006). Seven conversations about the same thing: Homophobia and heterosexism in the workplace. In A. M. Konrad, P. Prasad, & J. K. Pringle (Eds.), *Handbook of workplace diversity* (pp. 371–400). London, England: Sage.

Creswell, J. W. (1994). *Research design: Qualitative, quantitative, and mixed methods approaches.* Thousand Oaks, CA: Sage.

Creswell, J. W. (1998). *Research design: Qualitative and quantitative approaches. Choosing among the five traditions.* Thousand Oaks, CA: Sage.

Creswell, J. W. (2003). *Research design: Qualitative, quantitative, and mixed methods approaches* (2nd ed.). Thousand Oaks, CA: Sage.

Creswell, J. W. (2005). *Educational research: Planning, conducting, and evaluating quantitative and qualitative research* (2nd ed.). Upper Saddle River, NJ: Pearson Education.

Creswell, J. W., Plano Clark, V. L., & Garrett, A. L. (2007). Methodological issues in conducting mixed methods research designs. In M. Bergman (Ed.), *Advances in mixed methods research.* London, England: Sage.

Crittendon, A. (2001). *The price of motherhood: Why the most important job in the world is still the least valued.* New York, NY: Metropolitan Owl.

Cromwell, K. (2003). *Defining the future for the LGBT workforce.* Retrieved from http://www.kimcromwell.com/articles/SOMEWH-article.html

Croteau, J. M. (1996). Research on the work experiences of lesbian, gay, and bisexual people: An integrative review of methodology and findings. *Journal of Vocational Behavior, 48,* 195–209.

Croteau, J. M., Anderson, M. Z., Distefano, T. M., & Kampa-Kokesch, S. (2000). Lesbian, gay, and bisexual psychology: Reviewing foundations and planning construction. In R. M. Perez, K. A. DeBord, & K. I. Bieschke (Eds.), *Handbook of counseling and psychotherapy with lesbian, gay, and bisexual clients* (pp. 383–408). Washington, DC: American Psychological Association.

Croteau, J. M., & Hedstrom, S. M. (1993). Integrating commonality and difference: The key to career counseling with lesbian women and gay men. *Career Development Quarterly, 41,* 201–209.

Croteau, J. M., & Lark, J. S. (1995). On being lesbian, gay, or bisexual in student affairs: A national survey of experiences on the job. *National Association Student Personnel Administrators Journal, 32,* 189–197.

Croteau, J. M., Lark, J. S., & Lance, T. S. (2005). Our stories were told: Deconstructing the heterosexist discourse in the counseling profession. In J. M. Croteau, J. S. Lark, M. A. Lidderdale, & Y. B. Chung (Eds.), *Deconstructing heterosexism in the counseling professions: A narrative approach* (pp. 1–16). Thousand Oaks, CA: Sage.

Croteau, J. M., Lark, J. S., Lidderdale, M. A., & Chung, Y. B. (Eds.). (2005). *Deconstructing heterosexism in the counseling professions: A narrative approach.* Thousand Oaks, CA: Sage.

Croteau, J. M., Talbot, D. M., Lance, T. S., & Evans, N. J. (2002). A qualitative study of the interplay between privilege and oppression. *Journal of Multicultural Counseling & Development, 30*(4), 239–258.

Croteau, J. M., & Von Destinon, M. (1994). A national survey of job search experiences of lesbian, gay, and bisexual student affairs professionals. *Journal of College Student Development, 35,* 40–45.

Crow, S. M., Fok, L. Y., & Hartman, S. J. (1998). Who is at greatest risk of work-related discrimination—women, Blacks, or homosexuals? *Employee Responsibilities and Rights Journal, 2,* 15–26.

Dahr, J. (2009). *The will to resist.* Retrieved from http://www.truthout.org/083109R

Daly, E., & Simon, H. A. (1992). Sexual orientation and workplace rights: A potential land mine for employers? *Employee Relations Law Journal, 18,* 29–60.

Darwin, A. (2000). Critical reflections on mentoring in work settings. *Adult Education Quarterly, 50*(3), 197–211.

D'Augelli, A. (1996). Lesbian, gay, and bisexual development during adolescence and young adulthood. In R. P. Cabaj & T. S. Stein (Eds.), *Textbook of homosexuality and mental health* (pp. 267–288). Washington, DC: American Psychiatric Press.

D'Augelli, A., & Patterson, C. (Eds.). (1995). *Lesbian, gay, and bisexual identities over the lifespan: Psychological perspectives.* New York, NY: Oxford University Press.

Day, L. (1995). The pitfalls of diversity training. *Training & Development Journal, 49,* 24–30.

DeAngelis, T. (2002). New data on lesbian, gay and bisexual mental health. *Monitor on Pyschology, 33*(2). Retrieved from http://www.apa.org/monitor/feb02/newdata.html

Denzen, K. N., & Lincoln, Y. S. (1994). *Handbook of qualitative research.* Thousand Oaks, CA: Sage.

Deutsch, M. (2006, March). A framework for thinking about oppression and its change. *Social Justice Research, 19*(1), 7–41. doi:10.1007/s11211-006-9998-3

Diamond, E. (1987). Theories of career development and the reality of work. In B. A. Yutek & L. Larwood (Eds.), *Women's career development* (pp. 15–17). Newbury Rock, CA: Sage.

Discrimination. (n.d.). In *Merriam-Webster's online dictionary*. Retrieved from http://www.merriam-webster.com/dictionary/discrimination

Dixon, K. A., Storen, D., & Van Horn, C. E. (2002). *A workplace divided: How Americans view discrimination and race on the job*. New Brunswick, NJ: The State University of New Jersey, Rutgers, John J. Heldrich Center for Workplace Development.

Dohrenwend, B. P. (2000). The role of adversity and stress in psychopathology: Some evidence and its implications for theory and research. *Journal of Health & Social Behavior, 41*(1), 1–19.

Dometrius, N., & Sigelman, L. (1984). Assessing progress toward affirmative action goals in state and local government: A new benchmark. *Public Administration Review Journal, 44,* 241–246.

Driscoll, J. M., Kelley, F. A., & Fassinger, R. E. (1996). Lesbian identity and disclosure in the workplace: Relation to occupational stress and satisfaction. *Journal of Vocational Behavior, 48,* 229–242.

Dunne, G. A. (1997). *Lesbian lifestyles: Women's work and the politics of sexuality*. Toronto, Ontario, Canada: University of Toronto Press.

Eagly, A. H., & Carli, L. (2007a). Overcoming resistance to women leaders. In B. Kellerman, & D. Rhode (Eds.), *Women and leadership: The state of play and strategies for change* (pp. 127–148). San Francisco, CA: Jossey-Bass.

Eagly, A. H., & Carli, L. L. (2007b). *Through the labyrinth: The truth about how women become leaders.* Boston, MA: Harvard Business School Press.

Eagly, A., & Karau, S. (2002), Role congruity theory of prejudice toward female leaders. *Psychological Review, 109,* 573–598.

Elliott, J. E. (1993). Lesbian and gay concerns in career development. In L. Diamant (Ed.), *Homosexual issues in the workplace* (pp. 25–43). Washington, DC: Taylor & Francis.

Employee Assistance Programs Association. (2002). *EAPA online statistics.* Retrieved from http://www.eapassn.org/public/articles/EAPcostbenefitstats.pdf

Epstein, C. F. (1973, March). Black and female: The double whammy. *Psychology Today, 90,* 57–61.

Escoffier, J. (1975). Stigmas, work environment, and economic discrimination against homosexuals. *Homosexual Counseling Journal, 2,* 8–17.

Essed, P. (1991). *Understanding everyday racism.* Newbury Park, CA: Sage.

Fagenson, E. (1993). *The diversity advantage: How American business can outperform Japanese and European companies in the global marketplace.* New York, NY: Lexington Books.

Fassinger, R. E. (1991). The hidden minority: Issues and challenges in working with lesbian women and gay men. *The Counseling Psychologist, 19,* 157–176.

Fassinger, R. E. (1995). From invisibility to integration: Lesbian identity in the workplace. *Career Development Quarterly, 44,* 148–167.

Fassinger, R. E. (1996a). Notes from the margins: Integrating lesbian experience into the vocational psychology of women. *Journal of Vocational Behavior, 48,* 160–175.

Fassinger, R. E. (1996b). Validation of an inclusive model of sexual minority identity formation on a sample of gay men. *Journal of Homosexuality, 32,* 53–78.

Feagin, J. R. (1991). The continuing significance of race: Anti-Black discrimination in public places. *American Sociological Review, 56,* 101–116.

Ferrel, O., & Gresham, L. (1985). A contingency framework for understanding ethical decision-making. *Journal of Marketing, 7,* 87–96.

Fine, G. A. (2002). The storied group: Social movements as bundles of narratives. In J. Davis (Ed.), *Stories of change, narrative and social movements* (pp. 229–245). New York, NY: SUNY Press.

Foschi, M. (1996). Double standards in the evaluation of men and women. *Social Psychology Quarterly, 59,*
French, J. (2003). Interest in building bridges. *Out & Equal Spring Newsletter.* San Francisco, CA: Out & Equal.

Friskopp, A., & Silverstein, S. (1996). *Straight jobs, gay lives: Gay and lesbian professionals, the Harvard Business School, and the American workplace.* New York, NY: Touchstone Simon & Schuster.

Fukuyama, M. A., & Ferguson, A. D. (2000). Lesbian, gay, and bisexual people of color: Understanding cultural complexity and managing multiple oppressions. In R. Perez, K. A. DeBord, & K. J. Bieschke (Eds.), *Handbook of counseling and psychotherapy with lesbian, gay, and bisexual clients* (pp. 81–106). Washington, DC: American Psychological Association.

Fullerton, H., Jr., & Toosi, M. (2001, November). Labor force projections to 2010: Steady growth and changing composition. *Monthly Labor Review, 32-33*.

Gardenswartz, L., & Rowe, A. (2003). *What's next: Action steps for managers*. Retrieved from http://www.gardenswartzrowe.com

Gardyn, R. (2001). A market kept in the closet. *American Demographic, 23*(11), 36–43.

Garnets, L. D., & D'Augelli, A. R. (1994). Empowering lesbian and gay communities: A call for collaboration with community psychology. *American Journal of Community Psychology, 22,* 447–470.

Gay and Lesbian Victory Foundation. (2001). *Survey of the African-American community*. Washington, DC: Author.

Gay Rights Bill, H.R. 14752, 93rd Cong. (1974).

Gayle, S. (1997). *Workplace purpose and meaning as perceived by information technology professionals: A phenomenological study* (Unpublished doctoral dissertation). The George Washington University, Washington, DC.

Gedro, J. (2006, Winter). Lesbians: Identifying, facing, and navigating the double bind of sexual orientation and gender in organizational settings. *New Directions for Adult & Continuing Education*. Retrieved July 19, 2008, from Academic Search Premier database.

Gedro, J., Cervero, R., & Johnson-Faniel-Bailey, J. (2004). How lesbians learn to negotiate the heterosexism of corporate America. *Human Resource Development International, 7*(2), 181–195.

Gilley, J., & Eggland, S. (1989). *Principles of human resources development*. Reading, MA: Addison-Wesley Publishing.

Giorgi, A. (1985). Sketch of a psychological phenomenological method. In A. Giorgi (Ed.), *Phenomenology and psychological research* (pp. 8–22). Pittsburgh, PA: Dusquesne University Press.

Giscombe, K., & Mattis, M. G. (2002). Leveling the playing field for women of color in corporate management: Is the business case enough? *Journal of Business Ethics, 37*, 103–119.

Glazer, J. S., Bensimon, E. M., & Townsend, B. K. (Eds.). (1993). *Women in higher education: A feminist perspective*. Needham Heights, MA: Ginn Press.

Glesne, C. (1999). *Becoming qualitative researchers* (2nd ed.). New York, NY: Addison Wesley Longman.

Glesne, C., & Peshkin, A. (1992). *Becoming qualitative researchers*. White Plains, NY: Longman.

Glicken, M. (2003). *Social Research: A simple guide*. New York, NY: Allyn & Bacon.

Gomez, J. (2005). *Black queer studies: A critical anthology*. Durham, NC: Duke University Press.

Gonsiorek, J. C., & Weinrich, J. D. (1991). The definition and scope of sexual orientation. In J. C. Gonsiorek & J. D. Weinrich (Eds.), *Homosexuality: Research implications for public policy* (pp. 1–12). Newbury Park, CA: Sage.

Greenberg, P. (1999). Tackling costs one disease at a time. *Business and Health Journal, 5,* 31–37.

Greene, B. (1994a). *African-American women: Women of color integrating ethnic and gender identities in psychotherapy.* New York, NY: Guilford.

Greene, B. (1994b). Ethnic-minority lesbians and gay men: Mental health and treatment issues. *Journal of Consulting and Clinical Psychology, 62*(2), 243–251.

Greene, B. (1997). *Ethnic minority lesbians and gay men: Mental health and treatment issues. Ethnic and cultural diversity among lesbians and gay men.* Thousand Oaks, CA: Sage.

Greene, B. (2000). Beyond heterosexism and across the cultural divide. Developing an inclusive lesbian, gay, bisexual psychology: A look into the future. In B. Greene & G. L. Croom (Eds.), *Education, research and practice in lesbian, gay, bisexual and transgender psychology: A resource manual* (pp. 1–45). Thousand Oaks, CA: Sage Publications.

Greene, B. (2002). *Internalized racism among African Americans: The connections and considerations for African American lesbians and bisexual women in a clinical psychological perspective.* Retrieved http://academic.udayton.edu/race/05intersection/sexual01.htm

Greene, B. (2003). What difference does a difference make? Societal privilege, disadvantage, and discord in human relationships. In J. Robinson & L. James (Eds.), *Diversity in human interaction: A tapestry of America* (pp. 3–20). New York, NY: Oxford University Press.

Greene, B. (2004). African American lesbians and other culturally diverse people in psychodynamic psychotherapies: Useful paradigms or oxymoron? *Journal of Lesbian Studies, 8,* 57–77.

Greene, B. (2005). Psychology, diversity and social justice: Beyond heterosexism and across the cultural divide. *Counseling Psychology Quarterly, 18*(4), 295–306.

Greene, B., & Boyd-Franklin, N. (1996). *African American lesbians: Issues in couple's therapy—Lesbians and gays in couples and families: A handbook for therapists.* San Francisco, CA: Jossey-Bass.

Greene, K. (2006). *White men in diversity initiatives has become an essential component to successful diversity efforts.* Retrieved from http://www.pr.com/press-release/14745

Greene, V., Selden S., & Brewer, G. (2001). Measuring power and presence: Bureaucratic representation in the American states. *Journal of Public Administration Research and Theory, 11*(3), 379–402.

Guba, E. G., & Lincoln, Y. S. (1994). Competing paradigms in qualitative research. In N. K. Denzin & Y. S. Lincoln (Eds.), *Handbook of qualitative research* (pp. 105–118). Thousand Oaks, CA: Sage.

Guba, E., & Lincoln, Y. (1981). Effective evaluation. *San Francisco: Jossey-Bass.*

H.R. 14752, 93rd Congress House of Representatives Bill 14752 (1974). Gay Rights Bill.

Hackett, G., & Byars, A. (1996). Social cognitive theory and the career development of African-American women. *Career Development Quarterly, 4,* 326–339.

Hall, D. T. (2002). *Careers in and out of organizations.* Thousand Oaks, CA: Sage.

Hall, G., & Saltzstein, A. (1975). Equal employment in urban governments: The potential problem of inter-minority competition. *Public Personnel Management Journal, 4,* 386–393.

Hall, R. L., & Greene, B. (1996). Sins of omission and commission: Women, psychotherapy and the psychological literature. *Women & Therapy, 18*(1), 5–31.

Halley, E. (1999). *Don't: A reader's guide to the military's anti-gay policy.* Retrieved from http://dont.stanford.edu/regulations/pres7-l9-93.pdf

Harper, G., Jernewall, N., & Zea, M. (2004). Giving voice to emerging science and theory for lesbian, gay, and bisexual people of color. *Cultural Diversity and Ethnic Minority Psychology, 10*(3), 187–199.

Harris, J. I., Moritzen, S. K., Robitschek, C., Imhoff, A., & Lynch, I. L. A. (2001). The comparative contributions of congruence and social support in career outcomes. *The Career Development Quarterly, 49,* 314–323.

Haselkorn, H. (1956). The vocational interests of a group of male homosexuals. *Journal of    Counseling Psychology, 3,* 8-11.

Haverkamp, B. E., & Young, R. A. (2007). Paradigms, purpose, and role of the literature: Formulating a rationale for qualitative investigations. *The Counseling Psychologist, 35,* 295–327.

Heffernan, M. (2004). *The naked truth: The working woman's manifesto on business and what really matters.* San Francisco, CA: Jossey-Bass.

Hegstad, C. D., & Wentling, R. M. (2004). The development and maintenance of exemplary formal mentoring programs in Fortune 500 companies. *Human Resource Development Quarterly, 15*(4), 421–448.

Henderson, L. (2009). Between the two: Bisexual identity among African Americans. *Journal of African American Studies, 13,* 263–282.

Herbert, A. (1974). The minority administrator: Problems, prospects, and challenges. *Public Administration Review, 34,* 56–63.

Herek, G. M. (1990). Homophobia. In W. R. Dynes (Ed.), *Encyclopedia of homosexuality* (pp. 552–555). New York, NY: Garland.

Herek, G. M. (1991). Stigma, prejudice, and violence against lesbians and gay men. In J. C. Gonsiorek & J. D. Weinreich (Eds.), *Homosexuality: Research implications for public policy* (pp. 60–80). Newbury Park, CA: Sage.

Herek, G. M., Gillis, J. R., & Cogan, J. C. (1999). Psychological sequel of hate crime victimization among lesbian, gay, and bisexual adults. *Journal of Consulting and Clinical Psychology, 67,* 945–951.

Herr, E., & Cramer, S. (1996). *Career guidance and counseling through the life span: Systematic approaches.* New York, NY: Harper Collins.

Herrscaft, D., & Mills, K. (2003). *Workplace equality.* Washington, DC: Human Rights Campaign.

Herszenhorn, D. (2007, November 8). House approves bill outlawing workplace. *International Herald Tribune.* Retrieved from http://www.iht.com/articles

Hetherington, C., Hillerbrand, E., & Etringer, B. D. (1989). Career counseling with gay men: Issues and recommendations for research. *Journal of Counseling and Development, 67,* 452–454.

Hewlett, S., & Luce, C. (2005). Off ramps and on ramps: Keeping talented women on the road to success. *Harvard Business Review*, 43

*Hidden barriers.* (n.d.). Retrieved from http://www.workplacefairness.org/sc/discrimination.php

Hill, S. E. K., & Gant, G. (2000). Mentoring by minorities for minorities: The organizational communications support program. *Review of Business, 21*(1/2), 53–57.

Hirata, N., & Kleiner, B. (2001). New developments concerning sexual orientation discrimination and harassment. *The International Journal of Sociology and Social Policy, 21*(8–10), 92–100.

Hogue, M., & Lord, R. (2007). A multilevel, complexity theory approach to understanding gender bias in leadership. *Leadership Quarterly, 18,* 370–390.

Holstein, J., & Gubrium, J. (1996). Phenomenology, methodology, and interpretive practices. In N. Denjim & Y. Lincoln (Eds.), *Handbook of qualitative research* (pp. 262–272). Thousand Oaks, CA: Sage.

Hood, S. B. (2004). Learn from the best. *Canadian Business, 77*(24), 107–109.

Hornsby, E. (2006). Using policy to drive organizational change. *New Directions for Adult & Continuing Education*, Retrieved August 17, 2008, from Academic Search Premier database.

House, C. J. C. (2004). Integrating barriers to European American lesbians' career development and Super's life-span, life-space approach. *Career Development Quarterly, 52,* 246–255.

Human Rights Campaign. (2005). *Employment Non-Discrimination Act.* Retrieved from http://www.hrc.org/Template.cfm

Human Rights Campaign. (2006). *Employment Non-Discrimination Act.* Retrieved from http://www.hrc.org/Template.cfm

Human Rights Campaign Foundation. (2001). *Gay and lesbian families in the United States: Same-sex unmarried partner households.* Washington, DC: Author.

Human Rights Campaign Foundation. (2003). United States: Evidence from a national study. *Journal of Adolescence, 24,* 111–127.

Human Rights Campaign Foundation. (2007). *The state of the workplace for lesbian, gay, bisexual, and transgender Americans 2005–2006.* Retrieved from http://www.hrc.org

Human Rights Campaign. (2010). *Employment Non-Discrimination Act.* Retrieved from http://www.hrc.org/Template.cfm

Hunter, T. (1991). A different view of progress-minority women in politics. *The Journal of State Government, 64,* 48–52.

Hutson, B. (2009). The coming out challenge. *Diversity Watch, 40*(4), 55.

Ibarra, H. (1992). Differential returns: Sex differences in network structure and access in an advertising firm. *Administrative Science Quarterly, 37,* 422–447.

International Labor Organization. (2004). *Breaking through the glass ceiling: Women in management: summary.* Geneva, Switzerland: Author.

Irwin, J. (1999). *The pink ceiling is too low: Workplace experiences of lesbians, gay men, and transgender people.* Sydney, Australia: NSW Gay & Lesbian Rights Lobby.

Israel, T., & Selvidge, M. (2003). Contributions of multicultural counseling to counselor competence with lesbian, gay, and bisexual clients. *Journal of Multicultural Counseling and Development, 31,* 84–97.

Ivancevich, J., & Matteson, M. (1987). *Controlling work stress: Effective human resource and management strategies series.* New York, NY: Jossey-Bass.

Ivancevich, J., & Matteson, M. (1996). *Organizational behavior and management.* Boston, MA: McGraw-Hill.

Ivy, K. (2006). *African American female perceptions regarding career develop opportunities and career decisions: A phenomenological study focused on career decisions within the information technology industry* (Doctoral dissertation). Available from ProQuest Dissertations and Theses. (Publication No. AAT 3237072)

Jackson, L. C., & Greene, B. (2000). *Psychotherapy with African American women: Innovations in psychodynamic perspectives and practice.* New York, NY: Guilford Press.

Jaynes, G. D., & Williams, R. M. (1989). *A common destiny: Blacks and American society.* Washington, DC: National Academy Press.

Jernewall, N., & Zea, M. (2004). *Invisibility of lesbian, gay, and bisexuality people of color in psychological research: A content analysis of empirical articles over the last ten years.* Manuscript in preparation.

Johnson-Faniel-Bailey, J., & Tisdell, E. J. (1998). Diversity issues in women's career development. *New Directions for Community Colleges, 80,* 83–93.

Jones, B. (1996). *African-American lesbians, gay men and bisexuals.* Washington, DC: American Psychiatric Press.

Jones, J. (1996). Ensuring an ethical environment. *Journal of Security Management, 40,* 4–23.

Jones, W. (1984). Cost evaluation for stress management. *EAP Digest, 1*(11).

Kaiser, C., & Major, B. (2006). A social psychological perspective on perceiving and reporting discrimination. *Law & Social Inquiry, 31*(4), 801–830. doi:10.1111/j.1747-4469.2006.00036

Kalev, A., Dobbin, F., & Kelly, E. (2006). Best practices or best guesses: Diversity management and remediation of inequality. *American Sociological Review, 71,* 589– 617.

Kanter, R. M. (1997). *Men and women of the corporation.* New York, NY: Basic Books.

Kanter, R. M. (2000). Token women in the corporation. In J. Heeren, M. Requa, R. Lauer, & J. Lauer (Eds.), *Sociology: Windows on society* (pp. 152–163). Los Angeles, CA: Roxbury.

Kephart, P., & Schumacher, L. (2005). Has the glass ceiling cracked? An exploration of women entrepreneurship. *Journal of Leadership and Organizational Studies, 12,* 2–15.

Kerka, S. (2003). *Career development of diverse populations* (ERIC Document reproduction service No. ED482536). Retrieved from http://www.ericdigests.org/2004-4/career.htm

Kerr, B., Miller, W., & Reid, M. (2002). *Descriptive representation among Latinas, African-American women, and White Women in Multiethnic U. S. Cities.* Retrieved from http://plsc.uark.edu/csr/working/papers/paper15.htm

Kirby, S. (2006). American gay and lesbian student leaders' perceptions of job discrimination. *Equal Opportunities International, 25*(2), 126.

Kleinman, A., & Kleinman, J. (1991). Suffering and its professional transformation: Toward an ethnography of interpersonal experience. *Culture, Medicine, & Psychiatry, 15,* 275–301.

Kovan, J. (2002). *Sustaining passion: The experience of being an environmentalist in a small nonprofit organization* (Doctoral dissertation). Available from ProQuest Digital Dissertations. (AAT 3064258)

Krawiec, K. (2003). Cosmetic compliance and the failure of negotiated governance. *Washington University Law Quarterly, 81,* 487–544.

Lach, J. (1999). Minority women hit a concrete ceiling. *American Demographics, 21*(9), 18–19.

Laird, J. (1994). Lesbian families: A cultural perspective. In M. P. Mirkin (Ed.), *Women in context: Toward a feminist reconstruction of psychotherapy* (pp. 118–148). New York, NY: Guilford.

Lambda Legal. (2008). *Employment and rights in the workplace.* Retrieved from http://www.lambdalegal.org/our-work/issues/employment-and-rights-in-the-workplace/

Lambda Legal & Deloitte Financial Advisory Services. (2006). *2005 workplace fairness survey.* Retrieved from http://data.lambdalegal.org/pdf/641.pdf

Lent, R. W., Brown, S. D., & Hackett, G. (1994). Toward a unifying social cognitive theory of career and academic interest, choice, and performance. *Journal of Vocational Behavior, 45*(1), 79–122.

Lent, R. W., Brown, S. D., & Hackett, G. (1996). Career development from a social cognitive perspective. In D. Brown & L. Brooks (Eds.), *Career choice and development* (3rd ed., pp. 373–421). San Francisco, CA: Jossey-Bass.

Lent, R. W., Brown, S. D., & Hackett, G. (2000). Contextual supports and barriers to career choice: A social cognitive analysis. *Journal of Counseling Psychology, 47,* 36–49.

Leonard, J., & Levine, D. (2006). The effect of diversity on turnover, a large case study, *Industrial and Labor Relations Review, 59*(1), 547–572.

Lesbian. (n.d.). In *Merriam-Webster's online dictionary*. Retrieved from http://www.merriam-webster.com/dictionary/lesbians

Lester, S. (1999). *An introduction to phenomenological research.* Retrieved from http://www.devmts.demon.co.uk/resmethy.htm

Letellier, P. (2003). Tug of war: The relentless struggle for gay rights in 2003. *Lesbian News, 28,* 12.

Levine, P., & Leonard, R. (1984). Discrimination against lesbians in the work force. *Journal of Women in Culture and Society, 9,* 700–710.

Lewis, G. B., & Edelson, J. L. (2000). Congress votes on gay life course: A research agenda. *Journal of Gay, Lesbian, and Bisexual Identity, 2,* 202.

Lewis, R. J., Derlega, V. J., Berndt, A., Morris, L. M., & Rose, S. (2001). An empirical analysis of stressors for gay men and lesbians. *Journal of Homosexuality, 42,* 63–88.

Lingiardi, V., & Drescher, J. (Eds.). (2003). *The mental health professions and homosexuality: International perspectives.* New York, NY: Harrington Park Press.

Lipsett, L. (1971). Social factors in vocational development. In H. J. Peters & J. C. Hansen (Eds.), *Vocational guidance and career development.* New York, NY: The MacMillan Company.

Lorde, A. (1998). Age, race, class, and sex: Women redefining difference. In M. L. Andersen & P. H. Collins (Eds.), *Race, class, and gender: An anthology* (pp. 187–195). Belmont, CA: Wadsworth.

Lott, A., & Hutson, B. (2009). *Black enterprise what's keeping Black professional women from high-level Positions.* Retrieved from http://www.allbusiness.com/population-demographics/demographic- groups/12361373-1.html

Luthans, F. (2002). *Organizational behavior* (9th ed.). Boston, MA: McGraw-Hill Irwin.

Luzzo, D. A. (1996a). Exploring the relationship between perception of occupational barriers and career development. *Journal of Career Development, 22,* 239–248.

Luzzo, D. A. (1996b). Perceived occupational barriers among Mexican-American college students: Gender differences in college students' career maturity and perceived barriers in career development. *Journal of Counseling and Development, 73,* 319–322.

Lyddon, W. J., & Alford, D. J. (1993). Constructivist assessment: A developmental epistemic perspective. In G. J. Neimeyer (Ed.), *Constructivist assessment: A casebook* (pp. 1–30). Newbury Park, CA: Sage.

Lyons, H. Z., Brenner, B. R., Bradley, R., & Fassinger, R. E. (2005). A multicultural test of the theory of work adjustment: Investigating the role of heterosexism and fit perceptions in the job satisfaction of lesbian, gay, and bisexual employees. *Journal of Counseling Psychology, 52,* 537–548.

Majors, G., & Sinclair, M. (1994). Measure results for program success. *HR Magazine, 39*(11), 57–60.

Malcom, S. M., Hall, P. Q., & Brown, J. W. (1976). *The double bind: The price of being minority women in science. AAAS Report.* Retrieved from http://archives.aaas.org/docs/1975-Double%20Bind.pdf

Marschke, R., Laursen, S., Nielsen, J. M., & Dunn-Rankin, P. (2007). Demographic inertia revisited: An immodest proposal to achieve equitable gender representation among faculty in higher education. *Journal of Higher Education, 78*(1), 1–26. doi:10.1353/jhe.2007.0003

Marshall, C., & Rossman, G. (1995). *Designing qualitative research* (2nd ed.). Thousand Oaks, CA: Sage.

Martinez, M. (1996). Three strategies for successful business partners. *HR Magazine, 41*(10).

Matheson, K., & Zanna, M. P. (1990). Computer-mediated communications: The focus is on me. *Social Science Computer Review, 8,* 1–12.

Matias, J. (2005). *Building from the inside out: Empowering women of color nonprofit leaders.* Retrieved from http://www.jrimap.org/documents/WOC_Leadership_Forum_Report_6-05.pdf

Mays, V. M., Chatters, L. M., Cochran, S. D., & Mackness, J. (1998). African American families in diversity: Gay men and lesbians as participants in family networks. *Journal of Comparative Family Studies, 29,* 73–87.

Mays, V., & Cochran, S. (1988). The Black Women's Relationship Project: A national survey of Black lesbians. In M. Shernoff & W. Scott (Eds.), *A sourcebook of gay/lesbian health care.* Washington, DC: National Lesbian and Gay Health Foundation.

Mays, V. M., & Cochran, S. D. (2001). Mental health correlates of perceived discrimination among lesbian, gay, and bisexual adults in the United States. *American Journal of Public Health, 91,* 1869–1876.

Mays, V. M., Cochran, S. D., & Rhue, S. (1993). The impact of perceived discrimination on the intimate relationships of Black lesbians. *Journal of Homosexuality, 25*(4), 1–14.

McKenna B, Rooney D. & Boal K. B., (2009)). Wisdom principles as a meta-theoretical basis for evaluating leadership. *The Leadership Quarterly, 20*(2), 177–190.

McMahon, M. (2002). The systems theory framework of career development: History and future directions. *Australian Journal of Career Development, 11*(3), 63–68.

McMahon, M., Patton, W., & Watson, M. (2003). Developing qualitative career assessment processes. *The Career Development Quarterly, 51,* 194–202.

McWhirter, E. H. (1997). Perceived barriers to education and career: Ethnic and gender differences. *Journal of Vocational Behavior, 50,* 124–140.

Mertens, D. M. (1998). *Research methods in education and psychology: Integrating diversity with quantitative and qualitative approaches.* Thousand Oaks, CA: Sage.

Meyer, I. H. (2001). Why lesbian, gay, bisexual, and transgender public health? *American Journal of Public Health, 91*(6), 856–859.

Miles, M. B., & Huberman, A. M. (1994). *Qualitative data analysis* (2nd ed.). Thousand Oaks, CA: Sage.

Miller, G. V. (1995). *The gay male odyssey in the corporate world: From disempowerment to empowerment.* New York, NY: Harrington Park Press.

Moerer-Urdahl, T., & Creswell, J. (2004). Using transcendental phenomenology to explore the ripple effect in a leadership mentoring program. *International Journal of Qualitative Methods, 3(2)*.

Moore, J. (2003). Girls in Science Rule! *Science and Children, 40*(7), 38.

Morris, J. (1997). Lesbian coming out as a multidimensional process. *Journal of Homosexuality, 33,* 1–22.

Morrison, A., White, R., & Van Velsor, E. (1987). *Breaking the glass ceiling: Can women reach the top of America's largest corporations?* Reading, MA: Addison-Wesley.

Morrow, S. L., Gore, P. A., Jr., & Campbell, B. W. (1996). The application of a socio-cognitive framework to the career development of lesbian women and gay men. *Journal of Vocational Behavior, 48*(2), 136–148.

Morse, J. M. (1994). *Critical issues in qualitative research methods.* Thousand Oaks, CA: Sage.

Moustakas, C. (1990). Heuristic research: Design, methodology, and applications. Newbury Park, CA: Sage.

Moustakas, C. (1994). *Phenomenological research methods.* Thousand Oaks, CA: Sage.

Naff, K. (2001). *To look like America: Dismantling barriers for women and minorities in the Federal Civil Service.* Boulder, CO: Westview Press.

National Conference for Community and Justice. (2002). *Employment discrimination.* Retrieved from http://www.nccj.org/nccj/nccj.nsf/articleall/4547?opendocument&1

National Defense Research Institute. (1993). *Sexual orientation and U.S. military personnel policy: Options and assessment.* Santa Monica, CA: Rand.

National Gay and Lesbian Task Force. (2004). *Coalition against discrimination in the constitution.* Retrieved from http://www.thetaskforce.org/reslibrary/list.cfm?pubTypeID=2#pub165

National Gay and Lesbian Task Force. (2005). *Black same sex households census data.* Retrieved from http://www.thetaskforce.org/downloads/reports/reports/2000Bl ackSameSexHousehol ds.pdf

National Gay and Lesbian Task Force. (2010). *ENDA.* Retrieved from http://www.thetaskforce.org/reslibrary/list.cfm?pubTypeID=2#pub164

National Institutes of Health. (2008). *Conduct of research.* Retrieved from http://www1.od.nih.gov/oir/sourcebook/ethic-conduct/Conduct%20Research%206-11-07.pdf

Neely-Martinez, M. (1993). Recognizing sexual orientation is fair and not costly. *HR Magazine, 38*(6), 66–72.

Neisen, J. (1990). Heterosexism or homophobia: The power of language we use. *Outlook of Homosexuality, 3,* 37–38.

Neubeck, K. J., & Cazenave, N. A. (2002). Welfare racism and its consequences: The demise of AFDC and the return of the states' rights era. In F. F. Piven, J. Acker, M. Hallock, & S. Morgen (Eds.), *Work, welfare, and politics: Confronting poverty in the wake of welfare reform* (pp. 19–34). Eugene, Oregon: University of Oregon Press.

Neuman, J. (2007, November 8). House votes for protections for gay workers. *Los Angeles Times.* Retrieved from http://www.latimes.com/news

Newman, M., Thompson, C., & Roberts, A. P. (2006). Helping practitioners understand the contribution of qualitative research to evidence-based practice. *Evidence-Based Nursing, 9*, 4–7. doi:10.1136/ebn.9.1.4

Noe, R. A., Hollenbeck, J. R., Gerhart, B., & Wright, P. M. (1994). *Human resource management: Gaining a competitive advantage*. Burr Ridge, IL: Austen Press Irwin.

O'Conner, T. (2000). Managing employees' mental health: The emerging role of human resources professionals. *HR Magazine, 12*. Retrieved from http://www.shrm.org

Ogbu, J. U. (1990). Cultural model, identity and literacy. In R. J. Stigler, R. A. Shweder, & G. Herdt (Eds.), *Cultural psychology: Essays on comparative human development* (pp. 520–541). New York, NY: Cambridge University Press.

Oliveira, A. W., & Sadler, T. D. (2008). Interactive patterns and convergence of meaning during student collaborations in science. *Journal of Research in Science Teaching, 45*, 634–658. doi:10.1002/tea.20211

Organization. (n.d.). In *Merriam-Webster's online dictionary*. Retrieved from http://www.merriam-webster.com/dictionary/organization

Out & Equal Workplace Advocates. (2002). *Workplace advocates*. Retrieved from http://www.witeckcombs.com/show.news.asp?id=140&format=html

Out & Equal Workplace Advocates. (2006). *Harris interactive survey explored workplace attitudes toward LGBT people*. Retrieved from http://www.outandequal.org/news/pr/documents/2006_Workplace_Survey052306.pdf

Out. (n.d.). In *Merriam-Webster's online dictionary*. Retrieved from http://www.merriam-webster.com/dictionary/out

Palmer, G., & Johnson-Faniel-Bailey, J. (2005). The career development of African-Americans in the areas of training and organizational development. *Human Resources Training, 28*(1), 1–12.

Parker, P. S. (2001). African American women executives' leadership communication within dominant-culture organizations. *Management Communication Quarterly, 15*(1), 42–82.

Parrish. (2008). The experience of gay identity. *Journal of LGBT Issues in Counseling, 2*(1), 26–52.

Patton, M. Q. (1990). *Qualitative evaluation and research methods* (2nd ed.). Newbury Park, CA: Sage.

Patton, M. Q. (2002). *Qualitative research and evaluation methods* (3rd ed.). Thousand Oaks, CA: Sage.

Peavy, R. V. (1997). *Socio-dynamic counseling: A constructivist perspective*. Victoria, British Columbia, Canada: Trafford.

Peiss, K. (2002). *Major problems in the history of American sexuality*. Boston, MA: Houghton Mifflin.

Peplau, L. A., Cochran, S. D., & Mays, V. M. (1997). A national survey of the intimate relationships of African American lesbians and gay men: A look at commitment, satisfaction, sexual behavior, and HIV disease. In B. Greene (Ed.), *Ethnic and cultural diversity among lesbians and gay men* (pp. 11–38). Thousand Oaks, CA: Sage.

Pepper, S., & Lorah, P. (2008). Career issues and workplace considerations for the transsexual community: Bridging a gap of knowledge for career counselors and mental health care providers. *Career Development Quarterly, 56*(4), 330–343.

Phelps, D. (2003). *Supporters of same-sex benefits acknowledge loss.* Minneapolis, MN: Tribune.

Phillips, J. C., Ingram, K. M., Grant Smith, N., & Mindes, E. J. (2003). Methodological and content review of lesbian, gay, and bisexual related articles in counseling journals: 1990–1999. *The Counseling Psychologist, 31*, 25–62.

Podolny, J., & Baron, J. (1997). Resources and relationships: Social networks and mobility in the workplace. *American Sociological Review, 62*, 673–693.

Polkinghorne, D. (1988). Phenomenological research methods. In R. S. Valle & S. Halling (Eds.), *Existential-phenomenological perspective in psychology* (pp. 2–43). New York, NY: Plenum.

Polkinghorne, D. E. (1989). Phenomenological research methods. In R. S. Valle & S. Halling (Eds.), *Existential-phenomenological perspectives in psychology* (pp. 41–60). New York, NY: Plenum.

Polkinghorne, D. E. (2005). Language and meaning: Data collection in qualitative research. *The Journal of Counseling Psychology, 52*(2), 137–145.

Pollio, H. (1997). *The phenomenology of everyday life.* Cambridge, UK: Cambridge University Press.

Pope, M. (1995). Career interventions for gay and lesbian clients: A synopsis of practice knowledge and research needs. *The Career Development Quarterly, 44,* 191–203.

Pope, M. (2000). Preventing school violence aimed at gay, lesbian, bisexual, and transgender youths. In D. S. Sandhu & C. B. Aspy (Eds.), *Violence in American schools: A practical guide for counselors* (pp. 285–303). Alexandria, VA: American Counseling Association.

Powell, G., & Butterfield, D. (1994). Investing in the glass ceiling phenomena: An empirical study of actual promotions to top management. *Academy of Management Journal, 37,* 68–86.

Prince, J. P. (1997). Career assessment with lesbians, gays and bisexuals. *Journal of Career Assessment, 5,* 225–238.

Prochaska, S. (2003). Employee assistance programs: What does HR need to know? *HR Magazine, 5.* Retrieved from http://www.shrm.org

Raeburn, N. (2004). *Changing corporate America from inside out: Lesbian and gay workplace rights.* Retrieved from http://site.ebrary.com/lib/capella/Doc?id=10151274&ppg=271

Ragins, B. R. (1997). *The effect of legislation on workplace discrimination against gay employees.* Unpublished manuscript.

Ragins, B. (1998). Gender and mentoring relationships: A review and research agenda in the next decade. In G. Powell (Ed.), *Handbook of gender and work* (pp. 347–369).Thousand Oaks, CA: Sage.

Ragins, B. R., & Cornwell, J. M. (2001). Pink triangles: Antecedents and consequences of perceived workplace discrimination against gay and lesbian employees. *Journal of Applied Psychology, 86,* 1244–1261.

Ragins, B. R., Singh, R., & Cornwell, J. (2007, July). Making the invisible visible: Fear and disclosure of sexual orientation at work. *Journal of Applied Psychology, 92,* 1103–1118. doi:10.1037/0021-9010.92.4.1103

Ragins, B. R., & Wiethoff, C. (2005). Understanding heterosexism at work: The straight problem. In R. L. Dipboye & A. Colello (Eds.), *Discrimination at work* (pp. 177-201). Mawah, New Jersey: Erlbaum.

Ramsey, F., Hill, M. J., & Kellam, C. (2010). *Black lesbians matter*. Retrieved from http://zunainstitute.org/2010/research/blm/Blacklesbiansmatter.pdf

Redwood, R. (1996). *The glass ceiling working woman's summit*. Retrieved from http://www.inmotionmagazine.com/glass.html

Reinharz, S. (1992). *Feminist methods in social research*. New York, NY: Oxford University Press.

Renzetti, C., & Curran, D. (1992). *Women, men, and society*. Boston, MA: Allyn & Bacon.

Reskin, B. (1988). Bringing the men back in: Sex differentiation and the devaluation of women's work. *Gender & Society, 2*, 58–81.

Reynolds, A., & Pope, R. (1991). The complexities of diversity: Exploring multiple oppressions. *Journal of Counseling and Development, 70,* 174–180.

Rhode, D., & Kellerman, B. (2007). Women and leadership: The state of play. In B. Kellerman, & D. Rhode (Eds.), *Women and leadership: The state of play and strategies for change*. Hoboken, NJ: Wiley.

Richie, B. S., Fassinger, R. E., Linn, S. G., Johnson-Faniel, J., Prosser, J., & Robinson, S. (1997). Persistence, connection, and passion: A qualitative study of the career development of highly achieving African American-Black and White women. *Journal of Counseling Psychology, 44*(2), 133–148.

Ridgeway, C. (1993). Gender, status, and the social psychology of expectations. In P. England (Ed.), *Theory on gender/feminism on theory* (pp. 175–198). New York, NY: Aldine Press.

Robinson, T. L., & Howard-Hamilton, M. F. (2000). *The convergence of race, ethnicity, and gender: Multiple identities in counseling.* Upper Saddle River, NJ: Prentice Hall.

Rocco, T., & Gallagher, S. (2006). Straight privilege and moralizing: Issues in career development. *New Directions for Adult & Continuing Education. 112(2006),* 29-39.

Rostosky, S., & Riggle, E. (2002). Out at work: The relation of actor and partner workplace policy and internalized homophobia to disclosure status. *Journal of Counseling Psychology, 49,* 411–419.

Rowe, A. & Gardenswartz, L. (1999). *Workplace diversity tool kit.* Burr Ridge, IL: Irwin Professional Publishing.

Rudman, L., & Glick, P. (2001). Prescriptive gender stereotypes and backlash toward women. *Journal of Social Issues, 57,* 743–762.

Russell, G. M. (2000). *Voted out: The psychological consequences of anti-gay politics.* New York, NY: New York University Press.

Russell, G. M., & Richards, J. A. (2003). Stressor and resilience factors for lesbians, gay men, and bisexuals confronting antigay politics. *American Journal of Community Psychology, 31,* 313–327.

Rynes, S., & Rosen, B. (1995). A field survey of factors affecting the adoption and perceived success of diversity training. *Personnel Psychology, 48,* 247–270.

Sagaria, M. D., & Rychener, M. (2002). Women administrators' mobility. In A. Martinez Aleman & K. A. Renn (Eds.), *Women in higher education: An encyclopedia* (pp. 495–498). Santa Barbara, CA: ABC-CLIO Press.

Sandroff, R. (1988). Sexual harassment in the Fortune 500. *Working Woman, 12,* 69–77.

Sarra, J. (2005). Class act: Considering race and gender in the corporate boardroom. *St. John's Law Review, 79*(4), 1121–1160.

Saulnier, C. (2002). Deciding who to see: Lesbians discuss their preferences in health and mental health care providers. *Social Work, 47*(4), 355–365.

Savage, C. (1973). *Work and meaning: A phenomenological inquiry.* Unpublished manuscript, Boston College, Boston, MA.

Savickas, M. L. (2002). Career construction: A developmental theory of vocational behavior. In D. Brown & Associates (Eds.), *Career choice and development* (4th ed., pp. 149–205). San Francisco, CA: Jossey-Bass.

Savickas, M. L. (2005). The theory and practice of career construction. In D. Brown & R. W. Lent (Eds.), *Career development and counseling* (pp. 42–70). Hoboken, NJ: Wiley.

Schramm, J. (2003). Acting affirmatively. *HR Magazine, 48*(9). Retrieved from https://www.shrm.org/hrmagazine/articles/0903/0903schramm.asp

Schreiber, P. J. (1998). Women's career development patterns. *New Directions for Community Colleges, 80,* 5–13.

Schultheiss, D. E. P., Kress, H. M., Manzi, A. J., & Glasscock, J. M. J. (2001). Relational influences in career development: A qualitative inquiry. *The Counseling Psychologist, 29,* 214–239.

Scott, M. (2001). For women, the glass ceiling persists. *Black Enterprise, 32*(1), 30.

Sczesny, S. (2003). A closer look beneath the surface: Various facets of the think manager- think-male stereotype. *Sex Roles, 49*, 353–363.

Searles, B. (2009). *The seven simple secrets to building wealth.* Retrieved from http://www.timbooktu.com/searles/mirror1.htm

Shannon, J. W., & Woods, W. J. (1991). Affirmative psychotherapy for gay men. *The Counseling Psychologist, 19*, 197–215.

Siegel, K., & Epstein, J. (1996). Ethnic-racial differences in psychological stress related to gay lifestyle among HIV-positive men. *Psychological Reports, 79*(1), 303–312.

Signorile, M. (2003). *Queer in America: Sex, media, and the closets of power.* Madison, WI: The University of Wisconsin Press.

Simonsen, P. (1997). *Promoting a development culture in your organization using career development as a change agent.* Palo Alto, CA: Davies-Black Publishing.

Slevin, K., & Wingrove, R. (1999). *From stumbling blocks to stepping stones.* New York, NY: New York University Press.

Slobodzian, J. (2006, May 5). Breaking through the pink ceiling. *The Consulting Philadelphia Inquirer.*

Smoyer, J. (1998). A practical approach to the issues of drug and alcohol testing. *HR Magazine, 5.*

Snyder, K. (2003). *Lavender road to success: The career guide for the gay community.* Berkley, CA: Ten Speed Press.

Sobel, S. L., Westcott, K. S., Benecke, M. M., & Osburn, C. D. (2000). *Service members Legal Defense Fund Network.* Retrieved from http://www.sldn.org/templates/law/index.html

Society for Human Resource Management. (1999). *Workplace diversity.* Retrieved from http://www.shrm.org/diversity/buskit699.pdf

Society for Human Resource Management. (2001). *What is the business case for diversity?* Retrieved from http://www.shrm.org/diversity/

Solba, C. (2003). Lying in a room of one's own. Retrieved from http://www.iwf.org/iwfmedia/show/18327.html

Sommer, B., & Sommer, R. (1991). *A practical guide to behavioral research: Tools and techniques.* New York, NY: Oxford.

Srinivas, S. (1991). *Organizational commitment and job burnout among employees of non-profit organizations.* Retrieved from http://ca1.csa.com

Stanley, A. (2002, July 13). For women to soar is rare: To fail is human. *New York Times.* Retreived from http://www.nytimes.com/2002/01/13/business/yourmoney/13WOME.html

Stebbins, R. (1972). The unstructured research interview as incipient interpersonal relationship. *Sociology and Social Research, 56,* 164–177.

Stenius, V. M., Veysey, B. V, Hamilton, Z., & Andersen, R. (2005). Social roles in women's lives. *Journal of Behavioral Health Services and Research, 32,* 182–198.

Stokes, J., McKirnan, D., Doll, L., & Burzette, R. (1996). Female partners of bisexual men: What they don't know might hurt them. *Psychology of Women Quarterly, 20*(2), 267–

Stone, P., & Lovejoy, M. (2004). Fast-track women and the choice to stay home. *Annals of the American Academy of Political and Social Science, 596*, 2–83.

Strober, M. (1984). Toward a general theory of occupational sex segregation: The case of public school teaching. In B. Reskin (Ed.), *Sex segregation in the workplace: Trends, explanations, remedies* (pp. 144–156). Washington, DC: National Academy Press.

Subich, L. M. (1996). Addressing diversity in the process of career assessment. In M. L. Savickas & W. B. Walsh (Eds.), *Handbook of career counseling theory and practice* (pp. 277–290). Palo Alto, CA: Davies-Black.

Suzuki, L. A., Ahluwalia, M. K., Arora, A. K., & Mattis, J. S. (2007). The pond you fish in determines the fish you catch: Exploring strategies for qualitative data collection. *The Counseling Psychologist, 35*(2), 295–327.

Swanson, J. L. (1995). The process and outcome of career counseling. In W. B. Walsh & S. H. Osipow (Eds.), *Handbook of vocational psychology: Theory, research, and practice* (2nd ed., pp. 217–260). Mahwah, NJ: Erlbaum.

Swanson, J. L. (2002). Understanding the complexity of clients' lives: Infusing a truly integrative career-personal perspective into graduate training. *The Counseling Psychologist, 30,* 815–832.

Swanson, J. L., Daniels, K. K., & Tokar, D. M. (1996). Assessing perceptions of career-related barriers: The Career Barriers Inventory. *Journal of Career Assessment, 4,* 219–244.

Swim, J., Hyers, L., Fitzgerald, D., & Bylsma, W. (2003). African American college students' experiences with everyday anti-Black racism: Characteristics of and responses to these incidents. *Journal of Black Psychology, 29*(1), 38–67.

Szymanski, D. M., Chung, Y. B., & Balsam, K. F. (2001). Psychosocial correlates of internalized homophobia in lesbians. *Measurement and Evaluation in Counseling and Development, 34,* 27–38.

Szymanski, D., & Gupta, A. (2009, April). Examining the relationship between multiple internalized oppressions and African American lesbian, gay, bisexual, and questioning persons' self-esteem and psychological distress. *Journal of Counseling Psychology, 56*(2), 110–118. doi: 10.1037/a0013317

Takeuchi, D. T., & Uehara, E. S. (1996). Ethnic minority mental health services: Current research and future conceptual directions. In B. L. Levin & J. Petrila (Eds.), *Mental health services: A public health perspective* (pp. 63–80). New York, NY: Oxford University Press.

Tashakkori, A., & Teddlie, C. (1998). *Mixed methodology: Combining qualitative and quantitative approaches.* Thousand Oaks, CA: Sage.

Task Force on Sexual Orientation and the Legal Workplace. (1999). *Report of the District of Columbia bar task force on sexual orientation and the legal workplace.* Washington, DC: The District of Columbia Bar.

Technology Alliance. (2005). *Disaggregation.* Retrieved from http://www.technology-alliance.com/pubspols/dddm/disaggregation.html

Thiagarajan, S., Hou, L., Cain, N., & Perry, A. (2002). Hire with care. *Nonprofit World, 20,* 6.

Thomas, K. M., Bierema, L. L., & Landau, H. (2004). Advancing women's leadership in academe: New directions for research and HRD practice. *Career Development International, 23*(7), 62–

Tokenism. (n.d.). In *Merriam-Webster's online dictionary.* Retrieved from http://www.m-w.com/dictionary/tokenism

Trochim, W. (2006). Practical challenges of systems thinking and modeling in public health. *American Journal of Public Health, 96,(3),* --546.

Troung, F., & Kleiner, B. (2001). New developments concerning homosexual harassment in the workplace. *Equal Opportunities International, 20*(5–7), 32–36.

Trumbull, M. (2007, February 8). For women, glass ceiling still an issue. *Christian Science Monitor, 99*(51), 1–2.

Unity First. (2002). *Workplace discrimination.* Retrieved from http://www.unityfirst.com/ufthisweeknov182002.htm

University of California Los Angeles. (2006). *LGBT discrimination.* Retrieved from http://www.lgbt.ucla.edu/Discrimination.htm

U.S. Census. (2004). *How many gay Americans are there and what is their buying power?* Retrieved from http://www.focusondiversity.com/tools/articles/html/articledetail.php?id=42

U.S. Department of Labor. (1991). *A report on the glass ceiling initiative.* Washington, DC: Author.

U.S. Department of Labor. (2005). *The high cost of sexual harassment.* Retrieved from http://www.eurowrc.org/06.contributions/1.contrib_en/32.contrib.en.htm

U.S. Equal Employment Opportunity Commission. (2010). Retrieved from http://usgovinfo.about.com/cs/censusstatistic/a/aawomeneeoc.htm

USBE Diversity Watch. (2007). *Three in ten African American workers have experienced Discrimination.* Retrieved from http://www.Blackengineer.com/artman/publish/printer_740.shtml

Vaid, U. (1996). *Virtual equality: The mainstreaming of gay and lesbian liberation.* New York, NY: Doubleday.

Van den Bergh, N. (1994). From invisibility to voice: Providing EAP assistance to lesbians in the workplace. *Employee Assistance Quarterly, 9,* 161–177.

Van Manen, M. (1990). *Researching lived experience: Human science for an action sensitive pedagogy.* Albany, NY: State University of New York Press.

Van Puymbroeck, C. M. (2002). Career development of lesbian, gay, and bisexual undergraduates: An exploratory study. *Dissertation Abstracts International: Section B. Sciences and Engineering, 62*(12), 5982.

Vinnicombe, S., & Singh, V. (2003). Locks and keys to the boardroom. *Women in Management Review, 18*(3), 325–333. doi:10.1108/09649420310491495

Waldo, C. R. (1999). Working in a majority context: A structural model of heterosexism as a minority stress in the workplace. *Journal of Counseling Psychology, 46,* 218–232.

Walsh, W. B., Bingham, R. P., Brown, M. T., & Ward, C. M. (Eds.). (2001). *Career counseling for African Americans.* Mahwah, NJ: Erlbaum.

Walters, K. L., & Simoni, J. M. (1993). Lesbian and gay male group identity attitudes and self esteem: Implications for counseling. *Journal of Counseling Psychology, 40,* 94–99.

Walzer, M. (1987). *Watch with both eyes: Narratives and social science. Sources of insight into teachers thinking* (Unpublished doctoral dissertation). Harvard University, Boston, MA.

Warren, C. (1977). Fieldwork in the gay world: Issues in phenomenological research. *Journal of Social Issues, 33,* 93–107.

Welch, S., Karnig, A., & Eribes, R. (1983). Changes in Hispanic local employment. *Southwest Western Political Quarterly, 36,* 660–673.

Welch, S., & Seigelman, L. (2000). Getting to know you: Latino-Anglo social contact. *Social Science Quarterly, 81,* 67–83.

Wellington, S., & Catalyst. (2001). *Be your own mentor.* New York, NY: Random House.

Wells, B., & Hansen, N. (2003). Lesbian shame: It is a relationship to identity integration and attachment. *Journal of Homosexuality, 45*(1), 93–110.

Weyer, B. (2006). Do multi-source feedback instruments support the existence of a glass ceiling for women leaders? *Women in Management Review, 21*(6), 441–457.

Weyer, B. (2007). Twenty years later: Explaining the persistence of the glass ceiling for women leaders. *Women in Management Review, 22*(6), 482–496.

Wheeler-Scruggs, K. (2008). Do lesbians differ from heterosexual men and women in Levinsonian phases of adult development? *Journal of Counseling & Development, 86*(1), 39–46.

White, B., Cox, C., & Cooper, C. (1992). *Women's career development: A study of high flyers.* Oxford, UK: Blackwell.

White, E. (2007). Out of the corporate closet. *Black Enterprise, 30,* 64–66.

White, S., & Shoffner, M. (2002). Career counseling with lesbian clients: Using the theory of work adjustment as a framework. *The Career Development Quarterly, 51*(1), 87–97.

Wilkins, D. B., & Gulati, M. (1996). Why are there so few Black lawyers in corporate law firms? An institutional analysis. *California Law Review, 94*, 493–625.

Williams, C. (1999). African-American women: Afro-centrism and feminism: Implications for therapy. *Women and Therapy, 22*(4), 1–16.

Williams, D. (1998). *Discrimination*. Retrieved from http://www.macses.ucsf.edu/Research/Psychosocial/notebook/discrimination.html

Williams, D. (2009). *Corporate executives say more minorities in the suite is good for business*. Retrieved from http://www.allbusiness.com/population- demographics/demogr

Willmot, B. (2003). Accounting for people. *Personnel Today Journal, 5*, 1–2.

Wilson, B., & Miller, R. (2002). Strategies for managing heterosexism used among African American gay and bisexual men. *Journal of Black Psychology, 28*(4), 371–391.

Witmer, D. (2006). *Sex education in schools*. Retrieved from http://parentingteens.about.com/od/teensexuality/a/sex_education.htm

Wong, P. T. P., & Watt, L. (1991). What types of reminiscence are associated with successful aging? *Psychology and Aging, 6*, 272–279.

Woods, J. D. (1994). The *corporate closet: The professional lives of gay men in America*. New York, NY: The Free Press.

Wyatt, W. (1999). *The staying at work survey*. Retrieved from http://www.watsonwyatt.com/research/resrender.asp?id=W-875&page=1

Yoder, J. D., & Sinnett, J. (1995). Is it all in the numbers? A case study of tokenism. *Psychology of Women Quarterly*, *9*(3), 413–418. doi:10.1111/j.1471-6402.1985.tb00890.x

Young, C. Y., & Wright, J. V. (2001). Mentoring: The components for success. *Journal of Instructional Psychology, 28*(3), 202–206.

Zea, M. C., Jernewall, N., & Toro-Alfonso, J. (2003, March). Lesbian, gay, and bisexual psychology and ethnic minority issues over the last 10 years. *Communique*, iv–vi. Retrieved from http://www.apa.org/pi/oema/resources/communique/2003/03/february-special.pdf

Zunker, V. (2001). *Career counseling: Applied concepts of life planning* (6th ed.). Pacific Grove, CA: Brooks/Cole.

# APPENDIX A. CONSENT LETTER AND DEMOGRAPHIC FORM

2/16/09
**Dissertation Research Participant Request**
*Consent Letter and Demographics Form*

Hello, I would like to invite you to consider being a participant for a study being conducted by Denalerie J. Johnson-Faniel, a doctoral student at Capella University. This study seeks to describe the career development experiences of African American lesbian women. The research will explore their employment experiences as they relate to sexual orientation and professional career advancement. The research study is designed to learn about appropriate and effective work related practices for the lesbian community, specifically African-American women and their employers. The title of this dissertation research study is *The Lived Career Development Experiences of African American Lesbian Managers: A Phenomenological Study of Professional Advancement.*

Participation benefits include contributing to an understanding of the topic, adding to the knowledge, updating the research literature, and learning something about oneself by virtue of the interview process. There are no monetary rewards for study participation.

If you decide to participate in the study, which will last an estimated two hours, you will beasked to sign the consent form, complete the attached demographics survey, and return both to Denalerie Johnson-Faniel via toll-free confidential fax at 1-888 X-or privately mail to P.O. Box X. Only the researcher can access the confidential fax machine and private mailbox. **Entries must be received by 5pm EST, Friday, October 16, 2009.** Late or incomplete submissions will not be accepted. The criteria for participation include identifying as an "out," African-American lesbian between the ages of 32-72 with full-time managerial supervisory duties (not being retired from this capacity for less than two years). If you do not qualify, but know others that do, please forward this material to others that might qualify.

Those selected to be research participants will be contacted on or before January 1, 2010, to further discuss the study and set-up the interview. Participants will receive a copy of their signed consent form that will be kept on file in a confidential fireproof safe that only the researcher has access to. Study participation is completely voluntary and it is the participant's option to terminate participation at any time without penalty or prejudice to them. Participants may freely choose to avoid any specific question in the study and continue with the rest. Participants are encouraged to ask any questions at any time about the nature of the study and the methods used. Participants will also receive a copy of their transcription report so they have the opportunity to suggest changes to the researcher, if necessary. Participants will be able to read a copy of the final dissertation that should be approved before the summer of 2011.

The investigation involves two parts: (a) An explanation of this study and gaining the participant's informed consent, and (b) a discussion of the participant's experiences related to their being out at work. The length of the interview is anticipated to be approximately two hours, however, the timeframe is flexible to provide adequate time for the interview questions to be answered thoroughly. The interview questions will be open-ended, informal, and conversational in nature and the interviews will be scheduled weekdays after 5:00pm, for the weekend, or at a mutually convenient time. Interviews will take place in wheelchair accessible space at X or a mutually convenient location, such as the X, etc., if feasible.

Your participation in this study entails no unusual risks or discomforts. A dissertation based on this research will be prepared as partial fulfillment of degree requirements in a doctoral human services program. Knowledge gained from the research may be presented to others through published works and/or presentations and will be resourceful in future related scholarly work.

The only potential risk is your identification; however every effort will be made to protect privacy and confidentiality by using a self-selected pseudonym during the form completion, interview, and in the dissertation document. Neither you nor your place of employment, current or previous, will be identified. The interview process requires audio taping of the interview and researcher computer notation to allow for a transcription of the interview. Unauthorized persons will not access tapes or records and notes taken during the interview will only be used and seen by the researcher. The audiotapes, notes, signed consent and demographic forms, and transcripts will be rtained in the researcher's secure residential office location in a locked fireproof safe deposit in for a minimum of seven years with the key only available to the researcher. Seven years after publication of the dissertation, all tapes, notes, transcripts, etc. will be destroyed by erasure and/or shredding disposal. You will be asked to review the written transcript of your interview in order to check for accuracy. By returning the attached consent form with your signature and the completed demographics data survey form, you are indicating that you want to be a research participant, are agreeing to be audio taped, are agreeing to participate in the study interview and transcript review, and are agreeing to have your pseudonym responses included in this research project. By signing the consent form, you are agreeing that you have read the above statements and agree to participate in the research. In addition, you are aware that (You/My/I):

(1) My name and audiotapes will remain confidential.
(2) I am entitled to have any further inquiries answered regarding the procedures.
(3) Participation is voluntary and I may withdraw my consent and discontinue my participation in this study at any time and for any reason without penalty.
(4) No royalties, payment, fees, or monetary rewards are due the participant for any current or subsequent participation or publication.

For further information about this study, your role in it, or a report of findings contact: Denalerie J. Johnson-Faniel via email at djohnson@GBFresearch.com or this researcher's doctoral advisor, Dr. Bemker at Mary.Bemker@Faculty.Capella.edu. You may also contact CAPELLA UNIVERSITY, Institutional Review Board, 225 South 6th Street, 9th Floor, Minneapolis, Minnesota 55402 regarding your rights as a participant in this research. This research study has been reviewed and approved by the University's IRB Human Subjects Review Committee.

*This study has been approved by Capella University's IRB* 91568-1, *effective from* January 20, 2009 *through* January 20, 2010.

Thank you for your participation!

Denalerie J. Johnson-Faniel
Winter 2009

THE LIVED CAREER DEVELOPMENT EXPERIENCES OF
AFRICAN AMERICAN LESBIAN MANAGERS: A
PHENOMENOLOGICAL STUDY OF PROFESSIONAL
ADVANCEMENT

by

Denalerie J. Johnson-Faniel

**RESEARCH STUDY INFORMED CONSENT FORM**

By checking the box below and dating the form you acknowledge that you have been informed of and understand the nature of the study. You acknowledge that you freely consent to participate in the study, and that you meet the 32-72 age requirement, are African-American with full-time managerial and supervisory work duties (not retired from this capacity for less than two years), and are a lesbian that is out at work..

| |
|---|
| I agree to participate in the study as described in the attached cover letter _____ (✓ if you agree). |

| |
|---|
| I, _____, (printed name), have completed the attached demographics survey form and will mail or fax it and this completed consent form back to the researcher, Denalerie J. Johnson-Faniel, via toll-free fax 1-888-or mail to P.O. X, before April 20, 2009. |

| |
|---|
| Printed Name: _____ |

| |
|---|
| Signature: <br><br> _____ |
| Print Selected Name Pseudonym (fictitious alternative to a person's legal name): <br> _____ |
| Date: <br><br> _____ |

Questions may be directed to Denalerie J. Johnson-Faniel at djohnson@GBFresearch.com. Thank you.

THE LIVED CAREER DEVELOPMENT EXPERIENCES OF AFRICAN AMERICAN LESBIAN MANAGERS: A PHENOMENOLOGICAL STUDY OF PROFESSIONAL ADVANCEMENT
by
Denalerie J. Johnson-Faniel

**RESEARCH STUDY DEMOGRAPHICS COLLECTION FORM**

### (Please Type/Print)

| Name: | | | |
|---|---|---|---|
| Desired Pseudonym: | | | |
| Email Address: | Have You Lived in the U.S. the Majority of Your Adult Life? ☐ Yes ☐ No | | |
| Mailing Address: | Apt. #: | Phone #: ( ) | |
| P.O. Box: | City: | State: | Zip Code: |
| Do You Describe Your Ethnicity as Black/African-American? ☐ Yes ☐ No | Biological Sex: ☐ Male ☐ Female | Gender: Male ☐ Female | Do You Describe Your Sexual Orientation as Lesbian? ☐ Yes ☐ No |
| Occupation: | If Completed College, What Was Major Area of Study? | | Years Employed With Current Organization? |
| Job Title: | | | Years of Supervisory Manager Experience? |
| # People You Directly Supervise? | Brief Job Duties: | | Is Your Current Position an Entrepreneurship in which You are the Owner? ☐ Yes ☐ No |

| Birth Date: | Age: | Marital Status: | | # of Children: | |
|---|---|---|---|---|---|
| Total Years Work Experience: | Highest Level of Education: | To What Position Title Do You Report? | | Average # of Hours Worked Per Week: | |
| Employer Type: (☐ proper box) | ☐ For-Profit | ☐ Non-Profit | ☐ Government | ☐ Higher Education | ☐ Other _____ |
| I Am Out To: (☐ proper box) | Out to Close Friends. ☐ Yes ☐ No | Out to Acquaintances. ☐ Yes ☐ No | Out to Supervisor. ☐ Yes ☐ No | Out to Family. ☐ Yes ☐ No | Out to Co-Workers. ☐ Yes ☐ No |

THE LIVED CAREER DEVELOPMENT EXPERIENCES OF AFRICAN
AMERICAN LESBIAN MANAGERS: A PHENOMENOLOGICAL
STUDY OF PROFESSIONAL ADVANCEMENT
by
Denalerie J. Johnson-Faniel

**RESEARCH STUDY DEMOGRAPHICS COLLECTION FORM
(Please Type/Print)**

APPENDIX B. INTERVIEW GUIDE QUESTIONS

The research question is, "How does employment discrimination, or the fear of such discrimination, affect African American lesbian managers' perceptions of their career advancement?" The researcher will use the following questions as a semistructured guide in each participant interview to learn about perceptions of interviewees' career advancement. These questions will allow the research study participants to share their experiences. Please answer the following questions based on your own experiences as an African American lesbian manager.

1. Describe the type of work you do and your career development experience.
2. In as much detail as you can, tell me about your experience deciding whether to come out at work and any differences that you have experienced before and after coming out at work.

3. What role has having or not having a mentor played in your career development?
4. What are the measures of success in your careers?
5. What are the challenges/limitations/systemic barriers to your career path achievement?
6. Describe any experienced work related racism and any effects on career advancement.
7. Describe any experienced work-related sexism and any effects on career advancement.
8. Describe any experienced work-related homophobia and any effects on career advancement.
9. Do you think straight, White women are treated differently in positions similar or equal to yours? Straight, White men? White lesbians? Gay White men? Other lesbian minority women? If so, please describe how/why/etc.
10. What are the greatest pressures, strains or anxieties in the work that might be related to your being an African-American lesbian-how might this affect future career growth?
11. What are the common misconceptions about African-American lesbians working in this field?

12. How does your being an African-American lesbian affect your personal friendships, relationships, family life, etc.?

13. Are there regrets you have about how you made any of your career decisions? What suggestions can you offer other African-American lesbians as to how they might avoid having those same regrets?

14. What would you do differently in terms of diversity and staff career development if you ran your current place of employment?

15. Whom do you supervise and to whom do you report and how are those working relations affected by your sexual orientation?

16. Are there any pre-conceived stereotypes placed on you by coworkers because you are an African-American lesbian? Do you feel you can count on your co-workers and/or job resources for help and cooperation? Please explain.

17. Is there a dress code at work? If so, how does it affect your personal sense of dress and comfort level as African-American lesbian?

18. Are there any special concerns or issues for African-American lesbians in your field?

19. If you could do things all over again, would you choose the same path for yourself? Why? What would change?
20. Please explain whether you feel you have the necessary authority to do your job well.
21. How would you describe your overall satisfaction as an employee in this organization? How do you describe your company's benefits and diversity policy as it relates to sexual orientation? How does this affect you as an African-American lesbian?
22. What role, if any, does romantic love play in your career advancement? Please provide specific examples of the affects of your personal relationships.
23. How is professional advancement at work different for you as compared to that of other people who are not openly gay?
24. What is the affect of corporate and government policy development your career advancement?
25. Please feel free to expand on anything or share additional information.

Made in the USA
Lexington, KY
01 February 2012